THE
RISK TAKERS

PORTRAITS OF MONEY, EGO & POWER

JEFFREY ROBINSON

London
GEORGE ALLEN & UNWIN

Boston   Sydney

First published by George Allen & Unwin 1985
Second impression 1985

George Allen & Unwin (Publishers) Ltd
40 Museum Street, London WC1A 1LU, UK

George Allen & Unwin (Publishers) Ltd
Park Lane, Hemel Hempstead, Herts HP2 4TE, UK

George Allen & Unwin Australia Pty Ltd
8 Napier Street, North Sydney, NSW 2060, Australia

George Allen & Unwin with the
Port Nicholson Press
PO Box 11-838 Wellington, New Zealand

ISBN 004 658248 7

Set in 12 on 13 point Garamond by Columns of Reading
and printed and bound in Great Britain by
Biddles Ltd, Guildford and King's Lynn

Contents

For SJR
with love

Acknowledgements

There are many people I wish to thank for their help with this book. My agent Leslie Gardner, who believed in it from the very first. Nick Brealey at George Allen & Unwin, whose contribution went far beyond simply being an astute and sensitive editor. Liz Paton for her copy-editing, help and understanding. The editors of *Barrons*, for whom a number of the original interviews were done. The BBC Data Service for hours of research. Betty Powell at the Department of Trade and Industry, who never failed to offer her gracious assistance. And, for their loyalty, Constance Brown, Jack Greenwald, Adrian Shire, Marcelle D'Argy Smith and, of course, La Benayoun.

Also, friends and willing accomplices at the *Wall Street Journal*, the *International Herald Tribune*, the *New York Times*, the *Financial Times*, *The Times*, the *Telegraph*, the *Guardian*, the *Sunday Times*, the *Observer*, *Financial Weekly*, *Business Week*, the *Economist*, and *Euromoney Magazine*.

Plus, the dozens of people I spoke with – some of whom appear in the book but many of whom don't. They include the deputies and assistants, co-workers and even competitors of the businessmen who do appear. They also include all those secretaries who put up with my badgering for information and appointments, and who so kindly pleaded my case with their boss.

But most importantly, I wish to say thank you to the

risk takers who are portrayed here, all of whom at one point or another gave me some of their time. I trust they will understand that, while the chips have fallen where they may, at least they have fallen honestly and without malice. You guys really are more fascinating than movie stars and football players.

Introduction

It was back at the end of the '60s.

Through no fault of my own, I found myself stuck for a couple of weeks in a dusty, sage-brushed West Texas town called Lubbock. As the old joke goes, it was second prize.

Plunked down in the middle of flat, hot, cattle country, Lubbock was – and almost certainly still is today – a cowpoke town where young men walked through the main street wearing cowboy hats, jeans and with spurs on their boots. They'd probably have worn chaps as well, except it isn't easy climbing in and out of a pick-up truck dressed like that.

The motel where I stayed was owned by and named for a local hero called Donny Anderson. He grew up there, went to Texas Tech University there, and eventually turned into a big deal professional football star. He wore Number 44 for the Dallas Cowboys over several seasons. And just so that no one would miss the point, the swimming pool in the lobby of the Donny Anderson Motel was shaped like an American football helmet with the number 44 painted across the bottom.

In those days there were no such things as bars in Texas. The State licensing laws prohibited them. Instead there were private clubs – except they were open to anyone willing to pay the $1 one-night entry fee. You walked into the club at the Donny Anderson Motel and the smiling girl at the door asked you to sign the guest

1

book. She said, 'Hi, my name is Wilma and you'll be my guest at the club tonight. You'll have to pay for your own drinks, but you are welcome to use my drink locker.' Her drink locker turned out to be the club's bar. She and the bar tender might well have been the only legitimate members of this club – although I suspect the manager and owner were members too. Maybe Donny Anderson was also. I never asked.

Signing in one night, I followed a guy who wrote his name in the guest book as Frank something. I can't remember his last name. I have no idea what happened to him. I never saw him again. He may be, by this time, one of the best-heeled guys in America. Or he may be broke. I'd bet that he struck it rich.

It was the first time I ever met a Risk Taker.

He was in his 30s, well dressed, with a salesman's handshake and a salesman's grin. His particularly easy drawl gave him away as being from Georgia – it's a very different accent from what you hear in Texas. As it was early, and as the place was dead empty, we shared a table. I seem to recall that eventually other people came along and sat with us. I don't remember who they were, although if memory serves one was a flashy young woman whom he introduced as his secretary. That's what you had to do in America in the late '60s. Especially in places like Lubbock, Texas. Separate rooms please.

After the usual amount of small talk, coupled with a few Margueritas (besides beer that's what they like to drink in that part of the world), he mentioned that he was in town on business. And his business was chasing tornadoes.

Just one week before, Lubbock had suffered the wrath of the gods as a tornado ripped through the town. Seems they built the place in the wrong spot – tornadoes happened there with nasty regularity. And the tornado that smashed through Lubbock, Texas, in the early summer of 1969 had been one of the most devastating ever. Entire buildings were uprooted. The roads had flooded. Destruction was everywhere. Lubbock looked like Berlin at the end of 1945.

Frank was one of the first to reach the town. He was, in the purest sense, an asset stripper. He heard about the tornado, grabbed his chequebook, and got onto the next flight. He moved into the Donny Anderson Motel for as long as it would take him to buy up the town. A wrecked bridge. Steel girders. Iron fencing. The remains of a gas station. Junked cars. Twisted buses. He grabbed whatever scrap and junk he could lay his hands on. The insurance adjusters, who came through at about the same time, paid off claims and found themselves owning the spoils. In turn, Frank was willing to pay for everything the insurance companies didn't want. And they didn't want almost all of what they had paid for. Anyone who wasn't insured was also an obvious seller. Within a day or two word got around that some guy named Frank was in town with his pockets full of money. The motel switchboard lit up like a Christmas tree. Whatever anybody in the fallen city of Lubbock wanted to sell, Frank was willing to buy. If he had to pay 10 cents on the dollar that was fine. If he could get it for 5 cents on the dollar, that was even better.

In between buying sprees, which he did with a rented car, a line of credit at a local bank, a clipboard and preprinted contracts in hand, he stopped at what few phone booths were still standing to ring his office in Georgia and list the new inventory. His game was simple. Buy cheap and sell fast to someone, anyone, for more than he paid. The trick was to find someone who would know what to do with contorted steel bridge girders. It was your basic cash and carry . . . a big money business, he claimed, as long as he got all the ingredients right. But it could easily be financial disaster if he didn't. The last thing he wanted to do was get stuck with a bunch of battered telephone poles that he couldn't sell, wouldn't want to store, and didn't have the slightest intention of ever using. Added to that, he was also facing the competition – who knows how many other Franks were staying at other motels along the tornado's path, flooding the market with dollars to buy, and scrap to unload.

His particular type of risk taking relied heavily on instant turnover. Sure, he had regular clients on whom he could count to take a certain amount of scrap. And sure, much of what he bought was probably pre-sold. Much of what he bought that summer might even have changed hands several times before anyone came to take it away. Ideally, he wanted to sell before he bought, using the banks' money to purchase the scrap based on the contract to sell. The difference was pure profit. Of course, if he got his timing wrong, the difference was a flat loss. Then again, his business was built around so-called 'Acts of God'. He had to count on just the right number of natural disasters and just the right amount of destruction every year to keep him in silk ties and blonde secretaries. Too few disasters also meant scrap buying prices would be high and the cost of getting in the game perhaps prohibitive. Too many disasters would flood the sellers' market and diminish his profits.

It struck me, as he talked, that his act was a pretty exciting one. That his kind of wheeling and dealing was a terrific way to earn a living.

The idea for *The Risk Takers* began to germinate.

*   *   *

For many Americans, England is Europe without the pain.

This is a country where the plumbing works and where the food is familiar. Americans tend to find the British hospitable, honest, and almost always with a cousin living somewhere like Milwaukee. Because Great Britain is well known as a nation of retired Colonels, Americans are quickly reminded that every Brit over a certain age has served with Yanks, met Yanks, drunk warm beer with Yanks and usually likes Yanks. At the same time, we discover that most Brits under that certain age watch Dallas and Hill Street Blues, wear UCLA sweatshirts, and, thanks to Channel Four, know the difference between a quarterback and a defensive tackle.

We come here in droves, curious about cricket (it is unthinkable in the United States that any game could go on for five days, break for tea and then no one wins), admiring the Royal Family, amazed at how clean the Underground is, and in awe of a civilization that is so rich in history and tradition. A Beefeater at the Tower of London once told me that he was sorry the 'Colonies' broke away from the Crown back in '76. 'Had you stayed with us,' he said, 'today you would have been one of Britain's finest Dominions.'

The British may go to Miami in the summer – the wrong time of year – or New York in the dead of winter – just as wrong – and come back here star-struck at how big everything is over there. But you return to a country where Americans have, since Ben Franklin's day, visited and lived and felt right at home. We may have differences of opinion when it comes to the subtleties of politics and economics. You may wish you had never heard of McDonald's hamburgers or cruise missiles. And you may be one of those people who think that as a group Americans are loud, demanding, rude and forever wearing checked slacks with striped shirts. Americans individually may be any or all of those things. But as a group we are England's biggest fans.

If only we spoke the same language.

Because we think it's the same language, Americans expect the British think the same as we do. You don't. In the States, everything happens fast. Decisions are made right away. Time is money. If you've got the right deal, you can get anybody you want on the telephone and make your proposition. The class system is defined by money, not a birth certificate or school tie. The customer is always right. No parking, no business. And banks will take real risks. This is not to say America is better. It's merely to say that Britain and America are different.

I hope, in this case, I have been able to capitalize on those differences. Frankly, I don't think I could have had access to all the people who have given me their time if I had been a British writer. It's not only that I tried to approach these people with a different attitude, but I honestly feel that they reacted to me in a different way – Fleet Street brings out a mixed bag of emotions with these people, while the motives of an American writer seem to be more abstract and perhaps less threatening. One even told me that he believed I'd be much fairer than a British writer looking at British business because I'd have no grudge or cross to bear. I think he greatly underestimated many British writers, but I had no intention of arguing that point before the interview.

I would like to say here that this is not really a business book.

It's not one of those 'how to become a better manager' volumes, or any sort of British variation on 'In Search Of Excellence'.

It is basically a book about people.

But they happen to be very special people. They happen to be stars in much the same way that Redford and Newman and Sinatra are stars. They are individuals with a mess of special talents. They are men who are in the business of making money. Yet while they have made millions – in many cases more than enough money to last forever – it doesn't seem as if it's the money that counts. Almost to a man, they're in it for the game. It's an odd obsession. They are men who put their chips on the table and let luck have her shot. Winning becomes a pure drug. But they are not gamblers. Being a gambler and being a risk taker are two different things. Gambling is when you put your dinner money on the nose of a nag running at 12–1. That's hardly the same thing as plunking down £175 million to buy a company with assets worth twice that.

In describing a handful of men who also appear in this book, Kenneth Fleet, Executive Editor of *The Times*, so aptly wrote, 'All have established high reputations for their business acumen; they have built up very large corporate empires with considerable power in their industrial spheres; they are strong personalities; they have amassed personal wealth as well as created financial strength within their companies; they remain ambitious; and by virtue of all these shared qualities, they have the power of decision that few, in any around them, are likely to question.'

In addition to that, I would suggest that, to a man, the risk takers in this book exhibit an above-average intelligence, a startling sense of individuality, remarkable memories, unnerving stamina, an uncanny ability to smell a deal, a certain kind of personal presence that tastes like money and tends to ensure confidence, and a native talent to spot the real risks, which they then proceed to minimize.

The sole criterion I used in selecting the major portraits in this book was my own fascination. As I am not a financial journalist or a business writer by trade – in this case I'd rather think of myself as a portraitist – I began without any particular desire to draw any serious business conclusions. So, when I looked around for risk takers, I chose those who personally fascinated me. I therefore do not mean this to be a definitive listing of great British risk takers. I simply present these portraits for what they are – stories of and insights into men who do for real what so many people merely dream of.

*   *   *

It was eight or nine years later when I met my second Risk Taker. I was living in the south of France by then, writing short stories for the slick magazine market but relying heavily on the *International Herald Tribune* to buy my non-fiction features, which helped to pay the rent. I don't remember exactly how I met Marty Ackerman, but he and his wife Diane were in France that summer, having rented a gigantic villa on Cap Ferrat.

When I heard the Ackermans' story I realized that one of my fascinations with such high-flyers was how they get started.

In 1960, Ackerman was a young New York lawyer with an office on Park Avenue. He was 28 years old, married, living in suburbia, and the father of young children. But he was also a man burdened with an unnerving feeling that his life was a treadmill. One morning, he simply decided to change all of that. He walked out of his office and stepped into the nearest bank. With very little effort he was able to negotiate a relatively small $10,000 personal loan. Because the United States happens to be a lawyer-oriented society – the government is run by lawyers and so are a huge number of major corporations, even banks – Ackerman had no trouble getting in to see the loan manager, convincing him that he needed the money to fix up his office, and signing the proper papers. They wrote him a cheque right away. With that in hand, he headed for the next bank on the block where he opened a deposit acount for $10,000. The total time involved was less than an hour. Having nothing else to do before lunch, he repeated the procedure with another pair of banks. The interest on the $20,000 in term deposits was nearly enough to offset the interest accrued on the $20,000 loans. In other words, the cost of all this was relatively low – a couple of points per year. Except he didn't wait a year. Within a few months he paid off the loans and cleared his accounts. Now he had a proven line of credit with four banks. So he borrowed more, saved more, and paid off those loans. Then he borrowed more again. By moving increasingly larger sums of money between several banks, he was able to establish for himself a working relationship and credit record with so many banks that, within twelve months of that first loan, he was able to borrow, solely on his signature, over $100,000. That was the money he put down to purchase a struggling company in Philadelphia.

The climate was right for such things in America in the '60s. If you knew what you were doing, one company could get you two. And two could get you four. All you had to understand was that a pyramid can only stand when the base is flat and the top is pointed. Upsidedown it is guaranteed to topple. Throughout the '60s there were stories of upsidedown pyramids that came crashing down. But Ackerman's was built right and within eight years that ailing Philadelphia company was a $150 million conglomerate. He owned a private jet, a bank in Beverly Hills, and the once mighty Curtis Publishing Company.

As the '60s ended, Ackerman began thinking of opting out. What he did was what many risk takers always promise to do but never get around to. He decided that he had indeed lived all the ego trips of success in America, and now wanted something else. So he gave up risk taking. He retired. He divested himself of several homes – including a nine-storey Park Avenue townhouse, which he sold to the East German government. He packed up most of his modern art collection and with Diane, his second wife, and their new baby he moved to London.

As he said at the time, 'In those days, if I didn't work from 7 a.m. until 11 or 12 at night, I had guilt pangs. I was exhausted, too heavy and out of shape. My first marriage went bad. I had a permanent sore on my ear from the telephone receiver. I looked at myself one day and realized I was getting old. I had to get off the treadmill.'

Speaking as someone who knew first hand, he believed that 'The kind of money I made in the '60s can still be made today, but only by young people who are willing to take massive risks. It can only be done by young people who have no money and therefore nothing to lose. When you have money you become too conservative.'

Almost predictably, after a few sedentary years in Europe, Ackerman and family headed back to New York. When last heard from he was practising law – with a little bit of risk taking on the side, just to keep his hand in.

In many ways, the start of Sam Cummings' career as a risk taker is the same. In 1950 he had nothing to lose. Today he is the largest and single most important arms dealer in the world. His company, Interarms, is said to own so much equipment that, had he the soldiers to go along with it, he would be the fourth or fifth largest army on earth.

Cummings is a likeable man who tries, at every turn, to play down the idea that war is good for his business. 'As soon as there is any trouble in the world, the governments themselves get into the arms business and force the private dealers out. We've never supplied any nation, anywhere in the world, during a time of real or potential hostilities. But then yes, you'd be quite accurate in saying that my business, like war, is based totally on human folly and not on human wisdom.'

Cummings was born in Philadelphia in 1927. During the Korean War, he landed a job with the Central Intelligence Agency as a weapons expert. Strictly overt, he insists. Absolutely nothing spooky; 'You could even reach me on the phone there.' For three years he sat in an office looking at pictures of captured weapons, writing reports, explaining what those weapons were and where they came from. 'It didn't take too long before I grew very tired of looking at those same pictures.' So in 1953 he decided to go into business for himself. But the only business he knew was guns. He settled on the name International Arms Corporation simply because that had the right ring to it. His address was a post office box in Washington DC and his stationery listed him as Vice President. 'I couldn't afford an office and I figured I'd only be Vice President so that anyone I dealt with would think there was at least one other person in the company, and maybe a secretary.'

He wrote to governments all over the world offering to buy any surplus arms they had. His only response came from the police chief of Panama. 'That was especially fortunate because in those days Panama was one of the cheapest places you could fly to. The police chief had a stock of 5000–6000 weapons for sale. Forty years' worth of stuff they had taken off revolutionaries, bank robbers and drunken sailors. I offered him $25,000, he accepted, and then I was faced with the problem of where to get the money because I didn't have a nickle.'

He returned to the States and started ringing gun dealers around the country. He wanted $60,000 for the lot. One dealer in California said sure. Cummings used the dealer's acceptance to get credit at the bank. That paid for the guns. The Californian's cheque for $60,000 paid for the overdraft and expenses, and left him with a $15,000 profit. He then rushed back to Central America where his pal the Panamanian police chief put him in touch with other people who had guns for sale. As his business grew, military people started asking him where they could buy quality arms. He knew the manufacturers, thanks to contacts he had developed during his CIA years, and he found himself acting as a broker. 'This was during the years of the rearmament of Europe. The timing was right. There has always been a huge collectors' market, but the surplus arms market had never really been exploited in quite the way I was doing it. However, brains had nothing to do with my success. I fell into it. Dumb luck and serendipity.'

*   *   *

Dumb luck and serendipity is certainly an over-simplification. A better word might be control.

The gambler plays at the roulette wheel. The risk taker owns it. True, the risk element exists with both. But with the roulette player, luck is in control. With the risk taker, he must at least try to control.

A Texan named T. Boone Pickens is living proof of that.

Chairman of Mesa Petroleum Co., he is a tall, slender 56-year-old who looks more like an investment banker than the ruthlessly tough, oil baron the US financial press makes him out to be. The reason there might be some confusion is because Pickens doesn't seem to be very successful when it comes to actually acquiring companies through take-overs. He goes into the market but, on almost every occasion since 1973, someone else comes along to win the company.

However, it's the damnedest thing, every time he loses he also seems to make a lot of money.

Other people call it 'greenmail'. He insists that it isn't, and then adds that he is on record as being against greenmail – that is, going in for a take-over, running up the share prices, and then bailing out with a substantial profit. It's a faddish trick of many high-flyers these days. What Pickens does so very well is control the market in which he's a buyer. In some cases his mere presence is enough. At least that's what it looked like in the autumn of 1983 when he went after Gulf Oil. Pickens and seven partners started buying Gulf shares at $45. They had acquired some 21.7 million shares when Pickens announced his plans to revamp Gulf. That was more than enough to send the Gulf board into a frenzy. Obviously there was no place in the Pickens plan for them. They panicked, a take-over battle ensued, and Pickens kept the heat on. As long as he was on the offensive, he could control the game. It was up to the Gulf board to find a suitor who would be willing to save them from Pickens. As long as he maintained control – at one point he actually campaigned for uncommitted shares as if he was running for office – the Gulf board could do little but fend off the attack. Their last stand came when Standard Oil of California arrived on the scene to merge with Gulf. Beaten once more, Pickens relinquished control of the battle by selling those 21.7 million shares at $80 per. The battered and beaten Pickens limped away with a $760 million profit.

Another guy who has made a fortune by maintaining control over the various elements in his risk taking is Rupert Murdoch.

Recently cited as the wealthiest man in Australia, he and his family own a company called Cruden Investments. In turn, Cruden owns 46 per cent of the Australian-based News Corporation, which has two wholly owned subsidiaries – News Limited, an Australian holding company, and Newscorp Investments, a British holding company. News Limited owns a 50 per cent stake in Ansett Transport Industries, and owns and/or controls 51 Australian subsidiaries, including television interests and 27 newspapers. That company also holds 50 per cent of News America, which is made up of ten operating companies in the States, including newspapers like the *New York Post*, the *Chicago Sun-Times* and the *Boston Herald*. The British company owns 100 per cent of News International, which in turn owns and/or controls 28 British subsidiaries like *The Times*, the *Sunday Times*, the *Sun*, *News of the World*, and satellite television interests. Through News International there are holdings in Reuters plus the other 50 per cent stake in News America Publishing. Together with a 50 per cent stake in 20th Century Fox, Murdoch has credibility, and the power behind him to take the offensive.

In 1983, losses at Warner Communications (the former film studio turned entertainment conglomerate) had been running heavy. Murdoch spotted an opportunity and, before that year was out, he spent just over $100 million (then about £71.4 million) to acquire 7 per cent. By the first week of January 1984, Murdoch had filed his intention in the US to purchase 25–49.9 per cent of Warner's stock. His bid for the company was checked. However the fight to keep Murdoch out of Warner was hot enough to raise the value of the shares he was holding. He took a $40 million profit for his trouble.

Sir James Goldsmith is another one who understands how to make money by being in control. Cited by the *Sunday Times* as being worth £500 million – making him the sixth wealthiest man in Britain – he spends most of his

time these days in either New York or Paris. The
Goldsmith touch is recognizable: high risk, high gearing,
a complex structure. In 1984 he went after the forestry
and insurance group St Regis. He bought shares, panicked
the board and backed away with a $26 million profit.
(Unfortunately for the board at St Regis a number of
Goldsmith's pals followed him and they all walked away
with handsome profits. One of them later described that
three-act greenmail opera simply as 'gang rape'. Although
for once it did disprove Goldsmith's so-called motto: 'If
you see a bandwagon, it's too late.')

Two years before, he went after the forestry group
Diamond International, paid $752 million for it, dismem-
bered it and, at least on paper, became a billionaire. One
source says that he's made more than $500 million on their
land assets alone. In June 1984 he took a stab at the
Continental Group, a packaging, insurance and forestry
operation in Connecticut. He lost that take-over battle
too, but ended up $35 million richer for his troubles. By
the end of 1984 he was going after the Colgate Palmolive
Company and, even if he never winds up owning it,
because he is so very good at what he does it's almost a
sure bet he'll wind up with money enough for a lot of
toothpaste.

Of course, control itself is not the lone key to success.
Controlling the game and therefore being able to
minimize your risks is important. But the high-flyers
whose names have become household words in the City
and along Wall Street have all made money by combining
control with other factors. Much like the football player
who controls the ball, controls his opponent and helps his
team control the game, he also needs speed, know-how,
the right mental attitude, the best physical condition and
maybe even the luck of a dry pitch. However, also like
the football player, he will almost definitely lose by doing
nothing more than losing control.

Freddie Laker is the perfect example.

He began life in the airline business in 1938. He was

just 16. Jokingly he says he used to sweep up the hangars. His biography says he was in training as an engineer. It wasn't until after World War II that he actually began making some money. He got into the buying and selling of planes and parts, and when the Berlin Airlift came along in 1948, his planes were in the air. In 1951, when the Divided City was blockaded again, Laker was there flying cargo in and out. Also flying refugees out. A quarter-million of them.

Twenty-five years later, Laker took aim at what he knew could be the aviation world's most lucrative market. He wanted to do for trans-Atlantic travel what McDonalds had done for hamburgers. At its peak, Laker Airways had revenues of about $500 million. Shareholders' equity was a tenth of that. As he puts it, 'My company made a profit every year except 1981–1982. In fact, on March 31, 1981, we were in the black to the tune of £3 million. But in this business you only need to make one loss if it's big enough.'

By 5 February 1982 the loss was indeed big enough. And Laker was out of business.

A tall, pleasant man, Laker sounds something like Stan Laurel. He's got that same kind of accent. A folk hero and larger-than-life optimist, he became Sir Freddie in the days when he was champion knight of the skies. He had all the trappings of a wealthy man – expensive cars, a yacht, a farm – plus a face and name almost as recognizable as any pop star's. When the airline went under, he lost the cars, the yacht and the farm. He had to take the FLY 1 numberplate off the Rolls and transfer it to a Volkswagen. A travel firm paid the liquidator to use the name Laker on a holiday company, so the best he could do was remortgage his home to get up another stake and try again with a company called Skytrain Holidays. He got Tiny Rowland of Lonrho to go into partnership with him, and at least for a while it seemed as if he could make a comeback.

Whether Laker lost control of his airline or others

managed to take control away from him, is the object of several law suits. 'You have to understand that the anti-trust actions in the United States have nothing to do with me personally. They have been brought by the liquidator. Freddie Laker is not the plaintiff. But I'm very happy for the action to go on so that the truth will be told.'

Looking back, he says that, at least in the beginning, he wanted to produce a one-class airplane: 'DC-10s run with 380 people. Maximum seating on our DC-10s was 345, all economy.' He eventually did create another class on his planes, and now he admits that might have been an error: 'It probably was a mistake going into the other class of service the way we did at the end. We shouldn't have tried to fight the other airlines at the front of the plane, except they started to fight us in the back of the plane with their low standby fares. I felt that, by fighting them upfront, I might be able to get them out of the standby business.'

He didn't.

Another part of the problem was his commitment to buy more planes. 'I bought two A-300 airbuses. On hindsight, it might have been better had I not.'

Suddenly he could no longer control the fight with the major trans-Atlantic airlines. They had forced him to defend himself on their turf. Nor could he maintain control of his debt situation because he was in over his head on those two A-300s. It was all compounded when sterling took a nosedive and he lost control of his foreign currency exposure: 'The pound fell 26 per cent and that cost us $50 million. We survived the oil crisis and two groundings of the DC-10s. So it's kind of ironic, isn't it?' By not having hedged properly in foreign exchange, his profits turned into debt. Instead of minimizing his risks with financial futures and options – a mistake Richard Branson purposely tried to avoid when he started Virgin Atlantic – Laker become a sitting duck target to the whims and fancies of the dollar–sterling ratio.

*   *   *

When it comes to currencies, control means timing, and timing is everything. You find that out by spending one very hectic hour with another type of risk taker, a guy named Derek Tullett.

His company is called Tullett and Tokyo. And his business is foreign exchange.

The room in the City where Tullett does his thing is filled with men in shirtsleeves, more than a hundred of them, shouting at each other, then into telephones, and then at each other again. They sit around ten-sided tables, their neckties pulled down and their collars open, juggling three and four telephones while also trying to keep an eye on panels of flashing lights that mean more calls are coming in.

A man with a beard calls out, '86 I sell.' A colleague across the table answers, '81 I give.' Others at the table scream into their phones, '81 offered,' repeating it as they push buttons to open direct telephone links to banks all over the City. '81 offered . . . 81 offered . . . 81 offered . . .'

Then a man with two phones to his ears announces, 'Munich wants a quid.' The man with the beard lunges for his telephones, shouting, '74–86 overseas.' A man with glasses yells, '77 we bid a pound.' The Beard stabs a finger towards him, '77 you pay.' Glasses nods, 'B of A London.' The Beard nods, 'Yours. Done. County Bank.' At the same time, someone calls out, '73–85,' and someone else yells, '89 I sell,' and someone yet again barks, 'Munich wants a quid.'

Fifteen seconds have gone by.

And somewhere in the confusion £1 million has changed hands.

'The excitement generated in this industry is quite special,' Tullett says. He's a short, muscular man of 50, a former rally driver, and around the City these days he's known as a tough opponent on the squash courts. 'With so much money changing hands so very quickly, this is a high stress industry.'

High stress is an understatement. Guys at the dealing

tables burn out in their 30s. With so much money floating around, it takes a minimum of two years' training before Tullett will turn any of his brokers loose on a small handful of banks. Just as a side note, basic pilot training with the RAF is only 42 weeks.

'The minimum for a dollar/sterling deal is £1 million. And deals of £50 million–£100 million are common. It all happens at lightning speed. The broker is asked by a bank to sell some currencies for the highest price. But a broker on the other side of the table has been asked by another bank to buy some currencies for the lowest price. And timing is one of the major skills of broking. If you grab too fast, the bank you're dealing for may wind up paying more than they would have by waiting for the next deal one minute later. But if you wait 60 seconds too long, as other deals come in, as bids and offers change the market prices, then the bank you're broking for might wind up with less.'

Banks need to go back and forth between large sums of currencies, either speculating on their own account or buying and selling for clients. They come into a market – like the dealing room at Tullett and Tokyo – and expose themselves to the powers of supply and demand. That is the very backbone of foreign exchange rates. Heavy buying raises the price, heavy selling lowers it. It's no more complicated than that. Because the brokers and bankers know they're always talking in millions, they never actually say the word 'million'. They talk about a quid or ten pounds or twenty dollars. When the value of the pound is quoted in relation to dollars, the exact rate is carried out to four decimal places. As everybody in the marketplace knows that the pound is being traded at $1.25-something, they merely have to announce '75–85' to indicate that the spread for a pound is $1.2575–$1.2585. That's 10/10,000ths. On £1 million it represents $1000. On £90 million you're talking about a spread of $90,000.

In this case it's the banks taking the risks for their clients. The brokers at Tullett's place are merely the conduit for those risks. But Tullett is in his own right very much a risk taker. And a sense of timing was the talent that got him into the game.

London is the world's leading money broking market because there are so many foreign banks in the City. But the market is relatively young, only going back to 1953 when the Bank of England literally 'denationalized' foreign exchange dealings. Tullett came onto the scene in 1956, joining the currency brokerage house Savage and Heath. Within a few years he was a partner. Ten years later he was Managing Director. He always wanted to go out on his own however, but until 1971 the timing never seemed quite right. You don't really need anything to become a foreign exchange broker besides the skill of the trading business and a couple of telephones. Plus, of course, the confidence of your clients. Tullett had all of that. He had a reputation for being one of the best in the business. And, with hindsight, those who prophesied doom for Tullett now have to admit that he was the last entrepreneur who could have created a broking house to compete on the international scene. The trouble was, at the time, the pundits figured there were already too many well-established brokers in the market.

Tullett wouldn't take their advice. With immaculate timing he had spotted a window and crawled right through. 'It was a very difficult thing to do because by that time there were already a number of well-established brokerage houses in London. Getting a share of the market meant offering services to banks that other dealers weren't. In those days most of the broking houses concentrated on the Eurodollar markets. That's where the money was. So we decided there might be room for us if we emphasized the foreign exchange side of the business, while also providing dealing tables for Eurodollars and Certificates of Deposit.'

The day he went into business, the firm of Tullett and Riley (as it was then called) consisted of 15 people. Today the company employs well in excess of 750 with 15 offices around the world. They deal in Forex, the money markets, leasing finance, and financial futures. The product is money. The specific currency is irrelevant; the important thing is to put buyers with sellers and borrowers with lenders faster than his competitors. In return for arranging the deals, he takes a small commission – sometimes as low as 0.02 per cent. But the volume is enormous. He won't disclose the Tullett and Tokyo figures, yet one estimate for the five major broking houses (which includes Tullett's) puts the total daily foreign exchange business going through their offices at $25-$30 billion.

* * *

Looking at it closely, Tullett really only took a minimal risk because he knew the market and the market knew him. He had the patience to wait for his moment and the expertise to recognize it when it came along. But there was certainly more at stake than just his money. In this case he had his reputation to think of as well.

And, as long as reputation can at times be considered a commodity, some risk takers are very willing to use that as their stake.

By definition 'the company man' is not overly entrepreneurial. If he was, he would own the company. This is not to say there isn't risk taking in big business. Without risk taking there are no profits. But the Chief Executive Officer at a major public corporation like ICI or Unilever has decidedly less room for flamboyance. Many such companies, and Unilever is the perfect example, tend to promote from within, bringing management up through their own system. In the end they wind up with competent, albeit extremely dull, executives. Occasionally, however, a corporate man will seize an opportunity and become a kind of personal risk taker. In other words, he'll put himself on the line and risk the one thing that he has –

his reputation. The object of the exercise is almost always money.

Lee Iacocca made himself a millionaire by saving Chrysler against all odds. Like Laker, he found himself being cast in the role of the folk hero. Unlike Laker, he's still on top.

An engineer by profession, his first job was as a trainee with the Ford Motor Company. Public as it may be, Ford is still run by the Ford family, so even the most ambitious guy can only go so far up the totem pole. Iacocca was the most ambitious of men, is known in the industry as the father of the Mustang – one of the most successful automobile lines ever – and wound up, a mere 24 years after his debut, President of the company. He was there eight years before Henry Ford II gave him the boot. Just like that, Iacocca found himself on the dole. It was at a precarious time in his life – in his 50s, too old to start again, too young to call it quits.

There are few species more pathetic in the cut-throat world of American business than the unemployed corporate president. But Iacocca had a reputation and managed to get a job. A few weeks after he was fired at Ford – the Chairman's explanation to him was, 'It's just one of those things' – he went to Chrysler. But this wasn't exactly a promotion. Chrysler was in debt to the tune of $1.2 billion. Their cash flow was disappearing into the black hole of interest payments. The management was, as Iacocca puts it, 'In a state of anarchy. The company consisted of a cluster of little duchies, each one run by a prima donna.' In a real sense, he had nothing to lose. The ship was sinking and nobody in America expected it to be saved. Five years later he had cleaned up the company, replaced almost all of its upper management with old pals from Ford who knew his style, and paid off the debt. He took the risk of near-sure failure and turned it into the biggest success story in the history of American industry.

Some people even say that he was born to the job,

named Iacocca because it stands for 'I Am Chairman Of Chrysler Corporation (of) America'.

More recently, Howard Macdonald is trying to do the same thing at Dome.

The game might even be called 'no-lose'.

Any number of executives working for the 'Seven Sisters' (the major oil companies) might have fantasized about solving the problems of Canada's Dome Petroleum, but it took Macdonald to accept the challenge. And in the back of his mind he must have realized that this was a golden risk-taking opportunity. 'I wouldn't use the term no-lose. But I think it's fair to say that going into this job one is fire-proof, at least for a while.'

Macdonald was a company man at Royal Dutch/Shell for 23 years – although he doesn't like to be thought of as a company man, or an organization man, insisting: 'Shell happens to be the most free thinking and decentralized of all the oil majors.' He arrived in London from Scotland in 1958 as a founder of KCA, one of the original British drilling contractors. But money for drilling was hard to come by in those days – the North Sea bonanza was yet to happen – so after two years he joined Shell and rose through the accounting side of the business. He became Controller in 1974 and Treasurer in 1977.

While Macdonald was courting bankers in the City, a fellow named Jack Gallagher was making a reputation for himself in Calgary, Canada, as the risk taker who was Dome Petroleum.

Canada is of course an enormously wealthy country. Unfortunately many of the resources are buried under snow and permafrost. Gallagher had been a whiz-kid at Standard Oil of New Jersey, a geologist by profession, who at the age of 33 in 1950 was approached by a group of investors to manage Dome, then a very insignificant company. Gallagher didn't just join Dome, he became Dome. With Gallagher, Dome was the first oil company to drill an exploratory well in Canada's Arctic. Dome was considered the leader in High Arctic oil technology. As the '60s became the '70s, Dome participated in 11 wildcat wells in the Arctic islands, and made three important gas discoveries. That was also about the time they began preparing to drill in the Beaufort Sea, north of the Yukon territory and west of Victoria Island. By the Polar route it is almost exactly halfway between Montreal and Yokohama. It's so far north that the ice only begins to clear in mid-July. There is, these days, little doubt that the Beaufort will one day fulfil its promise. But Gallagher and Dome found out the hard way that the day was further off than they had led their bankers to believe. By 1981, Dome's oil exploration operation was so huge that it included the largest corporately owned marine fleet in the world and the biggest private air force in Canada. Gallagher was personally worth a few hundred million dollars. He was a wheeler–dealer of the old school, with all the flamboyance imaginable. It would be a tough act for anyone to follow, under any circumstance.

It was especially tough for Macdonald because by the time he got to Dome the company was nearly broke.

By 1982 the dice had turned. The Gallagher smile was no longer enough for the bankers. The company was up the proverbial creek. Not only didn't they have a paddle, but they'd already hocked the boat. It was like Burmah Oil, but three or four times worse. Their long-term debt stood at $6.3 billion (£4.4 billion). Mining and shipbuilding costs had skyrocketed by more than 12 times in under five years. Finance charges and interest had expanded nearly 14 times. Gallagher found himself on the outside; his personal wealth down by almost 90 per cent; his ego in tatters.

The story that went around Canada at the time – some swear it's true – is of Gallagher's right-hand man coming to see him, 'With good news and bad news.' Gallagher said, 'What's the good news?' The answer was, 'We can buy Gulf Oil for $200 million.' Now Gallagher asked, 'What's the bad news?' And he was told, 'They want $50 down.'

The bankers who found themselves owning Dome needed someone to put the company back together. But there weren't exactly long queues of applicants for the job. One financial writer likened it to flying kamikaze planes. Another said that the head hunters had to look for someone in Europe because no Canadian would be crazy enough. That's not exactly the way Macdonald saw it. In the back of his mind was a simple outline: if I win, I'm a hero; if I lose, they'll say, too bad but no one could have saved Dome anyway.

He started talking to Dome and their Canadian bankers in the spring of 1983. They offered him the Chief Executive's desk, and he took over that autumn. In between the initial meeting and his first day on the job, he had to think about problems on two fronts. First was Dome. He believed that the company was caught in a financial timing vice. There was an extremely strong asset base, but the mountain of debt was getting close to insurmountable. He had to get that down. Being able to talk the banks into rescheduling would help. He managed that to some degree. Selling off some assets would be necessary. He also managed that. Finally he would have to 'unfrock and eliminate the distrust factor'. Coming into Calgary clean, with his Shell reputation to back him up, was a big step in that direction.

Second, he had to establish for himself a minimal risk contract with Dome. After all, if he was going to put his reputation on the line it had to be worth his while. So he negotiated a five-year contract, with a clause to renew if both parties agreed. It also contained a 'break clause' at the three-year mark, giving him the chance to reassess his own risks during 1986 – a lifeboat clause just in case the ship is taking on too much water. Dome offered him $500,000 a year – decent by North American standards but enormous by British standards – plus a $4 million share option fund, which was set aside, out of any creditor's reach, just in case Dome did go broke. In that event, he could either get out on his lifeboat before doomsday, or simply stand in the ashes and shrug. In both instances, his pockets would be full. Or, if he manages to pull it off, if somehow he manages to raise Dome from the near-dead, then he will be an Iacocca-style hero. In both cases his future is assured. And only in the event of failure is anything at risk – his ego. But then, in forced retirement as he walks around the golf course, he can always say, I tried.

A similar type of personal risk was Dick Giordano's when he accepted to become Chief Executive Officer at the BOC Group in 1979.

Not that BOC was another Dome. Just the opposite. It's always been one of Britain's most solid companies. But Giordano put his reputation on the block and knowingly exposed himself to enormous personal risk because from the moment he arrived in London he was a star. The press was ready to put him under a microscope, the City fathers were sceptical, and not a few British industrialists were jealous. From his very first day of work he was Britain's highest-salaried executive.

Dick Giordano is the first-generation American son of Italian immigrants to New Jersey. Now just 51, he was educated at Harvard University and Columbia Law School. He spent some years as a Wall Street attorney, until 1963 when he decided he wanted to see for himself how the business world functioned. He signed on with an industrial gases company called Airco. It was near his home in New Jersey. It seemed like a good idea. Eight years later he was President of Airco. Then along came BOC (formerly the British Oxygen Company) under the direction of Sir Leslie Smith, and they tried to take over Airco. Giordano fought the war, but lost. However, Smith liked the way Giordano operated, and hired him. The idea was that in the boardroom Smith would be the boss. Outside, it would be Giordano. But the American said right from the beginning that he wasn't going to come to the UK on a British salary. So Smith – who had worked all his life for a British salary – convinced the

BOC board to pay Giordano by American standards. In 1979 that meant £479,000 – or more than twice what Smith was making.

'Being an American running a major British company', Giordano says, 'has sometimes meant walking a very fine line. BOC today is clearly less British. But not less British and more American. It's more international. A lot of people thought the first thing I'd do was turn BOC into an American company. And that was bound to be a source of resentment in this country.'

When he first walked into his office at Hammersmith, BOC share prices were running around 55p. Six years later they have been moving between £2.35 and £3.05. He helped give BOC a new image, and the City liked that. Undeniably, part of that new BOC image stems from the fact that Giordano is still the highest-salaried man in Britain, now earning £771,600 per year. Had he not been able to move BOC forward, he would have exposed himself to a great deal of personal criticism . . . you know, about how Americans come over here thinking they're worth so much money and then they don't perform. It would have been a very serious blow to anyone's ego. But by doing what the City had hoped he would, his gains should be substantial. And not simply monetary. Already, in January 1985, Leslie Smith retired and Dick Giordano became Chairman of the Board while still retaining his CEO title. Naturally he was always the frontrunner for the job. But because he's only 51, the City figures he also has one more major job move ahead. It may not come for several more years, but having taken his major risk while he was still in his 40s – an age when he might just be able to recover a loss – he's now begun to see the fruit ripen. The big risk having proved right, the next step could see him reap even bigger gains.

＊　　＊　　＊

In many cases, risk takers don't see themselves as taking risks. Giordano knew he was qualified for the job, had the background and intelligence to make it work, so where is the risk? It's the same attitude the Reichmann Brothers had when they bought New York City.

Albert, Paul and Ralph Reichmann are always portrayed as the great mystery men of Canadian business. They don't socialize the way businessmen are supposed to. They don't hand out photos and press kits every time a journalist calls. In fact, a good many journalists who write about them complain that they can't ever get beyond the extra-tight security that surrounds the Reichmanns. The problem turns out to be that many of those journalists are too lazy to try, or the Reichmanns know in advance they're not going to play straight. Getting an interview with Albert Reichmann was no more difficult than picking up the phone one Sunday afternoon in Montreal, and ringing his office in Toronto. He personally answered, and without any fuss a meeting was arranged. So much for mystery.

Albert Reichmann is President of Olympia and York (O&Y), the family's privately held company. His office is on the 32nd floor of the First Canadian Place building in the very heart of a newly built downtown Toronto. There is a round table near the corner windows of his office where guests are served coffee – he always drinks tea – and beyond the windows is Lake Ontario. What makes the vantage point unusual is that this is one of the few views of Toronto where you can't see most of the towering office blocks built, owned and managed by the Reichmanns.

They arrived in Canada via Tangiers during the '50s, refugees from Hitler's regime. Forced to flee Vienna in 1938 where Samuel Reichmann was a merchant, the family went to Morocco where they established themselves as bankers. In 1956 Reichmann père sent two of his sons – Paul and Ralph – to North America. They started in the carpet and floor tile business, and eventually became so

successful that the rest of the family followed. Samuel
Reichmann and Sons flourished. But by 1964 they
realized that the property boom was on its way. They set
up O&Y Investments, which was comprised of O&Y
Developments, O&Y Floor and Wall Tiles and a
company called Domus Engineering. And for the next 13
years they went about their business unobtrusively,
developing small properties, making a reputation for
themselves as solid players in the Canadian market.

In 1977 they took their risk and broke into the big
leagues. They went to New York and in one fell swoop
bought eight buildings in prime mid-Manhattan locations
for $320 million.

'We saw New York in the '70s as a city going broke,'
Albert says. 'But New York is the centre of the world.
We believed that would never change. So we went into
New York and found properties that were renting at
$9–$12 per square foot. We knew that if we could buy
good locations and good-quality buildings, it would pay
off when the demand came back. It has. New York City
real estate is now renting in the range of the high-$30s to
$50 a square foot.'

Canadian real estate developers going to New York
City is nothing new. They weren't the first, but they are
surely the most successful. Albert is now 56. His brother
Paul is 54. And the two of them jointly manage the real
estate side of their business. Ralph, 52, handles the
family's other interests. The three of them reportedly own
92 per cent of O&Y. The remainder is 'almost certainly'
divided amongst the rest of the clan. One says 'almost
certainly' because when you ask Albert he tells you in an
embarrassed and soft way, 'It's not important'.

Their over-zealous pursuit of privacy has, of course, led
to any number of stories about them. One Toronto real
estate analyst has literally made a career out of being the
Reichmann expert . . . even though he admits to never
having met them. But Albert says he doesn't care. He
feels that any information anyone truly needs about them

can be got. In other words, the serious players can find out what they need to know about other serious players. The rest of the world is irrelevant.

'We make all our own decisions,' Albert goes on, stressing that O&Y is more efficient for being private. Whatever he says, or whatever Paul says, or whatever Ralph says, goes. Some people consider Albert the financial expert and Paul the strategist, but Albert insists it's even simpler than that: 'We are brothers who share a common interest and a common trust. We work well together because we think alike. We always come satisfactorily to the same unanimous conclusion'.

They also always stand by their brothers' decisions. The tradition of the handshake is honoured, and their word is their bond. Much like the diamond business, when a price is decided and hands are shaken, that's the deal. For example, the Reichmanns built the Shell Center in Calgary, and the project was three-quarters finished before the final contracts were signed. 'When we make an agreement we proceed with it as if it were signed. Even if the economy has changed, we stick by our handshake. We were trained as bankers in Morocco and we learned that you have to live up to your word. The first time you don't honour a handshake is the last time anyone will shake hands with you.'

When they went into the New York market in 1977 they secured mortgages from a single lender covering a single building. But with large increases in recent years in both the size and price of commercial properties, the Reichmanns have discovered that their field of potential lenders is restricted to only the largest banks, insurance companies and pension funds. So a couple of years ago, when they were considering an $875 million refinancing of three New York office towers, they actually had to go to Solomon Brothers on Wall Street and ask them to put together a mortgage pool.

Their most major project to date is the development of Battery Park City on the tip of Lower Manhattan.

Encompassing the World Financial Center, the area will be a combination of space for business, retail shops, and residential houses for up to 25,000 people. Its projected opening is 1987, although it should be fully leased sometime in 1985.

But the Reichmanns have not confined their real estate empire simply to New York. Once their base was solidly established, giving them credibility as serious players, they methodically went about parlaying their success. It's the same old story of the first billion being the hardest. Today they own and/or operate real estate in all of North America's major cities, which ranks them as one of the top three North American real estate developers. They also own 100 per cent of English Property PLC in London.

One fair, albeit conservative, estimate of their total assets, is upwards of $13 billion Canadian.

*   *   *

With the Reichmanns it was a question of knowing what opportunity looks like, knowing what it sounds like when it knocks on the door, and knowing what to do about it after you open the door and find it staring you in the face.

Irvin Feld is one of the few people in America who ever managed it to the extent that millions of children will forever be grateful.

We met in the mid-1970s, in Monte Carlo, in the early days of the annual Monaco Circus Festival. Feld was there because he was a modern-day P. T. Barnum, the man *Time* Magazine once called 'the greatest showman on earth'.

I was there because some kids refuse to outgrow the circus.

A kind and gentle man, with a receding hairline, and glasses that he constantly readjusted even though they weren't falling off the end of his nose, Irvin Feld was raised in Maryland and once spent time as a young boy hawking snake oil at carnivals.

By the end of the 1930s, Feld went into snake oil merchandising on a much grander scale by opening a store in Washington DC. As racial prejudice was running rampant in the America of those days, and as Washington has long been a major black population centre, Feld was approached by the NAACP (the National Association for the Advancement of Colored People) with an offer to back him in a drugstore/soda fountain where blacks could congregate and feel at home. Feld argued that he wasn't a pharmacist but the NAACP said that was no problem. They said they would help him hire a black pharmacist. All they wanted was a store conducive to a primarily black trade. So Feld said fine.

Early on he saw a market amongst his black customers for music. Because in the States the customer is always right, he cleared out a corner of the store and opened his own record department. It was an immediate success.

'This was during the '50s', he explained over breakfast in Monaco that first time we met. 'I wanted to bring more customers in and I thought that the way to do it was to let them know what kind of music they'd find if they came inside. I put speakers onto the street in front of the shop and played loud music to attract business. Now every record store in the world does that. But nobody was doing it in those days. It worked so well that I decided perhaps the next step was to get the singer himself. I started booking acts. It helped to sell records.'

The drugstore became a record shop and the record shop became the Super Music City chain. Then he started his own recording label, Super Discs. Getting to know his artists, he quickly discovered that most of them were in need of personal management. He signed them up, then booked them on concert tours.

'I think the fancy word is impresario. I produced concerts with Paul Anka, Fats Domino, The Platters, Frankie Avalon, Fabian, Bill Haley and the Comets, and James Brown. When the Big Bopper, Buddy Holly and

Richie Vallens were killed in a plane crash, they were on a tour for me. I produced Errol Gardner's first recording. I bought Nina Simone her first gown for a concert she did for me. It was a very good education in show business.'

He booked his acts wherever he could, in whatever facility a city could provide. By the mid-1950s that meant large seating capacity arenas. Little did he know then just how good an education he was getting.

At the same time, the Ringling Brothers and Barnum and Bailey circus was in trouble. It was July 1956. The 'Greatest Show on Earth' was playing Pittsburgh, and when they struck the circus tent that summer, it could have been for the last time ever.

Feld heard the circus was closing and within 24 hours he managed to contact the man who owned and ran it, John Ringling North. Feld met with North and persuaded him that the circus should be promoted much the same way Feld was promoting rock and roll. North was willing to give it a try and within three months Feld had the circus back on the road. But now, instead of playing in a tent, Feld moved the circus indoors to those arenas where he had been booking concerts. By 1962 the world's largest circus was firmly on its feet again. Then John Ringling North moved to Europe. Before too long Feld grew tired of commuting to Switzerland or Spain to confer with North. He knew that changes were necessary to bring the show into the late-'60s and the '70s. And he wanted to make those changes. But North was of the old school where changes came slowly. The menagerie was de-emphasized because most cities had their own zoos. The sideshows of 700-pound ladies and two-headed tattooed giants were discontinued. The fire-eaters and knife-throwers were put to work in large production numbers. But still more had to be done.

'I woke up on the morning of January 1, 1967 and made myself a new year's resolution. I said, either I buy the circus or I quit.'

The next evening, Feld and North sat down to dinner

together in Switzerland. Feld said he wanted to buy the circus. North said it wasn't for sale. Feld refused to take no for an answer. North kept saying no. Feld said he couldn't continue running the circus unless he owned it. North said he wouldn't sell. And there they sat until 6 or 7 the next morning when one of them finally broke. It was North.

'He finally agreed to sell the circus to me for $7.5 million. But he had a long list of conditions for the sale. First of all, the sale had to be for cash. No credit. No time payments. Money in the bank on the closing day. Then he said I had to buy it as it was, which meant including a few law suits. Then he said he wanted to be able to change his mind right up to the last second.'

Feld came back to the States, put a group together who could finance the project, and offed to Europe with his backers. North was willing, until suddenly, out of the blue, one of the backers announced that the group would pay only $6.5 million. Feld was stunned. North was furious. The deal was ripped up and North threw them all out. It took months for Feld to convince North that he knew nothing of the counter-offer. When North finally said okay I believe you, he upped the price to $8 million. By September 1967 Feld had new backers. On 11 November, Feld, with his son Kenneth and daughter Karen, met John Ringling North in Rome's Colosseum and handed him a cheque for $8 million. For the first time in 96 years the 'Greatest Show on Earth' didn't belong to anyone named Barnum or Bailey or Ringling.

While North took his $8 million and bought gold at $32 an ounce, Feld set about creating a circus that would rival any spectacle in the world. He put together a second unit. Each unit tours for two years, alternating cities every year. Because each of them is a totally different show, every city gets a brand new circus every year. He sought young performers, lowering the average age from 46 to half that, assuring a future mine of talent. He created Clown College so that aspiring clowns could learn their trade. Then he filled his shows with clowns, more than five times as many as they used to have. He put acts in all three rings, and put performers in the air and along the tracks too. What had been a circus of 83 performers became a circus of more than 160. He even worked out a way to get children from the audience into the show.

In 1979, with his son Kenneth now his partner, Feld decided to branch out to other forms of show business. The Felds took over the management of two ice shows – The Ice Follies and Holiday on Ice – then combined the shows into the greatest ice extravaganza ever. Two years later, Feld Sr. hit upon the idea of using Walt Disney characters to bring plot and storylines into the ice shows. The result was 'Walt Disney's World on Ice', then 'Walt Disney's Great Ice Odyssey', and 'Walt Disney's Magic Kingdom on Ice'. At the same time they became associate producers of the smash-hit 'Barnum'. After conquering Broadway they aimed their sights towards Las Vegas and created 'Beyond Belief', a standing room only magic show at the Frontier Hotel that has broken all Las Vegas box office records since 1981.

Irvin Feld died in Florida in September 1984 at the age of 66. He came a long way from the snake oil and soda fountain days. But he knew what he was doing and he took his risks accordingly. The legacy he left is a world filled with children of all ages who will gasp and marvel for generations at just how wonderful life is when you're sitting in a seat at the circus.

✳   ✳   ✳

I must now admit to sins of omission.

As I've said, when I went looking for risk takers to portrait in this book, I made a series of totally personal choices. I wanted to write about people who fascinated me. The serious critic will quickly, and rightfully, say that all sorts of people are missing. Where for instance is Alan

Bond? He's the rather brash Australian who now owns Airship Industries but is better known as the man who footed the bill to win the 1984 America's Cup yachting trophy. Well, very frankly, he wouldn't talk to me. Bond is a strange guy. He was willing to risk millions backing the Australian entry in the race, but didn't particularly want to discuss exactly how much he spent or what he got in return for his money. The obvious dividend was an enormous amount of personal publicity. I assume that many businessmen watched Bond's team win, decided he was now a connected player on the international scene, and rang directory enquiries for his number. Let's face it, everyone loves a winner. I am sure that had he lost the Cup I wouldn't be alone in not thinking of him as important.

Robert Holmes à Court wouldn't talk to me either. At least Bond said no. Holmes à Court wasn't even polite enough to answer my requests. But then Holmes à Court has never been known on the British scene as being overly friendly, overly polite or overly accessible. Anyway, since taking over Lew Grade's Associated Communications Corp. he's had his hands full trying to sort out what could have been a less than wonderful purchase.

Alfred Taubman probably qualified to be in the book – he's the 'acceptable' American who won control of Sotheby's from the 'unacceptable' pair of Messrs Cogan and Swid. That battle was fiercely fought through the Office of Fair Trading, and Cogan and Swid made several million dollars in their losing battle. Had they won I would have felt remiss not having them here. As it happened, Taubman didn't seem anxious to participate and, after reading some things about him, I grew bored.

At one point the suggestion was raised, why not Lord Weinstock? He certainly has proven himself as one of the most successful businessmen ever in the UK. But this is not necessarily a book about business success. It's about personalities. Weinstock is very much an establishment figure. And somewhere in the back of my mind I think that, along with whatever other definitions I've put on risk takers, there is a sense of maverick about them. In a funny way, I see my kind of risk taker as a lonely hero. That eliminates the Weinstocks, Oppenheimers, Saatchis, Kings, and many more whose risks have indeed been as real as their successes. I do not wish to belittle them. But they didn't turn me on.

Conspicuous by their absence are women.

I would have been more than delighted to include as many female risk takers as I could find.

Come to think of it, that's precisely what I've done.

I looked. I rang people. I wrote letters. I searched the City. But I couldn't find a single lady wheeler–dealer to match up with the men in this book. Sure, there are women in business doing interesting things. And, yes, inroads have been made by women in some of those usual male-chauvinist worlds, such as investment banking. All too often, though, their presence around the Executive Suite is token. Begrudging concessions to changing times. Reluctant concessions by pin-striped, grey-templed men who believe that to give a little now will avoid having to give anything at all later on. Come on, they say, aren't we to be complimented for being liberated enough to consider a woman as our equal, to consider a woman capable of being able to keep up with us, to allow a woman use of the Executive loo, and anyway the girl has great legs!

I considered Laura and Bernard Ashley, but they operate these days out of Belgium and were spending time in the States. They were neither available nor, I felt, adventurous enough. They do what they do very well. I simply couldn't find that certain panache that makes some business men and women so very special. I thought of Debbie Moore and her success with Pineapple Dance Studios. But first there happens to be a very powerful Mr Debbie Moore behind her, and secondly they've run into a less than overwhelming reception by expanding into New York. She was a big star when Pineapple went onto the Unlisted Securities Market. Yet when they tried to finance their American adventure they had trouble finding backers. New York is a city filled with dance studios because Broadway is where dancers go to make their fortune. It's 'Chorus Line' and all that. I'm sorry but Debbie Moore didn't seem right. Then I thought about Jennifer d'Abo. There is no denying her success with the Ryman chain. Since buying it in 1981, she's turned it around from a loser to a profit maker. In December 1984 she told the *International Herald Tribune* that she is planning to open several new shops, will go for a Stock Exchange listing, wants to expand into Canada and is thinking about going to the United States. She said she is also seriously considering an investment in a bank that would cater to the specific needs of women. Maybe if she pulls it all off – and if anybody ever decides to write a book like this again – she'll be a prime candidate.

In the meantime, my sincerest apologies to the women of this world. Indeed, there are women in Britain successfully running companies. Unfortunately, none of them are doing their thing on a very grand scale. None of them have credibility on the international scene.

Even sadder is the fact of life that this is still a man's world and it isn't going to change very soon. A woman on her own, wheeling and dealing, simply can't get very far with the City. The City won't allow it. The City was built by men. The City is run by men. The City is a club exclusive to men. The only real chance she's got is if her husband – or any man – puts himself staunchly behind her. Then the response becomes, sure, we men in the City are liberated enough to let the lady take the glory but we'll do the real heavy business with her old man because men know how to talk to each other and anyway, if God wanted men and women to be equal, He would have given women a better understanding of Current Cost EPS.

Maybe television and the movies, and the bare-chested fantasies of after-shave ads have done some damage. We accept the sexy image of a man running around the globe, playing for millions. However there is something unflattering and aggressive in a woman doing the same thing. A man can be tough . . . that's a compliment. Being referred to as a 'tough bird' is not. Just because Britain has elected a woman as Prime Minister does not mean that British society has come very far. It was a fluke. The very fact that Parliament meets at hours designed to coincide with the business life of men in the City – conflicting quite blatantly with the hours a woman with children would have to keep – makes Mrs Thatcher the exception. The real test is not the first woman at Number 10. The real test is, how long will it be before there is a second woman at Number 10? Or, what would the City say to a woman as Governor of the Bank of England? Or as Chancellor of the Exchequer? Or on the Rota Committee at Lloyds? Or on the board of a major international British merchant bank? Even better, name one woman with some power around the City who isn't referred to by her male colleagues as 'a really bright girl'.

Too many men still feel women are meant to be pregnant, barefoot and in the kitchen.

I'm sorry to say that it will take a long time before a woman is ever permitted to find her way into a book like this.

1

Robert Sangster

It was a bank holiday weekend. Robert Sangster and his wife had house guests at their estate on the Isle of Man – ten friends who had come to play golf and go to the races. But that was also the weekend when Sangster had a horse running after a million-dollar prize in Chicago. So at 8 on Sunday morning, while his guests were still asleep, he flew from the Isle of Man to Heathrow to catch the 10 o'clock Concorde to New York. At JFK he changed for a flight to O'Hare and, at 1 p.m. local time, he was lunching with friends and watching the race. His horse finished second. At 7 that evening he boarded a Chicago to London flight, which brought him into Heathrow at dawn. He then got his plane back to the Isle of Man and arrived home in time for a morning's round of golf.

'I suppose I think of myself as a travelling salesman. Someone once wrote that I travel 100,000 miles a year. But I figure they're way off. If they said a million, that would be fine. I don't top them up. But I'm in an airplane five days a week, at least. Five or six days a week. Going to the Isle of Man and back. Going to America. Going to Australia.'

These days he reckons he's got globe-trotting down to a fine art. 'I only have a little bag. In the last four years I've stopped using the terminals. I only get there about a quarter of an hour before. I suppose if I miss the plane I miss it. You can take more of a risk if you travel lightly.

You can be in Los Angeles going to London and if Pan Am is delayed for three hours you can jump on TWA. But if you put yourself in the system, if you have luggage checked in, you're stuck. You know how you get those boarding passes with your ticket inside? The trick is to take the ticket out and put it inside the original ticket and then get on standby for somebody else.'

A few years ago, to make life easier getting to and from the Isle of Man, he bought a small charter airline, and one of those planes is always available for him when he needs it. He doesn't, however, fly himself. And the reason why might well sum up his philosophy of life: 'I tend to leave everything to professionals. I think I once said that the most important people in our lives were the pilot and the jockey. If you have a bad pilot, why have a jockey. Why train a horse if the jockey's no good. I tend to stick to the best jockeys.'

And to the best of everything else as well.

Robert Sangster is the kind of guy who believes that you can become the best when you're surrounded by the best. So he's always made a point of surrounding himself with the best horses and the best trainers and the best jockeys and the best breeders and the best vets and the best stable boys. In just about a dozen years he too has become the best. He is to the thoroughbred racing business what DeBeers is to diamonds – what Sinatra is to saloon singing. There is an enormous amount of jealousy surrounding his success. He is disliked by people who have never met him and frequently written about and misquoted by journalists who have never interviewed him. But he is revered by the people who work with him and know how skilfully he's managed his affairs. He is slightly stocky at about 5' 8", an avid golfer, and – in spite of the gossip columnists' opinions – naturally shy.

His father owned and ran Vernon Pools – of football fame, so Sangster grew up never having to worry about his next meal, more comfortable than most, working at Vernon until 1973 when he persuaded his father that the company should go public. And it was that 'mistake' that brought him into the horse business.

'I was inheriting the company then. I had a trust and when I was 30 I inherited a third. When I was 35 I inherited a third. When I was 40 I inherited a third. So now I'm 38. I owe the bank for inheriting share certificates, Vernon's paper, and I'm now owing capital gains tax of something like £4 million–£5 million. We'd had Labour governments – Wilson – and we've just got Heath in – you know, the three-day week – and I could see that when I hit 40 and inherited the third tranche, I'd be owing the bank £8 million plus. I'd own the shares and might be even worse. So I persuaded my old man to go public.'

Then Heath called an election. It was set for the very day Vernon was to go public. Sangster then had to spend a year in the City trying to do a reverse take-over. He tried to get together with Corals Bookmakers. When that didn't work after six months he went to Sears Group and Charley Clore. He had chats with the Rank Organization, and he had chats with Hanson Trust. The market was falling. And he was getting nearer to 40. He finally put a deal together with Ladbrokes and Cyril Stein which would have made him the largest shareholder in Ladbrokes. But when he went up to Liverpool and said, right, it's done now, and we're getting so much cash, we own this and that, and I'll be able to stay in England and pay off the capital gains tax, his father said he didn't want to know about Ladbrokes.

'So I said, well, it's now March and I've got three weeks to get out of the country. So I left and went down to Spain, to Marbella, it was my year out. And I thought about a business because I wasn't going to play golf with [Sean] Connery all my life. Then I went to Australia, trying to get football pools in there and I saw the terrific market potential for horse racing. I'm very glad I didn't stay in the country because I wouldn't be in the horse business. I'd probably be slogging away in Vernon Pools trying to get that going.'

To over-simplify, Sangster's business comes in two parts. There are the races; and there is bloodstock. You buy bloodstock to win races. When you win races you breed for bloodstock.

'You've got to win races. It's no good having the blood if you're not winning. You've got to be successful. People soon start knocking you if you're not successful. It's a slippery slope. And yet to be successful, as you know, in any walk of life, you're unpopular to a certain degree through jealousy. But to make the business work, you've got to win the races.'

The idea is to come up with a horse like Northern Dancer who has done it all. Unfortunately, Sangster says, it's not one of his horses. But Northern Dancer is the perfect example of how money is made with a horse. Bred in Canada, by Nearctic (son of Nearco) and out of Natalma (daughter of Native Dancer), he won the 1964 Kentucky Derby in record time, and followed that with a win in the Preakness. Although he lost the Triple Crown that year by failing to go the distance in the Belmont Stakes (Quadrangle beat him), he was put out to stud, having been syndicated at the then spectacular sum of $2.4 million. He proved to be the ultimate investment in bloodstock, being named UK Champion Sire in 1970 and again in 1977 – an unheard of feat for a foreign horse that had never stood in the UK. However, he was responsible for two Derby winners – Nijinski and The Minstrel – and also fathered Try My Best. These days Northern Dancer stands at the Winfield Farm in Kentucky where, 21 years after his racing career ended, the market in him continues to go up. Last year Prince Abdullah of Saudi Arabia was willing to pay $1.2 million for a share of a horse who is already past the age when most normal stallions start dropping back.

Northern Dancer is, of course, the exception. And breeding, Sangster admits, is not necessarily a sure thing: 'Seattle Slew and Spectacular Bid were Kentucky Derby winners and they were both bought for less than $50,000.

So yes, you do get the odd freak. But it isn't easy. And, no, breeding isn't a guarantee but it goes a hell of a long way towards it. Each year we try to get a quarter of Northern Dancer's crop to race for us. Well, statistically, he gets 22 per cent stakes winners to foals. So if you've got a quarter of his crop you know you're cutting the risks, you're eliminating a lot of errors. Percentagewise you're going to come up with four or five Northern Dancer stakes winners.'

*　　*　　*

His first horse was a gelding who won five races.

He figured he had the game knocked.

But then his next horse didn't win any races. In fact, he didn't see the winner's circle again for nearly two years. 'The first year I started a stud, before I left England, I lost £800,000. I remember seeing the figures and thinking, crikey, what the hell am I up to now. But I knew what I was doing. Obviously getting good horses has helped enormously. But it's always been very hard to explain the business to accountants and bank managers. Say you start with 20 horses and come up with two superstars, four very good horses, six fair horses that win an odd race, and ten bums that can't get out of their own way. Well then it's very easy to make a profit. Sell your two best and keep your worst. What I've done all the time is to sell my worst, those ten that couldn't get out of their own way. Of course that means your books sometimes show a loss. Say you average £10,000 a horse and you bought 20. That's £200,000. But your ten bottom ones could be worth only £2000 each. So by selling them you would be taking losses on paper. But your two top ones, which you keep, could be worth £200,000. It was always a struggle to explain that.'

He doesn't necessarily have to bother with such explanations any more because accountants and bank managers know very well who he is. They know that he owns more than 1000 horses. 'I got that figure off a computer. But they're having foals every day so the figure changes. If I say I haven't got a clue I sound so dreadful. You sound so blasé if you say you don't know. But honestly, I've never totalled them up. I really don't know.' Nor does he know what he's actually worth. One estimate tossed around the City is a billion pounds. When you mention that to him, he ponders it carefully for a few minutes. And instead of saying, 'A billion pounds? Are you crazy?' He shakes his head and says, 'A billion pounds? No. I think it's too high. But it's hard to say.'

In theory he's worth whatever his horses and the land under them are worth. But the racing game is based on the concept that winners are where the money is. And, to come up with a winner that's worth a fortune, you might have to begin by investing a fortune. Even then there are no certainties. Where racing and bloodstock are concerned, it's especially easy to throw good money after bad. Although, if you can get just one great horse, you can pay for it all. He proved that with a horse he bought in the States for under $250,000 called The Minstrel. 'We were having a bad year. We went to America in 1975 to buy yearlings over there, and say, just take a figure out of the air, I invested a million dollars. That's in July. In July 1976, they're just babies, two-year-olds and they haven't run. So you've got to invest another million on yearlings again before you've seen how your wine has matured. Then in '77 we came up with what we thought was a good colt and a good filly, The Minstrel and Cunara. She was a 6–4 favourite first time out and finished third. First time out The Minstrel finished third. Then we went to Ireland for the Irish 2000 and we got stuffed. The Minstrel was beaten there. The Derby was in June and we had the yearling sales coming up again in July and it looked as though we'd have to invest another one or two million. That's when The Minstrel won the Derby. That horse pulled the Derby off, and we recouped everything we spent. That one horse. But it's very lucky to win a Derby.'

Today The Minstrel stands at about $400,000 a service and earns $16 million a year.

Race horses are shared out in fortieths. Although, as broodmares can produce only one foal a year, Sangster keeps them down to three or four partners to avoid the complications that can arise when 40 partners each want to go with a different stallion. Much like shares in mines or oil wells, horse flesh is a very active commodity, traded worldwide. For the past four years, he says he's been buying horses at the average rate of about $9 million per year. In 1979–80, Sangster bought two-thirds of a dam from E. P. Taylor in the States for about $800,000. The dam was bred with Taylor's Northern Dancer and the result was El Gran Senor. In 1984 he won the Irish 2000 and everything else, and was unbeaten going into the Derby. He lost there by a short head. Still, the horse is today worth $40–$60 million because he is the likely heir to his father's throne. It was much the same story with a mare called Fairy Bridge – an unbeaten champion in Ireland. Sangster paid under $100,000 for her. He bred her to produce Sadler's Wells who, after winning the Irish 2000 Eclipse and the Irish Derby, was valued at $28 million – or $600,000 a share.

This part of the business is called syndication. 'Nearly all my colts are syndicated before they run, in that Stavros Niarchos has now come in with us. All the Irish horses across the board are owned by myself, Stavros Niarchos, the great trainer Vincent O'Brien, Danny Schwartz from Palm Springs, and John Magnier, an Irishman who runs a stud. We own every horse in the training yard between us. But not necessarily the same percentages of each horse. In Australia it's different. I'm in with people like the head of Pioneer Concrete in Sydney. In New Zealand I'm in with different partners. In South Africa I own 50 per cent with the leading owner there, a fellow called Graham Beck who's one of the biggest industrialists in South Africa. What they require of me is the expertise and general running around. They know I'm not going to be losing money so they back a proven horse really. All I do is back the proven horse with the proven trainer.'

If only it was so easy for just anybody. But, with such heavy money at stake, the days of racing simply for the fun of it are long gone. 'I get fun out of racing, but there isn't a lot of room for mistakes. Between the wars, or after the war, before crippling taxation hit the big racing empires, then you had the Dukes of Norfolk, Rosebury, Derby, and they all had terrific stables. They probably had 30–40 horses and they had a lot of fun no matter what the prize money was. Of course taxation crippled them. Today perhaps they could only afford to keep one or two horses in training out of earned income. It all costs so much. It's a very expensive luxury.'

It is, however, becoming a relatively popular alternative investment. 'You know, the most unsuccessful guy in racing is the one who has been a successful businessman. The entrepreneur who's got to the age of 70, and can't play golf any more, and can't play tennis any more, so he says let me buy myself some horses. He then proceeds to tell the trainer where to run and who's to ride them. And the worst enemy of a trainer is the owner's best friend. Because the owner has probably promised that his horse will win at Aquaduct or Ascot. When it gets beaten it's never his fault because he's a successful businessman.'

On the other hand there are syndicates open to anyone with the cash to buy a share. Syndication has grown popular in the States, especially along Wall Street. But most syndicates lose money and Sangster tends to regard such schemes as a bit of a gamble. 'It's a very special field. I'll give you an example. If we lose a race, I talk with the trainers and we try to analyse what went wrong. I might say, remember when a similar thing happened with a horse and we put a tongue strap on him and tied its tongue down and maybe that will work. By seeing so many races around the world, by travelling, one talks to all the leading trainers and learns the business. So the success of a syndicate depends on who's managing the syndicate. They've really got to know what they're doing otherwise you can get your fingers burnt.'

To keep from getting his own fingers burnt, the travelling salesman Sangster has divided his world into specific units. There is Europe (Germany, Italy, France, Ireland, and England), America, only Venezuela in South America, South Africa, Australia, and New Zealand. 'You've got to have your sales outlets. By having horses in training in various places like South Africa and New Zealand, then you know, this horse will suit so and so in Australia. That's why I have to travel. To meet the stud masters. To get to know people. By travelling around somebody might tap you on the shoulders and say our stallion is getting to 18, have you anything in the pipeline coming up. I say, I've got just the one for you, or I ask what kind of blood are you looking for? Are you looking for Northern Dancer blood? Or the Seattle Slew? Whatever. I can then produce the article. Maybe they can't afford El Gran Senor so I say, well, this one down the line in training met with an accident but he was a bloody good horse. And I can categorically assure you – because you're going to see me again and again – that he was a very good horse on the gallops but he broke down and never hit a race course. So therefore we'll take $100,000 for him. You've got to know where your market is.'

You've also got to know what the market will bear. 'You have to know what fits where. The top price an Australian stud could pay is about $4–$5 million for a top stallion, because they can't market their yearlings. They haven't got the entrepreneurial buyers for their yearlings so they can only import a $5 million horse. Whereas the Americans, at the moment, are up to I think $60 million. I mean, we were bid $60 million for El Gran Senor before the Derby. Seattle Slew is probably worth $80–$100 million for stud purposes. In Ireland we can do a horse for about $30 million. South Africa is improving. They bought a horse from us for $3 million.'

Before that, you've got to be able to come up with the goods. In England, Newmarket is the major market. But the centre of the bloodstock world is the Blue Grass state of Kentucky. 'Their sales are unreal. I remember one night when they sold something like 60 or 70 yearlings and they averaged over $800,000 a head. I said to my father, who is 84, you could buy four main Ford motor agencies in the North of England for one yearling and you know you'd have a successful production line. Or you could buy a chain of greengrocer stores for the price of one yearling. To average over $800,000 that evening – it's frightening really.'

And once you've got the goods, you've got to know what to do with them. 'Take some yearlings we buy in Kentucky. Say they cost $1 million. For that you'd get a very good-looking horse, out of a stakes winning mare by say, Seattle Slew, Northern Dancer, Mr Perspector, Alidar, one of the top stallions. Therefore they have the best handling from the minute they're bought. We send our Irish lads over to Kentucky immediately to look after the horses. They'll be flown back in a plane together so they're not next to other people's horses for disease and handling. They'll be broken in at our own stallion station, which looks after over 1000 mares from February through July. The ten or so yearlings which are bought come back in August. They have probably the most sympathetic upbringing of any yearlings in the world. Then they go to Vincent O'Brien. They're classed either 1st, 2nd, 3rd or 4th division. It's easy to sell the top ones – your El Gran Senors – people come to you for those. But you can't neglect the sort of horse that maybe is 15th best horse in Ireland, has won a Group 3, is a stakes winner with a beautiful pedigree. After all, you've got a million dollars invested in him, or maybe more with all the costs.'

The making of a commodity market in horse flesh is a fact of life that does not always please everyone in the business. And here Sangster is often criticized. He's accused of controlling the top end of the stallion market, much as the Hunts once tried to do with silver. Sangster's critics say he helped force the little guys out of the business by encouraging the Arabs to come in. He answers that with, 'I courted them because they had money to spend and I believed that an influx of money would stimulate the markets. It was money that could have gone into the theatre business or into making films. Instead it's come into the horse business and I think it's a good thing. Seven, eight, ten years ago when I first went to America, you didn't get many English trainers there. Now Concorde's jammed with English trainers. By that money coming into the racing industry, everyone's benefited. From the stable lads to the jockeys. Listen, jockey retainers are probably ten times higher than they were five years ago because the Arabs have made the business so much more competitive.'

His critics retort that, as long as only he and the Arabs can afford the best horses, they're going to win the best races and make the best money. But in a very real sense the making of a worldwide market was an idea whose time had come. Sangster might have been one factor. But jets and communication were decidedly another.

'We've all become much more informed about what everyone else is doing. We fly American vets in to do most of our major work. We've got American jockeys, like Steve Cauthen. I had the Australian champion Brent Thompson in Europe as well this year. Say 10–12–13–14 years ago there were probably only two or three breeders who went from Europe to America. We knew probably the top 10 stallions there. The Americans knew probably one of ours. Now I should think 12–13 years later we know the top 200 in America and they know our top 100. It has become a world business rather than a little insular business. I'm sure Lord Rosebury would never ever have dreamt of importing an American jockey or using American stallions. You know there's an awful lot of jingoism talked about wonderful British stallions, but to keep a stallion in England, in this day and age . . . I mean, as of today, your air fare is costing $5000. To go to Northern Dancer now, to get a nomination, just to get your mare covered, costs nearly $1 million. So what's a $5000 air fare?'

Simply by virtue of being the biggest in the business, Sangster would have quite naturally had an influence on that business. But he's also become one of racing's more knowledgeable spokesmen, and there's no denying that he has put his money where his mouth is. 'Because people are more informed, stallions coming to America are being picked out of South Africa and Australia. I've probably helped that. Or pushed it. Ten years ago, I took eight or nine fillies to race in Florida. Our season ends in October, November, and theirs was just beginning. We learned an awful lot even though we couldn't get on the course because it was trial and error adapting them to the climatical change. If you can run them five days from when they arrive in America, they'll run terrifically well. Then they'll lose their form. But we were I think the first to take a big team. Nowadays there are probably something like 200 horses that come from Europe to race in America. And every day you open the trade magazines, the *Blood Horse* or *Thoroughbred Record*, there's a horse that used to race here in Europe that is now in America. I suppose that's a major contribution, that Americans come over here and buy our race horses off the course. There's a great interchange of horses.'

There is, too, these days a great interchange of jockeys. In 1979 Sangster helped convince the then 19-year-old Steve Cauthen to come to England. Cauthen had been riding steadily in the States for two-and-a-half years. In his first full year on the American tracks he had 487 winners and had won $6 million in prize money. But Cauthen had got to the point where he himself felt burnt-out. His first year in England he brought in a mere 52 winners. His second, 61. In all it took him five years to win the English jockey's title – the first American to do it since 1913. Sangster has always believed that foreign jockeys mature in Europe, so, while Steve Cauthen was riding more than 100 winners in 1984, Sangster picked up the phone and rang Australia. 'I brought the Australian champion Brent Thompson to England to race here because I felt Thompson needed a serious challenge to help him improve on what was already a winning career. He had 30 winners. But then he's gone back to Australia never having been abroad before, he's only 25, and the confidence he'll have when he gets back . . . well, jockey-ship is confidence. If he thinks he's like Muhammad Ali he'll get on those horses and have the confidence of Muhammad Ali. When he was here he rode in France, Germany, I sent him all over the place just to get the experience. You might leave Australia as the champion jockey but you come back as a real man.'

As jockeys in England are under contract – it's not true of jockeys in America – Sangster worked out a deal with Thompson that, at least on the surface, appeared to be risky for Sangster. But he thought of it as an investment, and knew precisely what he wanted in return. 'I paid him a retainer of £10,000, plus all air fares, plus accommodation, plus a car. On top of that he gets the usual 10 per cent of winners, and jockey's fees for riding. Believe me, the risk for me was minimal. He rode 30 winners. We probably covered the whole cost of the exercise in those 30 winners. But that's not the point. Even if he hadn't had any winners, it still would have broadened his outlook. The risk to me was minimal because he'll be a better jockey when he races for me in Australia. After this year in Europe he won't get beaten in a tight finish.'

* * *

Sangster's office on the Isle of Man is fully computerized and he keeps in touch with his permanent staff of four no matter where he is. All you have to do is ask, at any time during the day, and he'll tell you: four winners yesterday, three horses going this afternoon, five tomorrow, had six on Saturday, had five winners last Saturday and three on Friday.

He personally attends race meetings whenever he can – usually three or four days a week. Normally he goes to Phoenix Park in Ireland every Saturday (he happens to be an owner of the track), and then to France for races there on Sunday. Nicely enough, he says when he's at a track he likes to have a flutter. 'I enjoy having a bet. But I wouldn't look at the paper. If I'm at a race meeting, sure, I'll participate. I'm really not a heavy better. It's just for fun. Probably a thousand dollars in Australia, something like that. In England you can't possibly win because the take is about 23 per cent, where in Australia it's only about 8 per cent so you've got a chance of winning. The bookmakers here take 23 per cent, including tax, which is roughly 10 per cent.'

With that exception, he feels that racing in the UK is very well conducted. 'We have the best horses in the world now racing here, purely because of the Arab influence. Of the top hundred yearlings sold in the world, most of those are sold in America. But probably 90 per cent are racing in Europe now, which is something new in the last three to four years. And what you're finding now is that your Kentucky Derby winners or Preakness winners are not the best bred because, apart from the private studs, most of the best animals come in through the sale ring. The best of the American horses are being bought by the Arabs or ourselves to race over here. So you're getting a very high competitive standard. I suppose it's like boxers. I mean if you have all the best coloured fighters from Detroit fighting in Europe then the standard will be much higher here, whereas the competition in America is so strong, our white hope, some British heavyweight, goes over and gets his name written on the soles of his feet.'

He is also partial to Irish racing. 'I suppose they're natural horsemen. They're natural tinkers. They're cer-

tainly the best judges. And like New Zealand, they have
the best climate. They also have a lot of good tax
concessions. I don't think there's any tax on a stallion
nomination in Ireland. I am, by the way, apart from what
a lot of people say about me being a tax exile, an English
company paying English corporation tax. It suits me
because I work under the double taxation agreements
with Australia and America, and if I had an Isle of Man
company there's no double taxation agreement. So, if you
pay English corporation tax you don't come under the
Australian umbrella, or the American umbrella.'

Yet there are some changes he'd like to see in UK
racing. And they begin with the prize money.

'Most of the time winnings simply go back to the
horses, to cover their expenses. Anyway, in America it's a
much more major factor than it is in Europe. You get
million-dollar races there. You get 2000-guinea races here.
In America, with the paramutual system, the prize money
is better. I win much more pro rata in America than I do
here. Although in America I miss the bookmakers. I like
their noise. I like the colour they add to racing. But the
problem here is that the money you bet with the
bookmakers doesn't come back into racing. Australia has
the best system in the world. They have bookmakers on
the course, with their satchel and just one pencil, and they
have the Tote off course in the cities. You can't bet with a
bookmaker in the cities. So they funnel all that money
through the Tote back to racing. And their prize money
makes ours laughable. I mean, second prize in the
Melbourne Cup is worth more than our Ascot Gold Cup,
which is the feature race at Royal Ascot. We won
something like £43,000 for winning it, whereas to be
second in the Melbourne Cup you get $100,000, which is
£50,000–£60,000.'

In other words, he wouldn't mind seeing some changes
here. 'The government has now got a tax of 10 per cent
and they'll never let it go. No government in England will
ever say, we'll give 5 per cent back to racing. But look at

Australia. Their tax is 3 per cent. The government gets
1½ per cent. And racing gets 1½ per cent. I don't think
any government, Conservative or Labour, will ever say,
okay, we'll reduce the tax in England to 4 per cent and
give racing 2 per cent. But what they don't realize is the
law of diminishing returns. In Australia the turnover per
head is so much greater that probably they get more for
their 1½ per cent than the British government gets from
their 10 per cent. There are many more winners that
reinvest in Australia. Everyone bets there. And you only
have to be half-smart to win in Australia. If you're getting
93 per cent return, if they're only taking 7 per cent,
you're betting against the pin-prickers who pick the horse
with a pin. If you know a little bit more you tend to win
money. Here you're betting against 23 per cent. You're
only getting 77 per cent back. It's very hard to win any
money. You've got to treat betting here as a bit of fun. If
I could change anything I'd change the betting format.
But people a lot more able than I have tried and you're
just banging your head against the brick wall.'

He'd also change the laws to allow racing on Sundays.
'We're trying to get it in Ireland, at Phoenix Park. We
actually came very close to getting it and will probably
get it next year. Funnily enough it's not the church who is
fighting it. I've always asked that, but I suppose France is
the biggest Catholic country and they race on Sundays.
Ireland would be a natural. And it would be very good
for England.'

Sangster's business is, by the way, built entirely around
thoroughbreds. He doesn't have jumpers, and gives some
sound economic reasons for that. 'It all gets down to the
end product. With jumpers you're talking about horses
that sell for £30,000. A really top jumper might go for
£50,000. Well, there's a member of the jockey club called
Brian Jenks. We both went in to racing in the late '60s.
We both spent say £150,000–£200,000. He bought 15
jumping horses and I bought 15 brood mares. Three years
later he was the leading jump owner with about £110,000

in prize money. Four years later all of those horses were in fields. Too old to race. There's no residual value. They're all geldings. Whereas my 15 fillies were all potential broodmares. Okay, they weren't all 15 good ones, but there were probably five really top broodmares. The investment is in the flats. The jumpers, you have the terrific satisfaction of winning the top races at Cheltenham, which is the big jump festival. He lived near Cheltenham and got a terrific thrill out of it. Nowadays he hardly has a horse in training. But he achieved his ambition in becoming the leading national hunt owner. And had a lot of fun doing it. But then to keep pumping money into the jumping business, you've got to have a bottomless pit.'

So the investment is in bloodstock and, of course, land. He has stables in Australia, and breeding farms in the US. There are also horse farms in France, England, and Ireland. But his most ambitious land investment is yet to be completed. He is in the midst of creating the ultimate horse training facility at Manton, a small village sitting quietly in the hills of Wiltshire. It's a 2,330 acre estate that will 'take to the turf' in 1986. With seven different gallops, the largest thoroughbred training facility in Britain will cost £10 million, and is being financed by Sangster alone – 'Just me and my bank manager.'

Besides those, he says he doesn't really have any other business interests. Although that doesn't mean he hasn't been thinking about some: 'I've been seeing bankers with a view towards diversification into other areas, mainly through the Vernon side. I think if one sold 49 per cent of the Vernon organization, which is probably valued at £35–£40 million, one would keep 51 per cent. We would probably go Unlisted Securities. I wouldn't mind having a crack at that. Then we'd use that money to build the Vernon group up and maybe try to buy successful small businesses with good management.'

He feels that one of the problems at Vernon is that he's neglected it for ten years. And he now thinks the time has come when he has to pay more attention to it.

'My father is 84. The managing director is 75. The chief accountant is 75. Well, you can't just start head hunting for a business in Liverpool, which is dead compared to London. I've got three boys, two are working in the City now, and this is the course I'd like to take to build the backside of a business. Maybe we'll give my oldest son another three years of experience stockbroking in the City and then say, right, I'll be watching you but this is what I think you should do. There's a lot of growth in the City. Some of those small companies are just about to mushroom.'

Under his own father there have been diversifications at Vernon. Much of Sangster's horse business is done through a Vernon subsidiary. Vernon also took lotteries overseas – one to New York State, although they were 'nationalized' there. 'The state took it over in 1984 because it was so successful. We had been doing it six years. What you need are the big prizes to make a lottery successful, and as soon as we got them in New York, they grabbed it. We've got another lottery in Sydney. We're in partnership with Rupert Murdoch and Kerry Packer. We do the handling of it and they do the TV and radio. We've also done some diversification in England into printing and Ford agencies. But that's been fairly static as an investment because the horse business has taken up most of the capital and the borrowings from the bank. I really must start devoting more time to Vernon. Over the past few years it's been only once a fortnight. Now it will be more.'

But what about his racing interests? 'I might still run those,' he says . . . then thinks for a moment about being stuck in an office in Liverpool instead of hanging out at paddocks in Sydney. And suddenly the travelling salesman says with more conviction: 'They'd keep going.'

2

David Thieme

As far as David Thieme was concerned, he was simply inviting a few friends to dinner.

Nine hundred friends.

Every February in London, just before the Institute of Petroleum held their annual banquet, Thieme would host a black-tie affair at the Royal Albert Hall. And the 1981 event was probably the best ever. He decorated the place with the colours of his Essex Overseas Petroleum Corporation – blue, red and silver. He hired Roger Verge to cook the meal (he's the three-star owner/chef of the Moulin de Mougins near Cannes in the south of France), while the Roux Brothers made the dessert. Because Thieme and Essex were, in those days, sponsoring Colin Chapman's Lotus racing team through the Formula One Grand Prix circuit, he figured it was only natural that the evening's door prize should be a Lotus Essex Turbo Esprit – about £22,000 worth of automobile. And then, just to make the evening complete, he hired Ray Charles to sing.

Less than six weeks later David Thieme was arrested in the boardroom of the Crédit Suisse Bank in Zurich. The charges were fraud and embezzlement of $4.5 million. On top of that, the bank said Thieme and Essex owed them another $40 million. Thieme said the charges were false and malicious. And he aimed to prove them wrong.

✻   ✻   ✻

David Charles Thieme was born in 1941, in Minneapolis, Minnesota, but he was raised in New York. His grandparents had come to the States from Heidelberg, Germany, just before the turn of the century. His father was an aeronautical engineer and at one point worked on the CG-4A and CG-13 gliders used during World War II. Thieme himself trained as an industrial designer. During the '60s he glossed and glittered trade shows for Mercedes, and jet-interiors for the Lear Corporation. 'I started my own design firm when I was 19. You don't need much to do that. One drawing board, one chair, one room, two pencils and no money.'

He made his first fortune before he was 30.

'I was sitting in a saloon in Dallas, Texas. After you spend any amount of time in Texas you can't help but smell oil everywhere. A friend told me about an opportunity, about a bunch of cowboys who drove pick-up trucks and who were looking for some backing in a small operation. They had a well they wanted to drill. Now you know what the chances are that anything like that actually works. Most of the time you kiss your money goodbye. Well, I sank $25,000 into this and believe it or not, they hit. It was dumb, blind luck. Of course it was fun for a gringo, but I knew I had been lucky once and that's where the fun ended. I sold out for more than my original $25,000. Considerably more. And then I went back to my design business.'

But the oil bug had bitten.

A tall, thin man, Thieme sports a goatee, square sunglasses and clothes in dark midnight blue. At first glance he appears mysterious. But he's an obsessively polite man whose only visible passions are music, motor racing and the oil business. His address is a hotel suite in Monte Carlo. A table is always waiting for him in the bar of the Hotel de Paris. If peroxide blondes ever interested him, he certainly doesn't show them off. In fact, his lady friends tend to be very unflashy. They're generally quiet women who stay with him for long periods of time and have not come from the international jet-set.

'It was in August 1973 when I sold my design firm because I wanted to take a leap into the commercial end of the oil business. I compiled whatever I could on the so-called spot market, because I wanted to know everything there was to know before sinking my money into it. Less than two months later war broke out in the Middle East. The fertilizer hit the windmill. There wasn't anything else to do but jump on a plane and go to Arabia. When you don't know anything about the oil business, the only way to learn is to get down on your knees and crawl around until you find out what you can. It doesn't take long though because it happens to be a simple business.'

What he learned about this 'simple business' was how to operate an independent oil company. He called it Essex Overseas Petroleum – although he never bothered to give himself a title. The scope of his business was, and is, the transportation, refining and marketing of petroleum products with leased shipping and refining capacity. In other words, he sits in his office in Monte Carlo with computers and telephones buying crude at the lowest possible rate and either selling it to someone else, or refining it himself and then selling the refined product to someone else. His game is one of percentages. He tries to get a small percentage somewhere in the middle of what amounts to a colossal sum. A mere half per cent of 2 million barrels at \$26 a barrel comes to \$520,000.

In the beginning his deals were modest. Most of them were nothing more than putting the supplier in contact with the receiver. As he grew more confident, he started financing his own deals, mostly joint ventures with first and second level independents. What eventually came about was an Essex network of a dozen or so trading companies, scattered around the world – although even in the best of times he never employed more than three dozen people.

In 1976 business was good and he began what he hoped would be a long-term relationship with the head office of the Crédit Suisse Bank, at 8 Paradeplatz, Zurich. He was making money, and so were they. He invited them to his parties. He got them reserved seats at the Grand Prix races. They saw him making money . . . a lot of money. But they also saw him spending money . . . a lot of money.

'Some people guessed I shelled out as much as $1.5 million for the party in 1981 at the Royal Albert Hall. And I've heard people tell me that the Lotus team must have cost me as much as $15 million a year. Frankly, I hope it looked like it cost me that much. I wanted it all to look expensive. But in all honesty, without saying how much it did cost, it was nowhere near that kind of money.'

As far as he was concerned, the parties and the racing cars were just his way of advertising to the people with whom he was doing business. 'If I took them out to dinner twice a year, separately, it would have cost me a fortune and taken up all my time. So I simply invited everyone to dinner on the same night. Look at it this way. If Proctor and Gamble could get all of the housewives who buy their soap together under one roof, they wouldn't need to advertise on television. As for the car races, I've always said that in Formula One only two things can happen. You can spend money and you can lose races. But the name Essex was everywhere.'

1979 was the year kings were made in the oil business. But Thieme insists he wasn't a king. At best he admits to having become a demi-baron. 'Oil is the last frontier. After being in the oil business, there can be no more fun anywhere else. Oil is like nothing else in the world. It's a game where you get in fast and get out fast. Fortunes are made on volume and velocity. But it's an extremely volatile game because fortunes are lost that way too. The market can reverse itself instantly with one gunshot or a few politically harsh words. To operate in the oil business you need chutzpah and luck and raw nerves steadied with Jack Daniels.'

Then came 1980. 'It was a tough year.'

And that was followed by 1981. 'That year was almost suicidal. It made the Bubonic plague look mild.'

To understand what happened, you've got to get deeper into the nature of the oil business – much deeper than Thieme's explanation, of it being 'a simple business'. On paper it is. In reality it is anything but.

The major oil companies – the Exxons, BPs, Shells and Mobils of this world – control 80–85 per cent of the business. The rest is divided among 50–60 independents – except that the top 25 independents divide up nearly 15 per cent of the market, leaving very little room for anyone else. Depending on consumption levels, those independents are fiercely vying for anywhere from 1 to 3 million barrels a day. The oil-producing nations, under the OPEC umbrella, set an official price. But everything is open to negotiation. Almost every standing contract or term-supply can come under discussion, revision or renegotiation if one of the partners smells a better deal somewhere else. When prices drop, as they did in 1980 and have continued to do with the oil glut, some companies find themselves sitting on oil for which there is suddenly no market at their committed price. It's known as a 'distressed cargo'. Some company chief goes to bed at night thinking he's made money but when he wakes up the next morning he finds that the price has dropped and he's suddenly facing a huge loss. It happens just that quickly. At the same time, there's some independent trader, like Thieme, willing to pick up that cargo. While it's impossible to say how much distressed cargo there is in the world at any given period, suffice it to say that in a soft market there are millions of barrels available for the trader who knows how to buy them and where to unload them. For the shrewd operator, they say, it's like hunting goldfish with a machine gun. The cargo itself can change hands any number of times between producer and eventual buyer, with prices going up or down at every step. If the last guy who gets it or delivers it is to make

money, he's got to have sold it or optioned it before he
ever sees it. In a slow slide of prices, or even in a slow
climb of prices, everyone involved with the cargo is very
careful. But in a rapid chute or a ferocious climb (which is
what 1979 was all about) there is big money to be made.
The trick is to be short in a slide and long in a climb. If
you are, you get rich quick. If you're not, you go bust
even quicker.

The prices for refined petroleum products are determined minute by minute in five major world markets:
Rotterdam, Houston, New York, Singapore and Tokyo.
They're the spot markets. In good years the price of a
barrel's worth of refined products was more than the cost
of a barrel of crude plus the various premiums the Arab
producers sometimes taxed on top. The difference was
profit. What happened in that 1980–1 period was that the
price for one barrel of refined products was actually less
than the price of a barrel of crude. The difference was
loss. Exxon and Texaco, BP and Shell could cushion their
losses by raising their prices at the petrol pumps. The
public complained, but the major oil companies own the
game and can make up the rules as they go along. In spite
of their pretentions, the majors have done little more than
give lip service to public attitudes. However, independents,
such as Thieme's Essex, have no pumps and no public.
They have no way of pawning their losses off on anyone.
A super-tanker riding the seas carries as many as 2 million
barrels. In the good days, that could mean profits for an
independent in the $1–$4 million range. In 1980–1, when
the dice turned against them, the $1–$4 million range fell
into the loss column. Although Thieme never divulged
how big he was winning in 1979, one fairly good guess
puts him over the $100 million mark. Perhaps as much as
$120 million. But when the market turned sour, it quickly
evaporated. Again, he won't say to what extent. He
refuses to talk about such things. The same way he won't
say how much he spent on parties and race cars. Because
he is such a private person, the element of mystery is

heightened. 'So what,' he likes to say. 'A little mystery never hurt anyone.'

Except that little bit of mystery was one of the reasons he was arrested.

＊　　＊　　＊

10 April 1981.

An article about Thieme appeared that Friday morning in the *International Herald Tribune*. It was a feature story titled 'David Thieme: Mixes Oil and Racing'. In the article he spoke about his lifestyle – about gloss and glitter – about the oil business, and about how he was looking forward to the Formula One season. There was a race scheduled that weekend in Argentina. As the Lotus sponsor, Thieme attended all the races, running around the globe to entertain clients on Grand Prix weekends. In the article he said he was looking forward to being in Buenos Aires. What went through the minds of the gnomes at Crédit Suisse when they saw the article that morning, no one really knows. But it's likely that the reference to South America raised some alarm. They knew the oil business was in a pretty awful state. Having financed an enormous number of deals with Thieme, it looked as if his bad luck could also be their bad luck. And there he was in the *International Herald Tribune*, pictured wearing his square sunglasses, looking mysterious, talking about big parties and race cars and South America.

Throughout that spring he had been meeting regularly with Crédit Suisse to reschedule and restructure his debt. He thought that, while the negotiations were tough, everything would eventually sort itself out. On 30 March 1981 the quarterly agreement between Essex and Crédit Suisse ended. The Essex debt was reportedly $20 million. According to documents later filed with the Swiss courts, the bank officials were already arranging Thieme's arrest. That's probably why they did not call in the quarterly loan agreement when it ended. Perhaps they needed some way to lure him back to the bank. Thieme of course wanted to extend the agreement. The bank demanded a show of good faith and got him to sign over to them a $5 million guarantee in his own name towards the Essex debt. Then they demanded more. They got him to put his signature on papers allowing the bank ownership of certain Essex assets – aircraft, specific commercial receivables, real estate and various vehicles, including the three-storey Essex bus that Thieme used as a hospitality suite at the Grand Prix races. The total, by Thieme's count, came to nearly $15 million.

When Crédit Suisse and Thieme joined forces in 1976, the Essex line of credit was $5 million. Over the years it grew to as much as $100 million. And both parties agree that between 1976 and 1981 Essex had borrowed and paid back with interest nearly $1 billion. But none of that mattered to Crédit Suisse that April. They might have liked him when he was flush, but the romance ended when they saw he wasn't. As far as Crédit Suisse was concerned, they had suffered through the likes of Bernie Cornfeld and the Investors Overseas Services scandal. They followed that by fumbling their way through a £543 million embezzlement by some of their own employees at the Crédit Suisse branch in Chiasso. Now they decided they had Thieme.

Taking charge for Crédit Suisse was a short, fat man named Joseph Muller. As Executive Vice President for 'Special Assignments', he was head of the bank's private C.I.A. He and Thieme met in a conference room one floor above the Paradeplatz, on the Bahnhofstrasse side. Thieme believed the meeting would go on all day, although he thought there would be a break for lunch. But, as lunchtime neared, Muller showed no signs of adjourning. Thieme remembers that Muller seemed to be dragging out the morning session, as if he was waiting for something to happen. Muller kept leaving the room, coming back in and then going out again. For most of the morning he was in shirt sleeves. Then, suddenly, he reappeared with his jacket on. With him was a group of men Thieme didn't know. They turned out to be the police. The officer in charge told Thieme in English that he was being arrested on charges of fraud and embezzlement. When the shock of that wore off, Thieme asked, 'Is manslaughter included?' The officer in charge looked puzzled, and mumbled, 'No.' Thieme asked, 'Do you want it to be?' The officer in charge said, 'Of course not.' So Thieme pointed to Muller and shouted in his anger, 'Then get that motherfucker out of here.'

Muller left the conference room convinced he was on top.

The police seized all of the assets Thieme had on his person – in Switzerland it's known as a 'pocket arrest' and it's often used in cases of debt so that those assets can be put towards the debt. They got some cash. Then the police escorted him to his hotel suite where they confiscated whatever else they could find. Finally, he was led off to jail.

Word immediately went out to the press that Thieme had been stopped on his way to South America. It was totally untrue. Whether anyone at the bank deliberately released false information or if some confusion evolved because of the South American reference in the *IHT* article is unclear. But certain journalists were told that Thieme had been arrested at the airport heading for Buenos Aires. That could have played some part in the judge's decision to refuse bail. Interestingly enough, Muller needed to be absolutely certain that Thieme would be immobile for several days. His case was riding on it.

Muller had built his reputation at the bank for being able to get something on anybody. While planning his battle with Thieme, he quite skilfully managed to unearth an employee at Essex who was susceptible to manipulation. Muller convinced her to come to Zurich, using the ploy that the welfare of the entire Essex staff depended on her. She agreed. On Monday 6 April, a Crédit Suisse representative in Monaco drove her to Genoa, Italy –

more than 90 minutes away – to meet a plane for Switzerland. The international airport at Nice is 20 minutes from the Principality by car, and only five minutes by regularly scheduled helicopter. Air France and Swissair provide daily services from Nice to Switzerland. Yet Crédit Suisse flew her out of Genoa. Then, Muller wouldn't see her that day. She was told he was too busy. It was the same story on Tuesday. She waited for him five hours until he cancelled the meeting. On Wednesday they did speak, but only very briefly, discussing Essex finances for five to ten minutes before Muller made an excuse to cut the meeting short. They did not meet on Thursday. And on Friday, while still hoping to see Muller, the woman was told about Thieme's arrest.

By Saturday morning she was in a panic, absolutely terrified of Muller.

That's when he announced that they were going to Monaco. Joining them were Dr Thomas Lehner, one of the bank's in-house attorneys, Dr Michael Werder, a Zurich-based attorney representing the bank, Patrick Lahusen, a Crédit Suisse Vice President who had handled the Essex loan account, and a minor Crédit Suisse employee who in the end had very little to do with any of this. The party checked into six adjoining rooms at the Loews Hotel Monte Carlo – literally a five-minute walk from Thieme's offices. All of the rooms were booked in the name of Michael Werder and paid for by him with a credit card. At no time did the name Crédit Suisse appear on the reservations, registrations or room service bills. Lehner, speaking for the bank, later claimed that the group had been invited to enter the Essex offices, escorted there legally by an authorized employee. He insisted that no papers were ever removed from those offices. He did however admit that photocopies were made of the papers found in David Thieme's desk, but added that this too was at the invitation of the woman employee. Werder would not make any comments. Lahusen has since met a less than cheerful fate at the hands of his former employers, being forced to resign. And Muller, quite purposely and consistently, has made himself totally unavailable for any comments whatsoever.

Yet, in a sworn statement before the Monégasque Prosecutor's Office, that woman employee paints another version of the events of that weekend. She says that the contingent arrived in Monaco on Saturday afternoon but did not go to the Essex offices until well after dark. She puts the time at about 10 p.m. when Muller ordered her and Lahusen to go with him. She says the two men had a list of documents they were looking for. She swears that Muller insisted on waiting outside, in the gardens facing the offices, until Lahusen and she had gone into Thieme's office, then raised and lowered the blinds twice to tell him the coast was clear. She says that the three of them spent about two hours in the Essex offices, with Muller and Lahusen rummaging through desks and files. It was midnight when they got back to the hotel and showed the bounty to Lehner and Werder. It's a curious point that neither Lehner nor Werder went along to Thieme's offices. Both are attorneys. Both are officers of the court. And both remained at the hotel.

The following morning, Muller told her that certain papers he had been hoping to find were not among the cache, and he ordered her back to the offices to find them. It was daylight. Lahusen went with her. Muller did not. But the two found nothing and, as they were both frightened that they would be caught, they returned to the hotel empty handed. Muller was furious. He was by now, according to the woman, showing signs of his own anxieties. He said they would check out of the hotel in. 'iately and go to Nice. There they piled into the office of a French lawyer where, the woman claims, she was forced to sign over to Crédit Suisse certain Essex assets for which she had control. Asked in an interview to confirm that this particular agreement was indeed signed in Nice on Sunday 12 April, Thomas Lehner, who was present, recalled that it was. The only problem here is that the agreement the bank later presented in their case against Thieme bears the dateline Zurich, 10 April.

✻   ✻   ✻

'I spent 13 days in jail. When I was finally released on bail, the bank officials were quite obviously upset. They were worried. They expected me to jump bail and run for my life. Instead I spent the next seven months cooperating fully with the Swiss authorities who were investigating the case. I don't think Herr Muller counted on me doing that. But I did because it was vital for me to prove to the Swiss authorities that I was not guilty of any wrongdoings.'

In presenting their case, Crédit Suisse set out to prove that Thieme had defrauded them of $3.8 million in a fuel oil sale, misappropriated some $490,000 of their funds, and embezzled a further 180,000 Swiss francs. While the Swiss authorities were studying the Crédit Suisse evidence, the bank was moving against Thieme in the Cayman Islands, trying to wrap up the part of the Essex empire registered there. They also filed suit against Thieme and Essex in New York.

Releasing Thieme on bail was the first indication Muller and the bank had to suggest the tide would possibly turn.

A little more than one month later, 29 May, Thieme produced evidence to prove that the fuel oil deal had nothing to do with Crédit Suisse, having been financed through the Banque de Paris et du Pays Bas in Geneva. Furthermore, the allegedly misappropriated and embezzled funds were sitting snugly in an Essex account with yet another bank, where they had been all along. And now Essex filed suit against Crédit Suisse in New York to the tune of $125 million – supposedly the largest single law suit ever brought against a foreign bank in the United States. He also filed against them in Switzerland and Monaco on behalf of Essex, including criminal charges against Muller, Lehner and Werder for what he claimed was the 'Watergate style' break-in of his offices. The worldwide claims totalled about 400 million Swiss francs (then somewhere close to £100 million).

The bank, in an effort to collect some of the money on the assets they had managed to seize, put the Essex plane up for auction. No one bought it. Then, a lower court in Zurich ruled that the pocket arrest of Thieme's personal property in the bank's conference room on 10 April was illegal. And exactly eight months after his arrest, the Swiss authorities announced that they were dropping all charges.

The next morning, in Zurich, Thieme held a press conference. The statement he read was brief: 'Eight months ago to the day, I was falsely arrested in the conference room of Crédit Suisse, main branch, Paradeplatz, in a desperate and malicious act of irresponsibility by my former banking partners. Today, I am pleased to inform you that by decision of Dr Gianpiero Antognazza, state's attorney of the Canton of Zurich, dated December 8, 1981, all proceedings against me based on the obviously unfounded charges by Crédit Suisse have been terminated. Both district attorney Dr Bruno Schadler and state's attorney Dr G. Antognazza have spent seven months thoroughly investigating and have concluded, as I have always believed they would, that there are no grounds for the Crédit Suisse charges. I have therefore instructed my attorneys to investigate the question of false arrest and malicious prosecution on the part of Crédit Suisse. Additionally, authorities in other countries continue their investigations and proceedings against specific officers of Crédit Suisse for criminal behaviour. Furthermore, we are continuing a number of civil actions in various jurisdictions. In particular, our New York attorneys are vigorously pursuing claims against Crédit Suisse in excess of $125 million.'

Many of the journalists present knew Thieme through his Formula One connections, had reported his arrest and were quite familiar with the bank's claims against him.

One of them had been in touch with the bank, and voiced their side of the story, saying that the charges had been dropped due to a lack of jurisdiction. Thieme answered: 'The charges were dropped because there was simply no evidence to support the bank's charges. I was arrested in Switzerland after the bank's lawyers and Herr Muller had plenty of time to plan their case against me. It's obvious they knew very well when they made their move where the jurisdiction lay. Had there been any jurisdictional problems, their legal staff would have seen that immediately. Had it only been a question of jurisdiction, the Swiss state's attorney's office would have handed down that ruling at the very beginning. No, the ruling they handed down is one of complete vindication.'

As the press conference ended, three rather burly men who had been sitting in the rear of the room – unnoticed by Thieme – came forward and introduced themselves as bailiffs of the court. They had with them a warrant for a pocket arrest. They said they were there on behalf of the bank to seize whatever assets Thieme had on his person and in his hotel suite. But this last-minute bit of histrionics proved fruitless. They found nothing. And Thieme was quoted in the Swiss papers the next day: 'Crédit Suisse certainly is a bunch of poor losers.'

Exactly six days after the Swiss dropped charges against him, the Supreme Court of the Canton of Zurich upheld the lower court decision in favour of Thieme concerning the first pocket arrest. The court wrote that seizing his assets inside the bank's conference room was 'in bad faith', adding that Crédit Suisse had 'violated the trust created by its own conduct. Such methods contradict the principle of good faith in business relationships and accordingly are not deserving of legal protection.'

For a Swiss court to say that about one of the country's major banking institutions was a slap in the face. Yet more was to come. The bank had 30 days to appeal against the Swiss prosecutor's decision to drop all charges, but they didn't. Instead, Crédit Suisse filed an appeal against the Essex suit aimed at them in New York, at the same time withdrawing their New York suit against Essex and Thieme. They now claimed there was no jurisdiction there for the suit against them. However, the New York courts felt differently, ruling that the Essex suit could indeed be heard there. Over the next year the bank appealed that decision twice – rising to higher courts each time – and they lost twice. Obviously frustrated, they finally moved against one of their own. Patrick Lahusen was charged with disloyal management and fired. The official line was that Lahusen had over-extended Thieme's line of credit. Lahusen's 'liquidation' brought on such severe depressions that he has been virtually eliminated from the case.

Thieme's feeling is that Lahusen was the scapegoat, slaughtered to cover up for others. 'Anyone who knows how a bank conducts business knows very well that Patrick Lahusen could never have acted by himself to approve whatever huge loans came across his desk. When requests for additional credit were sent to the bank, those requests had to go up the ladder. We're not speaking of a $3000 car loan. We're talking about a line of credit upwards of $100 million. That sort of business can only be approved at the very top. Don't think for a minute that the highest ranks of Crédit Suisse didn't know what was going on. It was their job to know. On the other hand, if the top levels didn't know, with such huge sums involved, as the bank now claims, then the crucifixion of Mr Lahusen is just as immoral because it means that the top-ranking men of Crédit Suisse are totally incompetent.'

At Crédit Suisse they have never seemed too keen to answer questions about Thieme's case. The official spokesman is the lawyer, Thomas Lehner. A tall, thin, German Swiss, probably somewhere in his mid-to-late 30s, he pounds loudly on his desk to demand that questions aimed at him be made softer. He doesn't care for most direct questions, choosing instead to give a long-winded and well-rehearsed speech about the bank's responsibilities. When he isn't banging on his desk and threatening to end the interview, he is laughing and shaking his head, insinuating that the questions being asked are stupid, irrelevant and based entirely on fallacies. For example: 'Did Crédit Suisse file charges against Mr Thieme and/or Essex in New York and then withdraw those charges?' For nearly five minutes he emphatically denied that to be true, saying it showed an ignorance of the case. What actually happened, he explained, was that, after charges were filed in New York, they were not withdrawn but rather moved to Switzerland where it would be more convenient for officers of the bank to testify.

When asked why Thieme had been vindicated by the Swiss courts, Lehner took the stance that it was only a matter of jurisdiction, which directly contradicts the bank's argument for moving the civil case from New York to Switzerland. To further support the bank's contentions against Thieme, Lehner pointed out that the Swiss authorities had not in fact let him off scot free. Thieme, he said, had been ordered to pay costs. Oddly enough, those costs after seven months of investigations amounted to a mere 3000 Swiss francs (something like £750). The way Thieme sees it, charging him such a sum was just a gesture: 'After all, I came to their town, to fight them in their language, with their own laws and in their own courts. And I won. Can you blame them for trying to save some face?'

Disregarding that, Lehner maintains that he could easily prove Thieme wrong, and would be quite willing to do so publicly, except that Swiss banking laws prevent him from speaking out. In fact, through a three-hour interview with Lehner, he spent an inordinate amount of time hiding behind those Swiss banking laws. At one point he said that, if only Thieme would release him from liability under the banking secrets act, he would happily make public a copy of the Crédit Suisse criminal charges against Thieme. 'It's very revealing,' he promised. But

Thieme himself quite willingly provided a copy of those charges, and, anyway, they were the same ones that the Swiss prosecutors had studied, investigated and eventually dismissed.

When asked about the entry into the Essex offices, Lehner said there was nothing at all illegal about that. When asked why it took place at night, Lehner said it was to avoid alarming any employees who might have been working there. When asked why, if it was a legal entry, neither he nor Dr Werder went along – attorneys could of course be subject to sanctions for taking part in any sort of illegal action – he said it was because they were otherwise busy. Doing what? He wouldn't say. When asked if the scenario of the woman (now a former Essex employee) was correct, especially her description of Muller waiting outside for the all clear signal, Lehner said that was ridiculous – in spite of the fact that he swore he wasn't there.

The bank tried, Lehner went on, to get Thieme to slow down when the oil market went soft in 1980. But, to their horror, Thieme seemed to prefer large parties and racing cars to 'good business sense'. And Lehner did not want anyone to forget that Thieme and Essex still owed the bank tens of millions of dollars, with the interest accruing daily.

Thieme has never denied that there is a debt. He just sees it differently. 'A commercial dispute does exist with the bank. But, by our calculations, the Essex debt is considerably less than the figure the bank continues to use. You must also understand that a great deal changed in our relationship with the bank when they had me slapped in a cell. That's why we have consistently maintained that, before anyone from Essex sits down with our former banking partners to discuss our obligations to them, they have several explanations to make about their own behaviour.'

Just about a year after Thieme's arrest, a BBC television crew from 'The Money Programme' tried to ask for some of those explanations. They were refused entry to the bank. When they started filming on the Paradeplatz – a public square – bank guards threatened to have them arrested if they didn't move away from the bank's front door.

The BBC crew was surprised. Thieme was not. 'I think the bank must realize that they've worked themselves into an awkward position. The last thing they want is anyone looking too closely at the way they've treated me. But if you study the records in Zurich, you can see that Crédit Suisse has in the past dealt rather heavy-handedly with a number of their clients. In a lot of cases those clients have not been able to fight back. This is not the case with me.'

For the past four years, David Thieme has been alive and well and running around the world flogging oil. Only a little of the gloss and glitter has changed. His wheeling and dealing was slowed down for two reasons: the market was awful, and admittedly he was commercially hurt by the arrest. Yet he managed to find other banking partners. Still in the wings is Thieme's personal suit against the bank for false arrest and malicious prosecution. That should easily amount to more than £100 million. Since Thieme's arrest, Crédit Suisse have continuously failed in their actions against him. They held a few commercial receivables, but never collected on them. The Essex plane is unsold. An Essex company was wound up, except that it was empty and worthless. In the end, for all the efforts against Thieme and Essex – and who knows how many millions of pounds in legal fees – the best Crédit Suisse have managed was the seizure and sale of a cache of 800 Cuban cigars they found with Thieme's name on it, sitting in a rented humidor in Zurich, exactly one block from their own front door.

3

The Roux Brothers

There's a recipe in Albert and Michel Roux's *New Classic Cuisine* for a pâte sablée – a shortbread dough. The reader is advised, while making the dough, to 'Work the mixture with your fingertips until the ingredients are thoroughly blended'.

It sounded like a minor point to Michel's wife Robyn the first time she tried it. So, when she got to the part where she was supposed to use the palm of her hand, she figured the hell with this, and reached for her food processor. This is why, she thought, God invented the Magimix. As far as she was concerned, the dough was perfect. She shaped it into shells, added a pear filling and tossed them into the oven. She was just taking the finished dessert out when Michel came into the kitchen, glanced, then mumbled as he walked by, 'You shouldn't have used the food processor.'

Her mouth dropped. 'How could you possibly tell?'

He shrugged.

Noblesse oblige.

* * *

Albert Henri Roux cooks at Le Gavroche on Upper Brook Street in London's Mayfair. It was the first restaurant in the UK to be awarded three stars by the Michelin Guide. Michel André Roux cooks at the

Waterside Inn, on the Thames in the small Berkshire village of Bray. In 1985 it became only the second restaurant in Britain to win the three stars award. With just 26 three-star restaurants in the world, Michelin therefore rates the Roux Brothers among the world's finest chefs. They don't look like brothers. But they're both quick to assure anyone who asks that they really are. In fact, they hardly ever refer to each other by name. They call each other 'Brother'. Together they rule over a group of five restaurants, an exclusive 54-suite hotel, and a slew of other interests in and around the food business in three countries. They employ nearly 200 people in England. Their first year at Le Gavroche they barely managed to turn over £75,000. This year, their restaurants alone will do more than £4.5 million. And some time within the next 12–18 months, they'll announce that they are going public with part of their group.

* * *

7:10 p.m. Albert in the kitchen is Olivier playing Hamlet. In the centre of his stage are four large ovens, surrounded by the various stations – sauce, vegetables, fish, hors d'oeuvres, salad and pastry. Facing the doors to the diningroom is the service bar where waiters hand in orders and collect highly decorated plates of food on silver trays. Every night there are three different kinds of canapé, and 130 of each kind. Tonight it's quail's eggs and foie gras and salmon mousse with chives. Albert stops to inspect the hors d'oeuvres station, nods and walks on. He stops to look at someone preparing a petit pâté de bécasse – a woodcock pâté. 'Bien,' he smiles. Then he asks loudly in French, 'How many pheasant pies are there tonight?' Someone answers in English, 'Fourteen.' No one seems to realize they're working in two different languages.

Dozens of copper pans in varying shapes and sizes sit on the stoves. Some with sauces. Some with boiling water. Some with vegetables. Two large frying pans have meat in

them. A couple of smaller ones await ingredients. Albert
inspects them all, just as the first orders begin to come in.
One chef takes the orders from the waiters. And calls out
loudly to everyone in the kitchen, 'Huit foies gras. Huit
toast. Deux papillotes. Deux menus exceptionelles.' And
like a Greek chorus, each cook at his station shouts back,
'Oui chef.'

※   ※   ※

Raised in the French region of Saône-et-Loire, Albert was
born in Semur en Brionnais in 1935. He's shorter, with
grey speckled hair and half glasses that are constantly
falling off the end of his nose. Michel was born in the
neighbouring village of Charolles in 1941. He's taller,
with blonde hair and a French schoolboy look in his eyes.
Their father, and his father before him, were both
charcutiers. At the age of 14, Albert began an apprenticeship as a pastry chef, spending five years to learn his trade
before accepting a post in London to cook for Lady
Astor. At about the same time, Michel began his
apprenticeship, also in pastry. He spent two years before
being appointed pastry chef at the British Embassy in
Paris. Then Albert went off to do his military service with
the French army. And eventually Michel was called for
his service. By the time they were both back to cooking
again, Albert was head chef for Major Peter Cazalet at his
stately home in Kent, and Michel was Chef de Cuisine for
Miss Cecile de Rothschild in Paris. But the two of them
had always wanted to go into business together. So Albert
told Michel to come to London, that they could find a
backer and open a restaurant. Michel arrived. It was 1967.
The original Le Gavroche on Lower Sloane Street was the
start of their empire.

'In a very real sense', says Michel, 'our risks are a
nightly affair. After all, we would not put our names on a
product which we didn't create. And every night we put
our name on our product. In our case, we've got to win

every game. But is goes further than that because cooking is our daily oxygen. It's got to be done in a grand place. Cooking is a day to day work. We couldn't go for long periods of time out of Gavroche or Waterside. It's a very personalized business. Like any show that's done every day, if the maestro is sick, he might be replaced for a day or two. But not for very long. So basically all of the things happening in our group get right back to what the two brothers are doing in the kitchen.'

The restaurant division starts with the 'flagships' Le Gavroche and The Waterside Inn. Michel says Waterside's profit – with around 600 meals per week – was nearly £150,000 last year, which is just ahead of Gavroche – with about 750 meals per week. 'While Albert's prices are higher, so are his costs; his percentage on food can't compete with Waterside.' Then there's Le Poulbot and Le Gamin in the City, and Gavvers, where the original Gavroche was. They created Le Poulbot to be the only restaurant in the City where one can eat grandly. Le Gamin is a less expensive restaurant near the Law Courts that offers a good value businessman's lunch. 'All we need to do there is phone once a day, to make sure the staff is all right, to see they've bought what they need in the market. You know, to have a chat with them. Then, once a week or so, either Brother or I go there for lunch. The two staffs have been trained at Gavroche or the Waterside. The Maitre d' at Le Poulbot has been with the group for 15 years. What we do with those restaurants is create the dishes and new ideas. Albert does their menu and planning. The wine list I do, and change it about every six months.'

Le Poulbot serves nearly 750 per week, not counting 450 lunches per week in the upstairs 'Francophiled' version of a snack bar. Yet Le Poulbot has never been able to come up with the profits the Rouxs hoped it might. Admits Michel, 'I don't think it's been looked after as it should be for the past two years. Albert is dealing with it now and things have been changed. We closed it last year and spent £150,000 on redecoration.

The Poulbot rent is over £20,000. On that kind of rent plus the rates, it's very tough. We only do luncheon five days a week. The turnover had been about £8000 per week. We're now doing £11,000 and I'd bet anything that the extra £3000 is practically all profit. So from £20,000–£25,000 profit last year which was miserable, I'd be surprised if it doesn't reach about £60,000 this year. That represents approximately 10 per cent of the turnover.'

As far as Le Gamin is concerned, serving 600 lunches per week, they're not certain what the profits look like there. The problem was that for the past few years the accounts for Le Gamin and their outside catering interests were combined. Although the results suggested that Le Gamin did a fantastic return – $13\frac{1}{2}$–14 per cent.

Gavvers is now the odd-man out. Four years ago when they moved Le Gavroche to Mayfair, the two brothers opened this dinner restaurant with a prix fixé menu. But while they cared enough to maintain the cooking standards, they were willing to settle for an operation that simply kept their cash flow going. Then they realized that they had an extremely competent chef working there named Denis Lobry. He was put in charge of the restaurant and Gavvers started making a little money. So the brothers cut Lobry in. 'We've made him a shareholder,' Michel continues. 'The deal is 70 per cent Roux and 30 per cent Lobry. It's unprecedented for us. We've never done this before. But he was a cook at the stove when we started Gavroche. We go there from time to time for dinner. Albert helps with the menu and I do the wine. But by making Denis Lobry a shareholder in Gavvers, by involving him much more with it, we're convinced the place is now going to show a very good profit.'

*　　*　　*

7:40 p.m. It's hot. Albert say it isn't. But it is. Very hot. He insists it's much cooler in his kitchen than most others. Some corners of the kitchen are less hot than others, but where it's hot – in spite of what Albert thinks – it is very hot.

A dish of scallops with creamy scrambled eggs is being made at the fish station when Albert says, 'Non, mes enfants. Mais non.' Heads turn. 'It must be done like this.' He moves the dish aside and starts to make another. The fish chef watches as Albert explains every step.

The chef at the meat station calls out orders non-stop. And in the middle of this panic Albert stops his *ad hoc* cooking school just long enough to ask, 'OK for that pheasant pie.' The clock in his head told him one of the orders was ready. Then, without missing a beat, he continues with the scallops, showing everyone what the dish should look like. 'You see it my children?' He hands it to the fish chef and goes to look at a plate being decorated with watercress. 'Put some ice on that watercress.' And all the time one chef is calling out, 'Canapés, huit. Scallopes, deux. Quatre menus.' And all the time the others shout back, 'Oui chef. Oui chef. Oui chef.'

☆   ☆   ☆

Outside catering began when the brothers realized that not everyone in the City could get out for lunch – and that the quality of food being cooked in some 'executive canteens' was pretty terrible. In a few cases, they supply pre-cooked dishes. In at least four other cases, they have taken over the running of those canteen kitchens. They've installed chefs full-time in bank head offices around the City, cooking strictly to Roux Brothers recipes. It's been so successful that the Banque de Paris et du Pays Bas has hired the Rouxs to do all the planning for the kitchen and food service in their new headquarters building currently under construction.

In 1973 they set up a patisserie in Wandsworth because they needed to supply their own group with pastry, bread, croissants, brioches, pains au chocolat, and cakes.

When they saw the potential of that business, they started taking in clients from the outside. Jacksons. Harrods. The Sheraton Park Tower. The Capital Hotel. Michael Chow. The Claremont Club. In all they've now got ten clients besides the Roux group. Nine years later they applied the same theory to their own butcher shop. Opened at the end of 1982, La Boucherie Lamartine on Ebury Street in London, represented an investment of £150,000. This year, with half their business wholesale and the other half retail, they're expecting turnover to reach £1 million.

There have, however, been a few failures. In 1973–4 they opened a charcuterie in Henley. But it didn't work – Michel thinks it might have been a little too sophisticated and that kept people away – so after a year they closed it and swallowed a £50,000 loss. Last year they lost again with a charcuterie. One of their sisters had been running Le Cochon Rose, near Gavvers, with her husband but she decided to go back to France. 'It was just as well,' Michel admits. 'We've got a sister who is so dreadful with people. She got rid of the clientele so beautifully that we found ourselves with a shop that is clean, with a great line of products and nobody wanted to buy from us. We're in a country where people like to be looked after nicely, and certainly not ignored. She turned the Cochon Rose from a profit maker into a loss maker. So, when she left, we didn't feel like going to find another charcutier. If she hadn't been our sister, we would have sacked her.'

Ever resourceful, when they closed the charcuterie they converted the kitchen there to handle all of their outside catering business. Then they made a few more adaptations so that they could begin an experiment which they now believe will be the future of the Roux organization.

* * *

7:55 p.m. There are two private parties upstairs. It's not a well-publicized fact but above Le Gavroche is the most discreet hotel in London. And the Roux Brothers have the management concession. It's called 47 Park Street. There is no hotel sign or a neon 'Vacancies' outfront. It's only 54 suites, with a kitchen in each suite. Tonight there is one party of 13 dining on the third floor, and one party of eight dining on the second floor. Albert has already checked their menus, but now he goes upstairs to speak with the head waiters assigned to those parties. 'Make sure we've got a carving board here.' Later he will return to carve the roasts at the table. Public appearances are part of being a star.

*   *   *

The future of the Roux organization could lie in vacuum-cooked food – a process that particularly fascinates Albert. 'It's not a complicated process but we've put three years of research work into it and have now begun to produce. Yet it's still very much of an infant. Vacuum packing of food has been around for a long time. You know, cooking in the bag. I simply took it a step further.'

The concept is to cook a dish under very high pressure, then deep freeze it immediately. That keeps both the taste and texture of the product fresh. The rest of the secret lies in the bag that's used. 'I wouldn't call this fast food,' says Albert. 'I would call it good bourgeois cooking. Some of the dishes will be worthy of a two star Michelin restaurant. We didn't have to create special dishes for vacuum cooking. We followed Escoffier. We tested it by serving some of this food in the City with our outside catering and it's been a great success. We tested it with merchant bankers and they liked it.'

They had an offer of £250,000 for the vacuum cooking method while it was still in the experimental stage, so they know there's a great future in it. They turned down that offer, and instead, some time this year, they're going public – probably using the Unlisted Securities Market – to create a chain of five to ten restaurants that will use this process. It won't be fast food by the look of it. But it will be fast food by the turnover. The restaurants will be in the style of Le Gamin but much cheaper.

'We can't expand without having the quality of our restaurants suffer,' adds Michel. 'But we can expand by using our skills to create recipes which we cook sealed into those plastic bags and then sell into appropriate markets. We're thinking of charging £2 or £2.50 for a main dish. A complete meal will be £6–£8 with a glass of wine. A sweet or starter will be 60–80p. We're going to popularize cooking which is called cuisine bourgeoise. It doesn't exist in England. You find a few places like that in France. But there is no chain in France of restaurants offering the quality of food which we are going to offer in this country. They will be run like a normal restaurant, except in the kitchen there will only be two or three cooks. All they have to do is boil the little bag, and perhaps make a few tartlettes. You must after all give them something to do or they get bored. We don't want to create a monster. We don't want to become Wimpys.'

＊　　　＊　　　＊

9:10 p.m. An order for a table of six comes in. Albert tries to speed things along because people are waiting for tables and it's not moving as quickly as he wants. In the midst of this a waiter announces, 'Adnan Kashoggi is in the restaurant.' Albert is busy with an order. The waiter tries again. 'Adnan Kashoggi is here tonight.' Albert merely nods. He's too rushed to be impressed. Then a dessert order comes in. Soufflé for two. And coming up is a chocolate roll filled with fresh raspberries and liqueured coffee beans, covered with a Melba sauce. Albert pokes his head around a corner and asks, 'Ready?' The English-born pastry chef says, 'OK for la rouleau.' Albert takes the tray with the chocolate roll. 'Le rouleau,' he corrects. The pastry chef shakes his head. 'La. Le. La. Le. Who cares?'

＊　　　＊　　　＊

The first two years of Le Gavroche in Mayfair were a disaster. The place was full. The first year's turnover was £1 million. But the cost of the move was £750,000 and that first year-end profit in Mayfair was under £50,000. It took a lot of work to make it a profitable success. Albert began taking orders later at night. Then he managed to fill the private diningrooms upstairs three, four, five times a week. That alone boosted turnover by at least one day more a week. So for the first time, last year, Le Gavroche showed a return of 12–13 per cent. But Michel believes that moving Le Gavroche from Lower Sloane Street to Mayfair came very close to being a mistake. 'It was a very bad move for the first two years. I don't think we should have gone for Upper Brook Street where the rates are so expensive. Although it shows now we did the right thing since we're managing 47 Park Street. But who knew at the time. Who knew that the fellow who owns 47 Park Street would suddenly realize that in his building he had people who were able to run and fill up the place?'

It was nearly a year after they moved to Mayfair that the majority shareholder of 47 Park Street realized what it could mean to have the Roux Brothers in the building. Until they came along, 47 Park Stret was a tired bunch of service flats. Albert discovered over lunch one day that the gentleman was most anxious to bring the brothers into his business. But Albert explained that the first thing they would want was a guarantee that money would be spent redecorating to their standards. He agreed to shell out more than £1 million just on redecoration. In the end he spent closer to £2 million. The Rouxs then took full charge. And profit has been up every month for the past three years.

*　　*　　*

9:35 p.m. Some cheese soufflés are taking too long to get out, so Albert moves in to help. A waiter tells him that two clients want to visit the kitchen. Albert wonders if

they're both pretty women. The waiter says no. Albert
seems disappointed but perks up when he hears that one
is a French chef. He finishes with the soufflés then goes
into the diningroom to meet his guests. A few minutes
later he brings them into the kitchen, making no attempt
at all to hide his enormous pride. The tour lasts only a
few minutes, but for those few minutes this is Mario
Andretti showing Nicky Lauda his winning Formula
One.

*   *   *

Dominique Rouxel was a barman at Gavroche who
wanted to go into the import/export business but didn't
have any money. So the brothers helped him form a
company they called Rouxel – after all, the R-o-u-x was
already there. When the banks said they wouldn't get
involved, Albert and Michel personally guaranteed £40,000.
They also did the original ground work. Albert went to
Paris and established contacts with the wholesalers. He
showed Dominique Rouxel around the markets, and an
import–export division was born. These days Rouxel goes
to Paris weekly, and fills up his lorry with 15 tons of
fruit, vegetables, and some poultry. He brings it back to
England where his biggest clients are Roux Restaurants.
They get fresh produce from France, and he's got a
business that now turns over nearly £1 million.

This was not the first time the brothers set up one of
their employees. In fact, over the past few years they've
actually helped to set up some of their own competition –
top-quality restaurants like Tante Claire, Interlude de
Tabaillau, and Paris House at Woburn Abbey.

They refer to these joint ventures as 'the children', and
the way it works is simple. The employee must have been
with the Rouxs for a minimum of five years. Then he
must have demonstrated great ability, confidence, trust,
skill and ambition. But they don't go to him and suggest
he should start his own business. If one of the staff thinks

he's ready, he must approach them. If they agree, the Rouxs line up banks, bank managers, lawyers and locations. Albert and Michel try to help them decide what kind of place they can best handle – 30 covers, 60 covers – the grading of their cooking, how many people they should have on staff, and which area of London they should be in. As soon as plans begin to gell, Albert and Michel invite a few of their best clients to become shareholders, to put some money into the restaurant.

Working closely with the brothers at this stage is Roux Restaurant Chairman Professor Michael von Clemm – who also happens to be Chairman of the investment banking house, Credit Suisse First Boston Ltd. He takes an active part in helping the 'children' to arrange for financing. Says von Clemm, 'The investors buy shares, and everyone who has ever put shares into one of the restaurants we've established for one of the Roux chefs has seen a profit, some of them as high as ten times their investment. But we insist that each of the "children" own at least 51 per cent of their business and that they maintain an option to buy back all the outstanding shares whenever they can. And I think you could say this has worked out well for everyone involved. The "children" have done well, and there isn't a week that goes by when one of the Roux's regular customers doesn't pull Michel or Albert aside and say, next time one of the "children" is going to set up, please let me know.'

In the spring of 1982, the first foreign joint venture was established. Christian Germain, a former chef at the Waterside Inn, wanted to return to France. So the brothers helped him to set up the Chateau de Montreuil – a hotel/restaurant near Le Touquet. Last year the Roux Brothers branched out again in France by investing nearly £100,000 in a factory doing vacuum packing of food. It is their highest-risk investment, and Michel is well aware of the high-risk element. 'We saved it from bankruptcy, and it's not out of danger yet. It is not inconceivable that we could lose our entire investment. On the other hand it can become one of the best investments we've ever done. They make pâtés and foie gras and we're using some of their foie gras in our restaurants. Our boucherie is selling their foie gras and their tinned pâtés. Hopefully we're also going to start selling those pâtés through a large British retailer. We've been discussing it with someone very big. We've also just done a contract to provide a small foie gras terrine to British Airways.'

Now they're expanding into the States with a restaurant called The Waterside Inn in Santa Barbara, California. It's a joint venture with an American who cooked for the Rouxs for five years and who, they claim, was one of the very best they'd ever seen. Like all the other deals, he owns 51 per cent with the usual buy-back option. And to give him some help, they've just sent three key men from outside catering and from Gavroche to spend time in his kitchen.

* * *

10:10 p.m. Paperwork is now piling up, so Albert goes into his tiny office to check some bills and make up his shopping list for the next day. This is the first time in nearly three hours that he's had the chance to sit down.

Twenty minutes later the last of the evening's orders is in.

Twenty minutes after that, the last of the main courses is out.

* * *

Their book, *New Classic Cuisine*, was a profitable venture in more ways than one. First, it helped to reinforce the idea that the Roux Brothers were the foremost chefs in Britain. Second, it sold 35,000 copies in hardback in less than a year – and as it's still selling, there won't be a paperback edition for another year or so. It has been translated into French for publication there, and a separate US edition has also appeared. Third, the books have helped in a small way to fill up tables in the restaurants during the winter, especially among American clients. But most importantly, the book has documented their skills and ingenuity. And business offers have come in because of it. Among them, British Airways. The Rouxs assist BA in supplying meals from their own recipes, act as consultants to assess food served on board – especially first-class meals on jumbos out of Heathrow – and have created new menus for the Concorde. More recently they've been asked by Marks and Spencer to rate existing products and to come up with some new ideas.

Already on the cards is a second book, due out by Spring 1986. They promise it will be the first and only major pastry book in England. Once that's done, Michel says, he and Albert might seriously consider opening an English restaurant. But not an English restaurant for England. Michel would like to open an English restaurant in France.

'English food is under-rated. We talked about it a few years ago. We had an offer which would have been fantastic. It was on the Champs Elysées and it wound up that Jimmy Goldsmith bought it for another £30,000 more than we were willing to pay. We would have called it The English House, and offered the best of Britain. Traditional English cooking with care, love and dedication. There are some dishes in English cooking which are as good if not better than some regional French cooking, such as steak and kidney pie with oysters. There are beautiful joints and roast beef. There's also chicken with bread sauce, grouse with bread sauce as well, loin of pork with crackling and apple sauce, and red currant jelly with nicely marinaded and roasted game. Shepherds pie is a lovely dish, simple and nice. Then there's black pudding from Scotland. And haggis is excellent. Serving English food to the French is still something I believe I someday want to do.'

11:00 p.m. The hors d'oeuvres chef is starting to clean up. The pastry chef will work at full speed for another hour. Albert checks that the washing up has begun – the kitchen must be made absolutely spotless for the next morning – and then looks at the orders remaining on the hooks above the service bar. A few salads. And some desserts. Content, the 'General' is now going home. He has been up since 8 that morning. They cooked 67 lunches and now 91 dinners. Except for a little siesta after lunch, Albert has worked his usual 15-hour day.

But just as he's ready to leave, the room service phone rings from one of the suites at 47 Park Street. Everyone else is too busy. Albert takes the order. A silver tray is brought over. So is a plate. So is a silver bell to cover the plate on the tray. The plate is decorated with watercress and one radish, which has been carved into a flower. And then, the man who is considered one of the two best chefs in the UK makes a room-service ham sandwich.

4

Richard Branson

Richard Branson started his career in a phone booth when he was just 15. Twenty years later, he is a most unlikely tycoon. Founder and 85 per cent owner of the Virgin Group – his cousin and long-time associate Simon Draper owns the other 15 per cent – he is £160–£170 million worth of record companies, book publishers, gay discos, straight pubs, cable TV, record shops, film production companies, recording studios, and an airline. He also likes to have his picture taken in the bathtub.

'I never actually set out to see how I could make the most cash. I've always merely tried to make the figures fit the ideas I've had rather than the other way around. I guess that's doing it backwards.'

The house that Branson built employs about 1600 people, most of them young, most of them fiercely loyal to him. Because he likes to promote from within, today's record shop cashier knows he or she could be tomorrow's group accountant. That sort of two-way dialogue between employee and benevolent monarch is, he believes, one of the reasons his business keeps growing. Because he feels high-rise office blocks defeat the purpose, there are never more than 50 people in any one of the Virgin offices, which are usually converted houses spread throughout North London. It may mean lots of switchboards and lots of messengers back and forth. It may also mean lots of rent. But he's comfortable that way and he says his employees are comfortable that way too.

The world according to Branson is loose, relaxed, and filled with perks – come up with a great idea and you get a slice of the pie, do your job and you get a week in Portugal, no wives, no husbands, no friends permitted. Just 600 fellow workers alone together for the first time, off for a romp in the sunshine. Whatever goes on, goes on. It's like an annual class trip. It's the 'one big happy family' style of Godfathering. Maybe IBM doesn't work this way. But Virgin does.

He himself used to work at home, which was a houseboat in a canal near a decrepit cement bridge that says 'Borough of Paddington, 1914' in raised letters, and all sorts of other things in spray can orange. But a year or so ago he had a bout of pneumonia and his doctor advised less damp accommodation. So he moved – live-in lady and their daughter in tow – to a nearby flat, but he kept the floating office. His desk – one tiny round table cluttered by papers, notes and four telephones – is in the centre of what would otherwise have been the wheelhouse. Two secretaries run up and down the gangway to find their captain on the bridge. There are plants and flowers scattered about. But this is not Sausalito, California. The climate is very different and houseboats in England are far from comfortable. Yet it doesn't stop Branson being, in many ways, something of a soft-core Sausalito. First names, sweaters and jeans. 'I don't change my style of dress when I go to lunch with my bankers. One of the special things about being successful is that you can afford the luxury of not worrying what money can buy. You can dress the way you feel comfortable. You can afford to drive a practical car rather than an ostentatious car. Sometimes I write out a cheque for something reasonably extreme like a couple of million pounds, and I chuckle. It seems unreal.'

Maybe that's partially because he remembers those cheques without so many zeros. 'I was a kid and I kept our company account at Coutts. Well, I had an overdraft

facility of, I think £350, and one day it went to £375. The
bank manager called me into a small room and sat me
down and gave me a lecture. I mean, you should have
seen how they looked at us when some of my people
would come into the bank to deposit money barefoot.
Anyway, he said to me, "Look after your bank and your
bank will look after you." Someone told me recently that
we're their largest single client. Hard to believe. It's hard
to realize that. Although I'm certain that the Queen has
more assets that we do.'

Branson left school (he went to Stowe and hated it) and
came to London in the middle of the swinging '60s.
Having been a student he saw the need for some sort of
national student magazine, so he decided to start one. 'I
called it *Student*. I needed £5000 in advertising to put out
the first issue, but I didn't have an office or anything like
that, so I found a phone booth and opened the yellow
pages and started selling.' The magazine came out
whenever he could raise the money for it over the next
four years. At the same time he started a student advice
service, which survives today in a slightly changed form.
'We had all sorts of people coming to us looking for help.
In those early days my office was in the crypt of a church.
My desk was a slab of marble above two coffins.' He
makes a face. 'Actually I think I was very lucky when I
started. I had absolutely nothing to lose.'

However, *Student Magazine* lost enough money that
its days were eventually numbered. In the final issue he
printed an ad offering cut-price records. It was a last-
ditch effort to somehow raise a stake. It proved an
overwhelming success.

So Branson became the first record discounter in the
UK.

Today there are more than a hundred Virgin record
shops throughout the UK.

From selling records he branched out to making them.
'Mike Oldfield came to us and wanted to record some
songs he did when he was a kid, but we didn't have any

money. We gave him a list with the names of every music publisher in town and sent him to see them. They all turned him down. A year later we had some money and decided to give record producing a try, so we made our first album with him.' It was called *Tubular Bells*, and has since sold more copies than any album since *The Sound of Music*. He followed that by giving the world The Sex Pistols. These days the Virgin label boasts some 75 acts, 60 of them to some measure a success. The other 15 are 'developing'. But in his stable are Genesis and Phil Collins and Oldfield and Culture Club, which features Boy George. 'He's probably the hottest act in show business today after Michael Jackson. Maybe you could say that Boy George helped Virgin Atlantic Airways pay for a wing or a tail section or something.'

Since hitting it, Branson has bought an island in the Virgin Islands and is spending £2.5 million to turn it into the world's largest recording studio facility and rock star tax haven hang out.

Since hitting it, he's bought a mansion in Oxford where he spends his weekends.

Since hitting it, he's put up the money for *1984* and *Electric Dreams* – and that means he's also in the movie business.

❊   ❊   ❊

When Virgin agreed to produce the film version of Orwell's *1984*, Branson knew that the score should be done by a musician whose music could also sell albums. Producer Simon Perry and director Michael Radford said, fine, but insisted that the music must be good for the film as well as for selling records. In April 1984 David Bowie was suggested by Virgin, but it turned out that he was too busy to meet the film's deadline. To make certain that they would have a score at all, Perry and Radford convinced Virgin to let them commission Dominic Muldowney, an experienced film composer. He wrote the score that August and it was recorded at the beginning of September.

That's when Branson announced he had signed the job over to a rock group called The Eurythmics. Perry and Radford were horrified. First, they felt The Eurythmics were quite wrong for the film. Second, they were worried about the time scale. The Eurythmics said they would deliver their music by 28 September, which was only one week before the first press viewing. Perry tried to make Branson understand that the risks were absolutely enormous. The Eurythmics had never composed a score before. He asked Branson to promise that, if the music didn't work, they wouldn't be obliged to use it on the film. Branson said, yes, I quite understand and oh, by the way, they can't come to London because they have tax problems so they want to do this in the Bahamas.

As far as Perry was concerned, the notion of a couple of film composers, especially as raw as The Eurythmics were, not even being able to come to London to work with the director, was outlandish. To top it off, they were on an American tour and wouldn't even be able to start work until 11 September. Radford phoned them in the Bahamas, briefed them, sent them a video cassette, and thought this hasn't got a hope in hell. But Branson was quite impervious. He said he was paying them a great deal of money and mentioned the figure of $600,000 – more than everybody of serious consequence on the film put together was going to be paid. (Richard Burton was contracted with a small fee and a percentage of the picture. The original budget was £3.7 million. Then the budget was revised during shooting and went up to £5.5 million. The actual cash cost to put it on the screen was £4.8 million.)

'Richard Branson is a very strange person,' Perry says. 'He has a great deal of charm. He's slightly extravagant, kind of mercurial, a rather appealing character because he's very unexpected. But he doesn't appear to have a solid, personal, heart-felt opinion about anything. It's very difficult to deal with that. He has no real passion. He's desperately shy, terrified of being caught out. A film is a complex artistic object. If the man who's got the purse strings, and in this country that means he's got all the power, doesn't have a firm opinion himself about what you're doing, you can't really have a dialogue.'

The Eurythmics delivered the music a day before schedule. Radford laid it roughly on the film that night, and had a showing for the Virgin execs the following day.

Perry continues: 'The music was quite horrendous. It was totally inappropriate. We thought it was prima facie inappropriate and that no one would be taking it seriously. But we realized as the viewing went on that, actually, the guys from the record company were very pleased with the results, that they thought it was very good.'

The Eurythmics' music was not used at the premier. The Muldowney version was the one that got the good reviews across most of Europe. Then a combined version was prepared by Radford using a little of The Eurythmics' music so that Branson could keep his rights to the soundtrack album. But The Eurythmics, or their management, changed their minds and said it would be all their music or nothing. That meant Branson had to re-soundtrack prints of the film around the world with the all-Eurythmics' version. Complicating matters, The Eurythmics' music was mixed onto the film in one night by some Virgin executives who, Perry says, had very little idea of what they were doing. He points out that there is camera noise on the film and some of the levels are wrong. Anyway, he wants the world to know it was the Muldowney version that won the *Evening Standard*'s Best Film award.

'A lot of dealing with Virgin reminds me of school,' Perry says. 'Branson is a bit like a school prefect. There's a great deal of yah-boo-sucks style of negotiation. A lot

of what happens is based on getting one back. Vendettas
go on a lot of the time. It's very strange, really. "Typical
Simon," they shout, when I point out that I've still got
the rights to do something. "Oh, you would say that."
It's that kind of stuff. Which on a good night can seem
quite entertaining. We heard a lot of jokes about the
Virgin inner-party and outer-party. Well, there is an inner
party and they're all related in some way. A cousin. A
brother-in-law. You know, like that. Our theory is that
Virgin is still finally and absolutely a record company.
And I think that they characterize us as the artist and his
manager. Mike being the rock'n roll performer who has
to be comforted and kid-gloved, given everything he
wants, flattered, and told he's wonderful. And then they
go out to the corridor and beat the shit out of the
manager.'

*   *   *

Branson says that the Virgin Group, as a whole, brings in
just over 10 per cent profit on turnover. His gimmick, if
there is one, might be an ability to maximize profits by
cutting Virgin in along every step of everything they do.
For instance, when they footed the bill for the film
Electric Dreams, Virgin recording star Boy George did
the soundtrack, which was released as a Virgin album.
Virgin books did the book. Virgin Film Distributions did
the distribution. Virgin's video game company is doing
the video game. While Virgin's video operation is putting
out the video.

The core business is music, accounting for nearly 70 per
cent of the group's total profits. Retailing is divided
between Virgin stores and a 75 per cent holding in Ames
Records Shops, a chain in the north of England. The
media business is 15 per cent of Radio Mercury, 45 per
cent of a cable rock'n roll channel called Music Box, video
cassettes, computer games, and films. Then there's
the venture capital side, which is pubs, nightclubs,

Virgin Atlantic and a home music synthesiser called Synthaxe.

The two things that all of the projects have in common are the basics of Branson's empire. One, he buys ready-mades. He sits in his houseboat and sifts through project ideas that come to him. Two, he changes those ready-mades to cater almost exclusively to the 'Virgin market' – the 15–35 year olds who know music, consider themselves 'in', and have money in the pockets to convince everyone else that they are 'in'.

On average, at least for the past few years, he's been setting up one new company per month. Although he's trying not to do that these days. 'You know when you're over the hump. And from there it's just a question of consolidating your position. Some people choose to take risks which will not consolidate them. We take calculated risks. All our risks are within a consolidated position. Such as the airline. But, no, I don't think I'm becoming more conservative as I get older. Not yet. I mean, I'm not a businessman like Gerald Ronson. He's older and he's had his time for learning. I'm still learning.'

He's also toying with a market flotation. Possibly 10–15 per cent on the Unlisted Securities Market. 'We would be the biggest company in the UK ever to go that route. Maybe we'll do it in a year or a year-and-a-half. To put the company on a sound financial footing with a valuation which we can use to possibly make acquisitions, possibly a bit of consolidation and acquisition. But I don't think I want people telling me what to do. Some advisers have been suggesting that we put some non-executive directors on our board. But that doesn't fit in with the way I see my company. I like my company to have the feel of being small and intimate. The only people who should be on the board are those people who are in the nitty gritty of it. Those people who are working every day in the company.'

In spite of appearances, it hasn't always been high times

for Branson. In 1971 he ran up against H. M. Customs and Excise. His discount record business was only just making it. He soon figured out a scheme to help it along. By declaring records for export at Dover, claiming purchase tax rebates and driving around the port a few times, he could head back to his discount store in London and offer cut-price records on the back of the tax man. It worked the first night. It worked the second night. It didn't work the third night. He spent that one in jail. His mother bailed him out. Having a grandfather who was a judge and a father who was a barrister and magistrate probably didn't hurt his case. The courts settled on a £60,000 fine and gave him enough time to pay it. When his debt was paid, Branson wrote to the authorities thanking them for their understanding. No one had to remind him that, had he been a poor black kid from Brixton, the story might not have had the same happy ending.

A few years ago he was reminded again that everything he touches doesn't automatically turn to gold. He tried to launch a 'what's happening' kind of magazine in London and failed within a very short time. This time he did have something to lose. It cost him £500,000.

He's written them both off to life lessons. They put his success into some sense of proportion and therefore, he insists, he has not let his fame and fortune go to his head. 'Does it surprise you that I don't fly first class?' (He does on Virgin Atlantic.) 'I won't let my rock groups fly first class so I don't and that way they can't argue about it. Frankly I'd rather spend the money on more practical things. And anyway, I can remember when £600 or so meant a lot to me. Maybe there's an element of the '60s left in me somewhere.'

However, when he named himself President of Virgin Atlantic Airways he learned something about the airline business he hadn't known. 'This habit of mine, flying economy, isn't such a dilemma any more. When you own an airline you're allowed to fly first class on everybody else's airline for nothing. And I'm not mad enough to turn that down.'

Although he quickly adds, almost apologetically, that in the end he's too shy to ring up Pan Am or British Airways and ask for his free first-class seats.

✻   ✻   ✻

Randolph Fields was born in Santa Monica, California, and moved to London in 1962 when he was 9. He says he met Richard Branson once when he was 16 and Branson was 17, but it was a very brief hello, and Branson doesn't remember. Educated in the UK, with one year at an American high school, Fields is a barrister who practised law for a couple of years in the States, and who came back to Britain two years ago with the idea of starting an airline.

He called it British Atlantic.

But right off the stick he ran into problems. Fields wanted to make the Gatwick–JFK run with an all business-class service. It was going for the jugular of the major carriers. He quickly saw the writing on the wall and opted out for Gatwick–Newark. That route had been assigned to British Air Tours. It was, Fields says, 'the most closely guarded secret in the world. Before People's Express came along, British Air Tours, which is a charter company of British Airways, wanted to show that it would be a disaster of a route. Which it was, for them. It ran with atrocious load factors and they pulled off at the end of January 1983. That route then became open for the British to designate a replacement carrier. But the climate at that moment in time was that if the world's most popular airline couldn't be successful there, nobody else could.'

Then People's Express arrived. It wasn't a new mousetrap. It was merely a cheaper one. Yet the world still beat a path to their door.

Fields then took another look at Newark–Gatwick. 'I'm a great believer in market segmentation, particularly on London–New York. It's such a large market that the best recipe for success is to appeal to a specific market and be overwhelmingly successful with that little bit of the market because it will fill your plane every day. There seemed to me to be two gaps in the market. One was that People's Express wasn't doing too well with the British visiting friends and relative traffic. They only did cold food. They didn't do hot food. Secondly, they weren't doing too well with youth traffic. Since Laker came off the route, youth traffic declined by two-thirds.'

He thinks Laker's appeal as a cult figure probably had a lot to do with it. 'With air transportaion, apart from the must-go travellers, we're selling a commodity that people actually do not need. Like Virgin selling pop records. People don't need records. They buy records because they have disposable income so they're able to buy the records, and because their interest is aroused. It's the same with air travel. We're selling a non-essential product.'

Fields knew that to sell his non-essential product, everything relied on his marketing approach. 'The reason I came up with Richard Branson was because I conceived of an airline that would appeal to the British visiting friends and relative market plus the youth market through the use of entertainment. It was possible due mainly to the development of new video projection systems. The classic problem with airplanes is that you've got all these people stuck in a metal tube getting bored out of their minds. There is no actual pleasure in the travel aspect of air transportation. After looking out of the window for five minutes (if you're lucky enough to have a window), you've had enough. So what you have to do is kill the boredom factor. With the newest video projection systems that have been developed, it struck me that you could show continuous entertainment throughout the flight, but you wouldn't have to darken the cabin. That's why the airlines only used to show one film. A lot of passengers don't want to watch films. So I conceived of this product where you would have entertainment and state of the art headphone technology. I had a lot of investor interest but I thought if you're going to have an investor you might as well get something from that investor. It occurred to me that if I got Virgin involved, not only would they serve as an investor, but also they would have the marketing expertise to reach the youth market.'

Fields simply picked up the phone and eventually got Branson on the other end. 'I told him, I've got an airline project that's about to take off and I think you might be interested. I talked to him for a couple of minutes about it and he said, have you got a business plan. I said yes. He said, well, send it round to me and send a copy to my financial director. And I did that. The next day he called me up and said, look, we'd like to talk about it. We met the following day and thrashed it around. Over the course of the next week or so we talked about it. And burnt the midnight oil for a couple of nights. And came up with a deal. And then announced it.'

British Atlantic changed its trading name to Virgin Atlantic on 29 February 1984.

Three months later they were in the air.

Within six months, Fields was no longer involved with the running of Virgin Atlantic. 'Well, yes and no. No, I don't think it was a boardroom fist fight. It had to do with the underlying circumstances. In Virgin I went to bed with a very highly motivated individual. And that individuality permeates thoughout all the companies. It suited both of our needs and purposes the way things developed. I committed myself to spending six months with it, getting it in the air, getting things running, and getting a chief executive. When we had a chief executive in place and we were able to agree that the guy we had should be made permanent, my job was pretty much done. Although Richard had asked me to stay on as chairman, I felt it was more appropriate that he should be chairman.'

In other words, Branson turned out to be a tougher

guy to do business with than he looks. 'He can be very easy, but Richard is a very shrewd businessman. He's an incredibly tough negotiator. He knows how to negotiate a deal. I still own 25 per cent. I'm very involved with it, except there isn't a hell of a lot to do right now. A lot of people saw our partnership as a good thing. And it was a shame that we weren't going to be partners in all things. But Richard is a very dynamic individual. I think he sees Virgin Atlantic and wants to see Virgin Atlantic as very much a part of the Virgin Group. Closely integrated. If we've split up, I have to say it's an amicable split. I think partners by definition have arguments, and we've had our arguments, but we haven't had an argument for months.'

When Fields presented him with all the facts, Branson took his usual approach to decision making. 'If you sit down with accountants and look at profit and loss projections, they'll manage to come up with all sorts of reasons why something won't work. Well I think if you've got a gut feeling about something then trial and error can produce the best results. I think the only way to learn is to give it a try.'

Like almost all the projects that come aboard the houseboat, within minutes of the launching they become Richard Branson's project. Randolph Fields was quickly and smartly escorted to a back seat. And the headlines echoed that effect. Branson takes on British Airways. Branson picks up where Laker left off. Branson introduces Virgin Atlantic Airways.

Almost on cue, the moment Branson got involved, opposition was raised by British Caledonian. They felt that Branson was too young and inexperienced. Anyway, Brit Cal argued, the success of an airline should not have to depend on how many pop groups made it to the Top 10. Branson's argument was a simple one. He compared Virgin's profits with Brit Cal's, and beat them two to one.

At the same time, Virgin Atlantic bought a 747 at a cost of just under $28 million. Included in the deal with Boeing for the three-year-old plane were all sorts of escape

clauses in case the passengers didn't flock in the way
Branson hoped. Actually all those escape clauses make it
look more like a leasing deal. Branson can sell the plane
back to Boeing at any time within three years, or sell it on
the open market if he chooses. The cost to him comes
down to £2 million a year. And he's covered that with his
company's cash flow and currency options against
distortion of the dollar/pound ratio. In fact, the way he
structured the business, the worst he could lose was two
months' profits on the Virgin Group.

It goes without saying that he took a risk. If nothing
else, Virgin Atlantic is a far cry from the music business.
But Branson doesn't see it quite that way. 'Yes, Virgin
Atlantic is the one that's not an obvious fit within the
group – although when we went into the music business
we knew nothing about the music business. The whole
way we got in was by cheap pricing and discounting and
appealing to a segment of the public. We're doing the
same with the airline. We're shipping tons of our records
over to America every day, with the airline, and I think
you'll find the market we're aiming at is the market we
know. The whole promotion, the whole decor, the whole
way our staff behave, the kinds of service, the fact that
our entertainments can now travel for nothing on the
airline – we can come up with all those sorts of things
because of our other businesses which other airlines
couldn't.'

However, running an airline has never been one of his
life-long passions. 'I only thought about it for the first
time when the idea was proposed. Originally I was
sceptical. I spent two weeks going over the figures and
finally decided that just because Freddie Laker went
down, it's no reason why we shouldn't have a go. I
figured we could learn from his mistakes.'

Those mistakes, he says, are fairly obvious, especially
with the benefit of hindsight. The fact that Laker went
first should, he hopes, make it easier for him as Number
Two. 'Laker didn't lose because he didn't have any

passengers for the North Atlantic run. No, he was selling seats. When he went under he was flying at 83 per cent capacity. He lost because he bought too many planes and found himself swamped by massive currency problems. The dollar swung and he suddenly found himself facing huge debts. The other problem is all that business about possible interference from the major airlines. Depending on how much of it you believe, whether or not it's true, I think it's unlikely that they would try anything like it with us. If they did it at all, I don't think they'd do it twice.'

Either he'll succeed, or those will go down as famous last words, alongside 'Hey General Custer, where'd all them Indians come from?'

5

Jacob Rothschild

The Honourable Nathaniel Charles Jacob Rothschild is a 49-year-old direct descendant of the legendary Mayer Amschel Rothschild. The old man is often described as having been 'an odd mixture of the philosopher and the entrepreneur'. His great-great-great-great grandson is the kind of guy that Mayer might have felt at home with. In fact, Mayer probably would have liked Jacob a lot. Six generations later the old family flair is alive and well.

'I drifted into business. I went to Oxford and nearly became an academic. There was a wish, I wouldn't say pressure, that I should go into N. M. Rothschild, which was our family business. So I went there. Then I trained outside Rothschilds as well. I spent some time at Cooper Brothers, the accountants. I spent six months there counting steel bars to help the auditors tidy up the accounts of some industrial company. That was the equivalent of starting in the mail room in the world of finance. I spent some time at Morgan Stanley, investment bankers in the United States. And I worked for a firm of West End financiers for a year. I was about two and a half years outside Rothschilds, and then I went back there. It was a fairly difficult place to learn as I was a member of the family. I was treated with too much respect and decorum. It's often easier to learn the hard way.'

In 1980 Jacob Rothschild and his cousin Evelyn de Rothschild disagreed as to how N. M. Rothschild & Sons should be run. It has often been described as a very bitter fight. When the dust settled, Jacob went out on his own, away from the family umbrella, a man determined to prove himself.

'I don't mind the description investment banker. I think it depends on where you live. In America, Wall Street houses call themselves investment banks. They don't like to be called stockbrokers. In London, people traditionally call themselves merchant bankers. It's a kind of elegant description that some people would like to carry. I don't really mind what I'm called. Although I don't care to be called a stockbroker. But investment banker is fine. Or, I'm running a financial services company. I don't think it matters what the label is, too much. But the sector I fit into is financial services. Or, diversified financial holding company.'

It was September when Jacob Rothschild left N. M. Rothschild, taking with him a small investment branch called RIT (Rothschild Investment Trust). Within a year he convinced David Montagu to join RIT, adding a definite heavy-weight to his team. Montagu had built his own reputation as Chairman and Chief Executive at Samuel Montagu & Co. (his own family's merchant bank), Chairman and Chief Executive at the Orion Bank and Chairman of Merrill Lynch and Co's international bank. Six months later RIT pulled off the first of several successful, and often thought of as 'flashy', deals – a £97 million absorption of the Great Northern Investment Trust. Before the end of 1982 they added a 29.9 per cent stake in the London-based stockbroker Kitcat & Aitken where they were able to call on the expertise of Nils Taube, one of the City's most respected traders and investment managers.

Now called RIT & Northern, in August 1983 Rothschild looked to the United States for his next buy. It was the New York investment bank, L. F. Rothschild, Unterberg, Towbin. Interestingly enough, the bank's founder, Louis F. Rothschild, is no relation whatsoever of the European

Rothschilds – the name is strictly a coincidence – but the purchase of a 50 per cent share for £42 million was significant in a most personal way. It seems that Evelyn de Rothschild was also looking at the bank and wanted to pick up a controlling 51 per cent. Jacob was willing to settle for an even half, and the bank's Robert Towbin sided with Jacob. It was not only a good acquisition for RIT & Northern, it was without a doubt a substantial moral victory for one cousin over another.

Now the City started to see Jacob Rothschild in a new light. He was very quickly becoming someone important, not for a family name but for his own financial skills. And if there were any remaining doubts about those skills, the following six months took care of them. In November 1983 Rothschild merged RIT & Northern with the Charterhouse Group. It was a £400 million deal that brought into the stable a merchant bank plus a whole group of industrial investments, and created Charterhouse J. Rothschild (CJR). Exactly six months later, Rothschild really dropped the bomb when he announced that CJR owned a 25 per cent stake in Mark Weinberg's Hambro Life Assurance group, and was planning a merger. The new company, with over £1 billion in capital, would be called Allied Rothschild Charterhouse.

The idea was to create a financial services empire, the likes of which the City of London had never seen.

'At the time we acquired our original stake of 25 per cent, we thought two things. We thought first of all that 25 per cent would be a good investment and that we would take that risk. Secondly, we hoped and believed that we would end up merging fully with Hambro Life. It didn't work out, which was a disappointment and a setback, for all sorts of reasons. One of them was that to have imposed a merger on an unwilling stock market would probably have resulted in a lower share price, and scepticism by the market for a number of years. That wasn't in our shareholders' interests. So both of us [Rothschild and Weinberg] decided to step back. Having stepped back, we had to demonstrate that the decision to acquire 25 per cent of the capital was in fact a good investment.'

That 25 per cent stake in Hambro Life also represented one-quarter of CJR's assets – a pretty hefty chunk to cram into one basket. 'Yes it was,' Rothschild agrees. 'It was a risky investment. But it was a measured risk and with good fortunes it proved worthwhile.'

Those good fortunes materialized when the British American Tobacco Company (BAT) came along wanting to buy Hambro Life. Rothschild sold CJR's stake with Weinberg's approval in mid-December 1984. The bottom line showed CJR with a £40 million profit.

'Let's face it, we took a risk. Now we believe that the risk was a reduced risk because it was undoubtedly the best-managed retail financial services company in this country. It's a quality business. The financial services area is one in which everyone is intensely interested and therefore the possibility of it being acquired by a third party, because it had these characteristics, was always there. In this particular case that third party indeed turned out to be there. I'd rather think that we controlled our own destiny, through backing people of quality instead of trying to impose our wishes on personalities.'

Once BAT announced that they were serious players in the game, the decision to recommend an offer by BAT was, Rothschild notes, a very very difficult one for people like Weinberg, who had built up Hambro Life. He feels that in making that decision, a bunch of entrepreneurial businessmen actually suppressed their own egos for the sake of doing what they came to believe was the right thing for everyone involved.

'If you can make those types of difficult decisions then hopefully that demonstrates a quality of independence and objectivity which I think is very important. In a sense you have to change horses, don't you, because most companies are created by driven-ego types. But very often their ultimate destiny should be the very suppression of the egos that helped to build them up. In the case of Hambro Life they're not stepping away from it, but are putting their shareholders' interests in front of their own. They're accepting a value for their company but they're continuing to work for that new company. Because they're honourable and good people they will continue to do that. Although it will be a subsidiary of another company which will own 100 per cent of its equity. So their direct economic interest in its affairs is reduced or even eliminated. That quality is most unusual in corporate life and is not as easy to live up to as it sounds.'

Interestingly enough, had the Hambro Life merger actually come off, Rothschild himself would have stepped down as Chairman in favour of Weinberg. 'If Mark had run the company, and he would have run the company, then his style would have applied. That's very different from my style. We happen to get on exceptionally well as individuals and I would have hoped I would have still had something to offer him. But he would have run the company.'

And he insists, he could have done it easily. No ego problem at all. 'I have plenty of other interests. No problem. The attraction of Hambro Life was that he is a superb businessman whom I happen to like very much, so whatever was created would have ended up in very good hands. The Hambro Life exercise would have been a perfectly satisfactory way for the company I helped to create to have become independent of me, just as we've made other businesses independent of us. I would have found it difficult a number of years ago. But not now. I find it rather satisfactory that one can be as objective as that about it.'

He admits, however, he might have found such a move difficult to accept if he wasn't independent, if he didn't have a lot of other interests. And both sentimentally and ideologically, he would very much have liked to merge Charterhouse J. Rothschild in some shape or form with Hambro Life. 'But realistically it wouldn't have made sense for either their shareholders or our shareholders because you're living in a period when financial conglomerates, or financial holding companies, whatever you'd like to call them, will sell at relatively low prices and relatively low multiples. So, to have disposed of our interests in Hambro Life to British American Tobacco on a basis which was very acceptable to Hambro Life's management and also resulted in our shareholders being endowed with a significant capital profit in the course of a few months, seemed to us to be the right way to behave from the shareholder interest point of view. I can talk about the ideology of financial services but can't ask people to invest in it if the two don't happen to coincide. So I discipline myself to that approach.'

Within a month of selling his Hambro shares, Rothschild stunned the City by divesting CJR of his merchant banking arm. He sold Charterhouse Japhet and CJR's UK, French and Canadian development capital interests to the Royal Bank Group for £155 million. A few weeks later CJR was renamed J. Rothschild Holdings (JRH).

The business press labelled it 'a retreat'.

Businessweek noted that Rothschild's 'Attempt to build a British global investment bank able to compare with such giants as Salomon Brothers or Nomura Securities has foundered.'

But not everyone believed that it was a defeat. Rothschild, the analysts said, was simply going back to what he does best – betting huge sums on risk arbitrage and buy-outs.

'We intend to concentrate on those aspects of our policy upon which CJR and its predecessor companies have principally built their reputation, namely the risking of capital,' he wrote to the shareholders when the sale of Charterhouse Japhet was announced. 'As a transaction-oriented company with a small, entrepreneurial management team we will stand in marked contrast to the many service oriented companies which have developed in the City of London. Other investment bodies, such as investment and unit trusts, operate under specific regulatory constraints, while banks and insurance companies are not only regulated in the management of their assets but are also obliged to devote their capital to the support of their deposit and actuarial liabilities.'

Not so with JRH.

'More and more, the profile of our company is one with a big enough capital to attract opportunities in America and England and elsewhere. We're risk orientated. I think that's a more capitalistic approach than perhaps if I read back to what we said at the time of the Charterhouse merger or the Hambro Life attempted merger. I think with hindsight there was too much philosophizing about creating a new financial services empire. I think that's what, to some extent, my colleagues and I have withdrawn from. We're now saying we must at all times discipline ourselves to not indulge in a philosophy that won't benefit our shareholders.'

While the sale of Charterhouse was not initiated by Rothschild – it was the Royal Bank that thought of it first – the fact that Rothschild agreed at this time might not be such a coincidence. The City is, like it or not, becoming 'Americanized'. Wall Street firms are moving into the Stock Exchange, and winds of change are in the air. In the City, almost all of the big security groups have a merchant banking base. But in the States the trend is towards a more streamlined approach. None of the major investment banks, such as Goldman Sachs or Salomon Brothers or Morgan Stanley, is a bank in the traditional sense.

As David Lascelles asked in the *Financial Times* at the time of the Charterhouse sale: 'As long as you can do deals, trade in the capital markets, and run venture capital and investment portfolios, why encumber yourself with a highly regulated and not particularly profitable deposit and loan business?'

Significantly, one very important part of the Charterhouse Group that JRH has kept is called CHUSA, a US-based leveraged buy-out operation which is concentrated on the $0–$100 million leveraged buy-out, management buy-out type of acquisition. 'That's an area of risk, of transaction orientation rather than relationship orientation that we want to develop and foster. In America, for example, where because of high interest rates you have relatively low stock markets so that the values placed on certain companies are far below their real values in stock market terms, we might well take advantage of that situation. We certainly don't want to cut ourselves off from that.'

In other words, if the price was right, he'd go for it. But it's not only the price that matters. The management of the company being acquired would almost certainly have to go for it too. 'Let me say that I have an aversion to doing things on a hostile basis. As do most of my colleagues. And that's quite a disadvantage at times. Lots of people have made money out of hostile take-overs, so sometimes they're worthwhile in materialistic terms. But sentimentally or temperamentally, I'm just rather squeamish about hostile bids. I think on the whole that they have not been industrially constructive in the last few years. We feel we have the ability to analyse and research a company and see what its true worth is. Therefore, if the deconglomeration of a company can result in far greater values for the shareholders than the stock market would put upon that company, sure. But as I said, if it's something of significant size, I think to work with a partner with more industrial experience than ourselves is the approach we would usually adopt. As we build our own management competence in our leveraged buy-out sector, we'll have more self-confidence about tackling those situations ourselves.'

JRH's resources will be allocated between financial services, leveraged buy-outs, investment holdings, strategic investments and dealing. He plans to dispose of CJR's few remaining industrial subsidiaries, using that capital to expand CHUSA and bring some of its techniques and skills into the UK market.

Again, the 'American' approach. 'In the case of the successful UK conglomeration, they're really putting together a collection of diverse industrial interests under the umbrella of a holding company. It works extremely well under strong management and direction. But it's a kind of curious architecture, isn't it, because you have no theme in it. You have a neoclassical room, a renaissance room, a rococo room, whatever you like. You're living in that mixture, that melange. It's a curious phenomenon, that this type of conglomerate is being embraced in the UK whereas in the United States deconglomeration is in fashion in what one might call the post-Geneen (ITT) era.'

So, the 'melange' that Allied Charterhouse Rothschild might have been is not where Jacob Rothschild is at these days. One associate has been quoted as saying, 'Now he is going back to the kind of thing that comes naturally to him.'

And what comes naturally to him is being quietly opportunistic.

He is definitely opportunistic and makes no qualms about saying that there are some deals he just can't pass up. For example, he is not necessarily against a little good old-fashioned 'greenmail'. At the beginning of 1984, CJR together with Sir James Goldsmith, Australian financier Kerry Packer and Italian automobile magnate Gianni Agnelli put $100 million into a pool as part of an 'investment' in the US-based paper, insurance and energy company, St Regis. Goldsmith held 60 per cent, Rothschild's stake was 30 per cent, and the other two divided the remaining 10 per cent. The mere presence of Goldsmith was enough to panic the St Regis board. He left Britain years before and quickly discovered that there is a major difference in the way American banks play. Unlike British banks, which tend to allow borrowing based on the wealth of the borrower, American banks believe it's the assets of the bid target that matter. So

Goldsmith found financing easier on that side of the Atlantic, where he borrowed what he needed to make take-over bids. A few years ago, he asked the banks for £661 million, snatched up the forestry conglomerate Diamond International, and a year or so later sold it for enough to pay off the debt and also claim a £350 million profit. It's a modern form of swash-buckling, very much to the liking of guys such as T. Boone Pickens and, lately, Rupert Murdoch. Murdoch went after Warner Communications, made as tough a stand as anyone could, walked away without the company, and wept all the way to the bank. The skill and sang-froid under pressure that Murdoch showed in that particular bit of greenmail – or, 'investment' if you will – led Goldsmith to be quoted as saying, 'Rupert is the only man I know who makes me feel like Liberace.' So Jacob Rothschild found himself in the right kind of company when the St Regis opportunity arose, although he and his three pals didn't come onto the scene with guns ablazing. They were most charming – which can be most menacing – and the St Regis board paid them to go away. Their $100 million very quickly became $150 million.

'I think there are once-in-a-lifetime risks that occur and then you've got to have the courage to take those risks. Those that are spread don't normally do very well. It puts a lid on their upside if they're spread too much. So you have to have the courage from time to time to take important risks. But there's a difference between gambling and risk taking. They're totally different. Gambling means that you can really lose everything you've staked in a short period of time. And the chances of your losing everything you've staked are quite significant.'

Call the game that Rothschild likes to play 'calculated risk taking', where the bets are placed only on quality and only after all the homework has been done to minimize the risks. 'They should be macro-risks where you go wrong. I mean if suddenly the American economy collapses or there's no steel business, or interest rates go through the roof, or there's a war, whatever, those are things that could occur. When you take any kind of investment risk you should think about that. But in the normal course of business you should be able to analyse out most of the risks. Especially if you risk a significant amount of the capital of the company you're running, which is earned after all by people who don't expect you to lose it. Due diligence, the soundness of the assets, the quality of the management, those are all things that are integral in the course of assessing risks. It's quite distinct from gambling.'

Here of course, he's referring to the responsibilities of running a publicly quoted company. That, he insists, is not necessarily the same game for people who run privately owned companies. 'They have a divine right or royal right to behave as they please. But once you're out of that domain and into the arena of being owned by widows, orphans, institutions and pensioners, then you've got a quite different set of responsibilities. And those responsibilities are paramount.'

Nicely enough, Rothschild is fast to admit that he's not the world's best businessman. But he's extremely proud of the fact that, internationally, he enjoys a reputation for being a straight and honourable businessman. But then he is a Rothschild, which means he not only has a long-standing family reputation he must live up to, he is also financially independent. Personal gain is hardly his primary motivation. In other words, he can afford to be an honourable man. 'I think it's certainly partially that. Obviously, it's easier to be objective if one is independent. I'm fortunate enough to have been born independent in a materialistic sense. I think it makes it much easier for me to, if you like, adopt the attitudes which I've spoken about. I think as a family, hopefully, we have a tradition of putting objectivity, particularly with other people's money and assets, as an extremely high priority. Perhaps the highest priority. So certainly, there's a family tradition and history. And as I said before, that independence is also very helpful.'

When the Hambro Life deal was still on the cards, *Businessweek Magazine* featured Rothschild in a major cover story, calling him 'London's New Financial Whiz'. The article's subheading was 'Jacob Rothschild rebounds from a family feud to thrive on risk'. But rather oddly they described his style as 'aggressive and arrogant'. It's then surprising to meet him because he doesn't appear to be either. He is absolutely not arrogant – 'Let's hope that you're right and they're wrong.' Nor does he seem very aggressive. 'I think we're prepared to work extremely hard. But I don't think that makes one aggressive. I enjoy working hard and seem to have done without many holidays for 20 years or so. I think those measures of hard work probably apply. I'm not sure it is always fun, but if you're looking for an answer as to why I do it, there can't be a very rational reason other than I enjoy it. We all need an element of therapy in our lives, but it would be exaggerated if I were doing it purely for therapeutic reasons.'

Anyway, he adds, he is a man of varied interests. In mid-1985 he took over as Chairman of The National Gallery. He describes that as a public service commitment which he takes very seriously. But there are others, equally serious in their own right, just perhaps slightly off-beat. 'I dabble at businesses that are, if you like, inappropriate for a public company. For instance, I own Clifton Nurseries, which I hope is the best nursery garden in London.' (He interjects here that he's not a gardener now, but hopes to be, 'When I'm older.') 'Also, Terence Conran and myself are developing Butler's Wharf together. He is by far the biggest shareholder and the controlling shareholder, but we're hoping that it will eventually be the Covent Garden of Docklands in a few years' time. So, I have those kinds of interests. They're personal interests. I don't see life as disintegrated between work and other things. I find these dividing lines that perhaps the English system tends to put on people are not necessarily valid in my case. There isn't something which is work between 9 and 5 and then something which is something else after 5. Although I have a family and children which is absolutely different from one's work. So I think life is something that goes on all the time.'

Another interesting description of Rothschild comes from Michael von Clemm, Chairman of Credit Suisse First Boston, Ltd. He sees Rothschild as 'A combination of long-range thinker on the one hand and an opportunist on the other.'

Now Rothschild chuckles. 'It's nice of him to say it. Let's put it another way. I think one of the most important characteristics of someone who is in the field of business is to correct his mistakes. So it may well be that you make a decision and it doesn't come off for one reason or another. We've spoken about Hambro Life in that context. Then you have a very big responsibility to correct it. If you take Michael von Clemm's kind phrase, maybe you make some decisions and it looks to outsiders like long-term strategy but to correct the mistake you have to be an opportunist.'

At the *International Herald Tribune* they see him in yet a different light. They wrote that he was a gunslinger who was good at pulling off 'flashy deals'.

But here he disagrees. 'I don't think of myself as a gunslinger. Obviously not.' Nor does he care to think of himself as merely the sheriff who heads up a posse of gunslingers. 'No, not that either. If you take a point I made earlier, we have an aversion to being involved as principals in hostile bids. The gunslinger somehow gives you a picture of someone who is endlessly making take-over bids of a hostile kind, and we're not that at all. It is perfectly true to say that we have bought and sold companies which we have developed. But I think that's a constructive thing to do. I think the building up of a conglomerate empire can be very successful over a period of many years. Ultimately, there seems to be a tendency for such companies to end up being deconglomeratized by somebody else. You see that over and over again with the process of deconglomeratization in America. In our case, what we aim to do is stick to what we know quite well. We don't really have it in our mind any more to create some huge edifice.'

In many ways, Jacob Rothschild is something of an enigma. Having come to the City with financial independence, at least in the beginning he was seen perhaps as a dilettante. He's tried very hard to prove them wrong. He has, without any doubt, outshone his cousin, and brought a certain flamboyance to the modern Rothschild family image. Yet, meeting him and speaking with him, the first thing you notice is that here is a man not at all out of the high-flyer mould. His ego, if there is one, seems insulated with old money, much like seven layers of fibre-glass wrapped around the water tank to keep the heat in. There is nothing of the self-publicist in Jacob Rothschild. He'd rather talk about almost anything than himself. Yet, when he refers to certain people with whom he has done deals, such as Jimmy Goldsmith and the St Regis affair, there is almost a glint of envy that flashes in his eyes. It's not hero worship but it could be a bit of 'I wish I could be ruthless too.' Pressed on that he quickly says, 'But I'm much too squeamish.' On the other hand, when he was told about this book and promised that his personal life would not be a part of it, that no skeletons in the cupboard were of interest, he muttered with slight astonishment – as if everyone should know – 'I have nothing to hide. There are no skeletons.'

Not everybody in this book can be as frank.

Then, too, not everybody in this book repeated with such consistency and such conviction that his reason for playing the game was mainly the satisfaction derived from seeing his shareholders make a good return. It's almost as if each share is a kind of personal vote in one man's campaign to prove, at least to himself, that Mayer would have been proud.

'We don't have a five-year plan or a ten-year plan. We see ourselves as calculated risk takers with the features I've described. Of course we must build a company with a constructive purpose. I have no interest in JRH becoming a personalized vehicle for wheeling and dealing. Hopefully we'll see a number of opportunities in the next few years. We've held ourselves out to investors and our existing shareholders as a company which has a track record of success in that area of endeavour and who may, therefore, in the future continue to be successful. If people want to invest with us, they can. And if they do, well, hopefully they will profit from it. It's no more ambitious than that.'

6

Ashraf Marwan

The 'mysterious Dr Marwan' doesn't think of himself as being mysterious.

'Why mysterious? I'm not mysterious. Everything is open. When you buy shares you buy them through stockbrokers and banks and everything is registered. So what's mysterious?'

But maybe you're mysterious if other people think you are. And lots of people think he's mysterious.

Sic semper Egyptian risk takers.

* * *

Mohamed Ashraf Marwan has an office on Piccadilly, in a less than fancy building, behind a glass door marked Mestimo Investments. Dr Marwan is, it turns out, a minority shareholder in this Nassau-registered company from which he leases his office.

You step out of the lift, and face a glass door looking into the reception. A not-necessarily mysterious middle-aged Arab gentleman vets you before unlocking the door. He takes your coat while a secretary explains that Dr Marwan will be right with you. Coffee or tea is offered. Everybody seems busy. People are constantly moving about. The waiting area turns out to be someone's private office – crowded for space, the secretary apologizes.

When you are finally ushered into the corner office – a

large room with Islamic art on the walls – the mysterious Dr Marwan turns out to be a tall, starkly serious, but otherwise cordial man. His receding hairline makes him look older than his 41 years. And at first it would be easy to mistake his character for a chilly dose of xenophobia.

'I have my PhD in Chemistry.' His voice is low, laced with the sort of thick accent that gets used in films about the Middle East – used by actors who are trying to sound, yes, mysterious. 'My BA and my Masters are also in Chemistry. It helps a lot in business because in chemistry you cut things short. One plus one equals two. Never two-point-one. Hydrogen plus oxygen gives you water. You see, I don't go for theoretical or hypothetical things.'

He says he is a man who prefers to deal with facts. And one fact of life – as far as he's concerned – is that the British tend to think foreigners are mysterious. 'If you are a foreigner in this country, and make no mistake about this, if you try to become too successful, you will be absorbed by the financial establishment. You will be killed by them. You cannot fight them as long as you are a foreigner. You are single-handed. You know, we have a saying, if you cannot fight them, join them. Well, I have applied that system here but with a slight modification. If I cannot join them, I avoid them'.

In 1965, the 21-year-old Marwan was a Lieutenant in the Egyptian Army. Four years later he was named to a very minor information and intelligence post in the Nasser government. A year after that, following Nasser's death, Anwar Sadat brought him to real power as a personal adviser, asking him to head an office that in the west might be called the President's Advisory Board for National Security. He also served Sadat as Secretary for Foreign Contacts, a job that gave him instant access to all of the political and financial leaders in the Arab world.

He was still in his 20s.

Around Cairo they referred to him as 'the miracle child'.

By having shrewdly built up friendships with the most influential men in the Arab world, Marwan was appointed Chairman of the Arab Organization for Military Industry in 1976. It was a £1 billion joint venture between several Arab nations that Sadat hoped would establish an arms industry in Egypt. But it fell apart in 1979 when Saudi Arabia and some of the Gulf States decided that the Camp David Agreements had turned Egypt into an Israeli ally. Feeling changes about to happen in Egypt, Marwan came to live in the west. He said at the time that he wanted his children educated in England. His official residence is Monte Carlo. But he maintains a home in England.

Although you wouldn't know it by the way his name is bandied around the city – suggesting he's had a long-standing influence on certain share transactions – he's only been doing business here since 1980. But then he didn't come to England penniless. The 'wonder child' was already a millionaire.

'I started in the 1970s by selling a piece of land in Abu Dhabi. That's where I first made my money. But I have to say that I was lucky. You know, business is all about knowledge and luck. Both must be combined. It's like two different people having two different oil concessions 500 metres apart. One drills and finds oil. One drills a dry well. I was lucky because I had the land at the right time and there was a buyer. Sometimes you have some merchandise and there is a buyer. Sometimes there is no buyer. When there is no buyer you keep it. If you have good-quality material, there is always someone who will buy it. Like having a flat in Eaton Square. You can put any price tag on it. You can sell it in one day. You can sell it in two years. But eventually you will sell it.'

Unlike many wealthy men who love to tell you how smart they are, Marwan is almost alarmingly frank about the role luck has played in his own life. 'I'm not necessarily a bright man. It was a big piece of luck that President Sadat picked me for a job as his adviser.'

But not quite.

It just so happens that his father was a well-known Egyptian General, so as a family the Marwans had a sort of pedigree. It was most certainly a name respected enough that the dashing Lt Ashraf Marwan could meet, fall in love with and wind up marrying President Nasser's daughter. Treated kindly by his father-in-law, his associations at the highest levels led him to the friendship with Sadat.

'He chose me, yes. But then I had to perform. He gave me the chance and I took the chance. But if he didn't give me that chance I would have stayed where I was. A small, young clerk in one of the government departments. I would have been like anyone else in the country. That's the way it is.'

Because he knows what it's like to be on the inside, he doesn't hide the fact that he feels the cold all the more in England where he is decidedly on the outside. 'In the UK, everything is a club. If you want to go to a gym, you must belong to a club. If you want to get a good meal, you must belong to a club. If you want to meet the right people, you must belong to a club. Everything here is a club. It is a kind of discrimination, especially between the foreigners and the locals. In this country, if you do some small business, okay, they will leave you alone. But if you are a foreigner and you start touching the cream, the business establishment will close in on you. They won't let you. The individual is not welcomed as part of the establishment.'

Frankly, it's a good bet that very few people would ever have heard of Dr Marwan (or thought of him as being mysterious) had he not got too close to the cream when he bought a sizeable holding in the House of Fraser. 'The establishment didn't like me for that.' When the establishment looked around and realized that Marwan knew Tiny Rowland – 'another individual' – the establishment did what he always knew they would.

They closed in on him.

*   *   *

A 'concert party' has nothing to do with the Royal Philharmonic and crumpets.

It is, instead, an 'arrangement' between at least two parties to circumvent certain procedures laid down by law in regard to share holdings. The Companies Act says that notification must be given to a company if it is the object of 'a meeting of minds' between two or more parties for buying, using, retaining or disposing of shares. As an example, say someone has 29.9 per cent of a company's shares and for whatever reason is not permitted to acquire more than that. Then say that person meets another person and offers to buy shares of a company through that second person or buy the shares already held by that second person, some time in the future when he is legally allowed to do so. Or, say that first person agrees to purchase those shares when the second person agrees to vote with the first in a certain matter before the annual general meeting. In other words, a concert party is a type of conspiracy.

It is, of course, illegal.

But everyone knows it's illegal and you'd have to be pretty stupid to get caught at it. There's no need to say, 'Let's conspire' when anyone with a good nose can smell a fast profit. Case in point. One well-known businessman was, some time ago, engaged in a take-over battle. It was hostile, and a block of shares that would be potentially important for that person's victory was pledged against him. In fact, the owner of those shares let it be known that he would sell them to anyone in the world except the person leading the fight for the take-over. So another person – and it must be pointed out that neither one of them is Dr Marwan – heard about it and rang the first person. Despite the fact that there has never been any love lost between the two, the second was willing to buy those shares in his own name, with the intention of voting for the take-over, then pass them along to the first person once the take-over had been completed. He was willing to do it because it would be profitable for him to do it. A verbatim account of the entire conversation, as reported by that second person, went like this:

Second: 'Hi X, this is Y.'

First: (Laughter)

Second: (Laughter)

First: 'Thank you for calling. But I think I can manage it.'

Second: 'All right. Goodbye.'

First: 'Goodbye.'

So much for concert parties.

Where Ashraf Marwan ran up against the establishment was when someone decided there must have been a concert party between Lonrho's Tiny Rowland and Marwan concerning several million House of Fraser shares held by Marwan and needed by Rowland to split Harrods away from the House of Fraser. De-merger would eventually bring Harrods into the House of Lonrho. Well, it was bad enough having foreign-born Tiny Rowland trying to run British-born Professor Roland Smith, Chairman of the House of Fraser, out of town. But having an Arab do it as well was simply too much. Foreigners should know their place. After all, we're not talking about a Pakistani buying a corner newsagents or a Greek going into a High Street souvenir shop. This is Harrods. HM The Queen shops there. So does her daughter-in-law. So does Jackie Onassis. What did it matter if Harrods made money and the rest of the House of Fraser wasn't up to the same snuff. By God and Union Jack, we can't have these immigrants telling us British what to do with Harrods. Anyway, the Professor obviously wasn't ready to accept as compensation just any old job at some medium-sized nationalized industry. Why shouldn't it be Sir Professor of Knightsbridge, or, even better, Lord Smith of the Food Halls. So someone rang the Department of Trade and Industry to profess that Marwan and Rowland had acted in concert.

The DTI appointed John Griffiths, CMG, QC, to investigate. While he proceeded, Lonrho discovered the somewhat awkward fact that Griffiths had accepted a brief for and had appeared in court on behalf of the National Coal Board Pension Fund. Among the gentlemen connected at the time in one way or another with the National Coal Board Pension Fund were: Mr Hugh Jenkins, manager, Sir Ronald McIntosh, adviser, and Mr E. H. Sharp, member of the Investment Advisory Panel. Mr Sharp is also a director of the House of Fraser. Sir Ronald is also a director of S. G. Warburg, a merchant bank advising the House of Fraser and a supporter of Professor Smith. While Mr Jenkins – controlling at the time some 4 million shares – is also one of the more vocal House of Fraser investors in favour of the Professor's position against Lonrho. Naturally Lonrho objected. However Norman Tebbit, Secretary of State for Trade and Industry, ruled that this did not constitute any sort of conflict of interest.

According to the Griffiths' report, Dr Marwan built up a holding of 2 million Fraser shares between 19, 20 and 23 May 1983. Subsequently he bought 1.2 million more. Another investor with an interest in House of Fraser shares at the same time was Mrs Adriana Funaro. It turns out that she is a member in good standing of the Al-Fayed family who on 2 November 1984 bought £138.3 million worth of Fraser shares – the 29.9 per cent stake owned by Lonrho. It also turns out that Marwan bought his 1.2 million share parcel from her.

Marwan had, Griffiths revealed, previous links with Lonrho. Tiny Rowland held a directorship on a Swiss company called El Sara and the office Marwan uses on Piccadilly had been bought by Mestimo Investments from El Sara. But that was pretty minor compared with the discovery of a Marwan/Rowland joint venture. Ah hah, Griffiths must have thought, the plot thickens. The two had known each other when Marwan was in Sadat's office. In 1980 they cemented their 'friendship' when Marwan purchased a 40 per cent stake in Tradewinds Air Holdings, Ltd. Lonrho had the other 60 per cent . Yet by

1983 there were cracks in the cement. Marwan was coming to realize that all that glitters Tiny is not necessarily gold. He wanted out. So he wrote to Rowland saying that he was going to sell his shares to a certain Libyan who would be a thoroughly objectionable partner from Lonrho's point of view. Rowland quickly suggested lunch. The matter was resolved with Rowland eating one vanilla ice cream, drinking a Perrier and a coffee, and Marwan selling his 40 per cent to Lonrho for £500,000. Marwan's original stake in the company was worth £1.3–£1.4 million. Mr Griffiths never said what Dr Marwan had for lunch. Nor did he explain who paid the bill.

But Griffiths did look into Marwan's wealth. He found out that since 1978 Marwan had invested in real estate, banking and other ventures in a number of countries. Marwan told Griffiths that, in the summer of 1983, he was worth about $20 million.

What worried Griffiths, among other things, was the motivation and the percentages behind Marwan's stake in House of Fraser. Marwan stated that his decision to invest nearly one-third of his wealth – some £4 million – in HoF was based entirely on a newspaper article that appeared in the *Sunday Telegraph* on 15 May 1983. Titled 'Slater's Tip', one-time high-flyer Jim Slater was quoted as saying that anyone buying 1 million Fraser shares for the sum of £1.86 million could then use those shares to tip the balance in favour of Lonrho at the annual general meeting the following month. Slater figured that, if Lonrho were indeed successful in splitting Harrods away from the Group, those shares would rise to £2.5. It would not only be a good profit, but it would also be a fast profit. And the article promised, 'It cannot go wrong.'

Marwan said he read the article, liked the idea and bought the shares.

Griffiths didn't believe him.

He asked Marwan if he knew Mr Slater, or had ever heard his name. Marwan said, no. Then he asked, 'If you did not know who Mr Slater was, merely four short paragraphs to invest £4 million – it seems unusual.'

Marwan answered, 'Why? Last week I invested over £1 million – against the advice of everyone, even against the advice of my broker. . . .'

But Griffiths firmly believed that there was more to Marwan's interest than the 'Slater Tip'. It was that 10 May luncheon. The Harrods de-merger battle had been in all the papers. Griffiths was convinced that the two must have discussed it that day.

Question by Griffiths to Marwan: 'Did he [Rowland] say anything about House of Fraser?'

Answer by Marwan: 'No, but I was reading what is written in the newspaper for the past four or five years.'

Another question by Griffiths: 'There he was in the middle of a very sensational incident reported widely in the newspapers, midway between two meetings of House of Fraser and you did not speak at all?'

Answer by Marwan: 'I did not speak. Why speak? As I said, I had a very bad experience with Lonrho which cost me dear.'

Then it was Rowland's turn.

Run-on sentence by Griffiths: 'Again, I would find it surprising if, in the middle of this foray, in the newspapers it seems to have been, you meet him, having done your business, and you do not move on to discuss this foray.'

Response by Rowland: ' . . . It is possible that he asked me about the House of Fraser, but I do not know whether he raised it, I raised it, or whether it was raised at all. But it was not an issue. If you are trying to suggest that I said to him, "Look, I will pay you £500,000. It would be a good idea if you were to buy House of Fraser shares," you can dismiss that from your mind. That was not said by me and it was certainly not said by him.'

After further prodding by Griffiths, Rowland made this remark: 'I would not want to do business with Ashraf Marwan. We did the Tradewinds business and that was a

disaster . . . because I would never know from day to day
whether he was still my partner or whether he had sold
his shares to a third party. Mr Griffiths, I have told you, I
meet a lot of people – a lot of rich people. It may surprise
you. It would have been easy for me to persuade a lot of
people to buy shares in House of Fraser. I would not be
such a fool – after all, we had given undertakings to the
Minister – as to say to Dr Ashraf Marwan, who is totally
unreliable when it comes to business . . . "Buy shares
in House of Fraser and support us." I could have done it
with reliable people. In terms of business Dr Ashraf
Marwan is totally unreliable. . . .'

And later still he added: 'I would not dream of asking a
man like Dr Marwan to buy shares in the House of
Fraser. . . . I could have asked Robert Anderson to buy 10
million shares. I could have asked D. K. Ludwig to buy
10 million shares. I could have asked half a dozen or a
dozen or dozens of people to buy 100,000 shares in the
House of Fraser. Why pick on Marwan?'

When Griffiths questioned Marwan as to why he had
used his votes to support Rowland's plea for the de-
merger of Harrods from the House of Fraser, he got this
response: 'Because if there are, say, 130 shops and one
shop is producing 50 per cent of the profit, there must be
something wrong with the management of the other 129
shops.'

Concluding on the testimony by Dr Marwan, Griffiths
wrote that certain areas did not carry 'the ring of truth'.
He could not accept, for instance, that the sole reason
behind Marwan's decision to buy those 2 million shares
was the article by Jim Slater. He could not accept that the
de-merger topic was not raised at lunch. Without much
more than his own gut feeling, Griffiths decided, 'I
believe he concealed the discussions over lunch and the
real origins of his purchase because of his misguided fear,
induced perhaps by reading the press comments about
himself or about concert parties, that his involvement was
somehow unlawful under English law. Assuming the

conversation went no further than I have concluded it did, then he had, ironically, nothing to fear by telling the truth, for no concert party agreement has been proved.'

When Marwan received his copy of the report, he says, 'I put it in the dustbin. I don't care a damn what they think about me. That investigation was a waste of time and money. It led to nothing because there was nothing. You see, you can go to Hyde Park now and make a speech, allegations about anyone, right? Okay. That's what Professor Smith is doing. He makes defensive allegations to gain time. The Griffiths report was just Speakers Corner.'

At one point Rowland wrote to Griffiths, 'If Dr Ashraf Marwan's position in England were equivalent to his place in Egyptian society, you would unhesitatingly accept his word, which is also supported by his financial and natural independence.'

But the report stands. Interestingly enough, it seems that Mr John Griffiths, CMG, QC is the same John Griffiths, then merely QC, who in 1980 was involved as Attorney General in Hong Kong with the inquiry into the death of Police Inspector John MacLennan. Two years later, an editorial in the *Hong Kong Law Journal*, reviewing his wisdom in that case, notes 'errors of judgement' and a public statement that was 'grossly misleading in a material respect'. Oh well. Can't win 'em all.

※   ※   ※

'It's very true that the first million is the hardest,' Marwan says. 'After that you see more chances. You can act. If you don't have anything and you see chances, what can you do? You are helpless. That is the whole issue about business. You can buy any assets if you have the money. When people know that you have money, a lot of propositions are coming to you. Offers are coming to you. But when people know you don't have money, who comes to you then? That's the way it is. It's better to face the realities of life than to talk in hypothetical terms. That's the way life is. When you have money, people know that you have money. You will have a lot of chances. People will talk to you.'

So when you're wealthy, people come to you looking for deals. Marwan is wealthy. Therefore people come to him looking for deals.

No. Most of the time, he says, he gets his ideas out of the newspapers. 'I do my homework. By reading. I read over 30 publications a day. If you read, you know. People don't call me with a tip. No national in a country where I am would ever give me a tip because he will never trust me. Because I'm a foreigner. And another foreigner would only have a second-hand tip. When it reaches a foreigner it's passed through too many nationals. That's the way it is. It's a private club. Social. Financial. Either they accept you or they don't accept you. Here in the City they don't like individuals. Individuals don't abide by the unwritten rules.'

In other words, it all gets back to being a member of the club. You play by the established rules. Especially in the City of London. He says that's one reason why he much prefers doing business in the United States. 'America is completely different. There are no unwritten rules in America. You just have to assemble a group of people to take over whatever you want. You can do what you want if you have the financial pull with the banks. I put it to you in another way. Did you ever hear in England of a leveraged buy-out?'

Not long ago he found himself in San Francisco, meeting with some local bankers and stockbrokers. 'I told them, if you come to England, you will do a leveraged buy-out every day. They would sell their money very quickly. Listen, go to any bank here and talk with them about a leveraged buy-out and they will say, no. Why? Don't ask me, ask the establishment. England is 50 years behind America. At least. There are very solid banks in the City but the rules are completely different. Here they loan you one to one. In America you can go three to one or four to one, depending on the project itself. So with the same amount of money you pick up more growth in America.'

In Britain he confines himself solely to share speculation. But abroad, he's getting heavily into real estate. In America he's holding land and is building residential units on the outskirts of Chicago. In Monaco he's involved with building apartments. And in Mallorca he owns the five star hotel, Son Vida Castle. 'I bought Son Vida after a dinner. I had an operation on my back, so I went to Spain for a vacation with my wife, and I met some people, some friends there, who invited us for a dinner. There was a Spanish guy talking about a transaction he was doing for a Spanish group. I asked him how much he wanted for the hotel. He told me. Suddenly in the morning I called him and asked, is that figure true? He said, yes. I said, okay, you have a deal. Just like that. It was cheap. For a piece of real estate you can make a quick evaluation. For a company you have to dig. Look at any publication of any company. Are you going to believe it all? The hidden reserves and the real evaluation of the assets and the book value? You know how things are done. Creative accounting. But when you buy a building, it's a building. You can appraise it.'

Although, at least in America, he has not been quite as successful as he has been lucky. 'The project in Chicago. I admit we have not yet made much money there. But for me it is special. There is emotion involved. It is the only time I will let emotion into my business. But this was my first project. With some land in Kentucky it was different. That was luck. Some other guys drilled and found nothing. We bought the land to drill, to try our luck, and there was oil. People buy concessions, and all the studies and all the geologicals give indications that there is oil. But the final test is when you drill. British Petroleum lost a lot of money in Alaska. So that's life. I was lucky. But I know I can't be lucky all the time.'

In fact, he readily admits that he isn't lucky all the time. 'Sometimes I have bad deals. I don't say that all the deals I touch are good – 80 per cent good and 20 per cent bad. Like the only deal I ever did with Lonrho when I lost money. I went into a business where I don't understand anything and there was a recession. So now I know that when you do something you don't understand, you will never manage it properly. Unless you are very lucky, you will lose money. Now I only go into a deal after I study it. What's my high. What's my real risk. What's my down. You have to look at it all ways. I never do business like Mr Nadir, in risky places. I only do business in places like Spain, America and Monaco.'

There are, however, a few projects in Egypt – not exactly a low-risk part of the world. He's sunk money into a textile factory there, and also a chemical factory there. But, he says, 'That's home, so the risk element is less. I did it because I wanted to do something for my country. This is the only reason. It's not a marvellous investment, but you feel you have to do something for your country.'

He also feels the need to explain that he is not a wheeler–dealer. 'No. Wheel and deal I don't do. I never do trading. Because if you trade, you have to go to the door of someone to sell your goods. You have to understand the way most Arab investors think. They follow each other. Even if they are competitors, they do the same thing. If one of them goes into real estate, they all go into real estate. If one of them buys horses, they all buy horses. But they don't buy computers. Would you like to know why the Arabs have never invested in computers? Because computers don't look like anything. They can show off their horses and they can show off their real estate, but you can't show off a computer. I like creation. So we build things. After we build it, sometimes we sell it. Like an office building. Or we lease it. But we build things.'

At least, he builds things when he's not speculating in shares. 'I buy so that I can sell at a profit. If the shares go down, so I keep them. I don't sell them like that. I never work on margins. I have the strength to keep the shares as long as I want. I sell when I feel like it. If I'm making anything over 20 per cent, I start thinking about selling. But it depends on the market. If the market is bullish, why sell. If the market is bullish, it's not bullish for just one day. If the market is bad it's not bad for just one day. It takes weeks.'

In this case he's not interested in anything but speculation. 'Take-over is not my point.' Yet late in 1984, when someone was quite definitely poking through the back yard at Trafalgar House, picking up shares and making the numbers move, there was a blurb in *The Times* suggesting that it was all part of a Marwan Take-over. 'I have nothing to do with Trafalgar House. The whole article had nothing to do with me. If I would buy to take over, I'd want to spin it off after that. Not to keep it. I would sell it off as divisions. To asset strip. We call it asset spinning. Whether or not it's a good thing to do depends on the assets. You must do your homework quite well. But with the Trafalgar House story, nothing is true. I never bought one single share in Trafalgar House.'

Marwan has his mysterious reputation to thank for that sort of thing. There was a very strong market rumour at the time that Marwan had taken an interest. The options dealing made it seem that someone was making a large presence in Trafalgar. Marwan wasn't answering his telephone. He wasn't prepared to deny it. Nor was his stockbroker prepared to deny it. So the story ran.

But Marwan's answer is simple. 'You know, I must tell you this. It is not always easy to do my business discreetly. I would like to, but sometimes when I buy, other people get wind of it and the prices go up. When that happens, I sell. The problem is this. If other people know my intentions, they will try to outsmart me. That is business. Or they will try to finish me. So I have to keep my intentions to myself. But I am not mysterious. I bought House of Fraser shares, I bought Polly Peck shares, I bought Fleet Holdings shares. I declared them. Whatever else is absolute bullshit.'

He sold Fleet. And he sold House of Fraser. 'I always said I was going to sell House of Fraser when I have my price. Because there is a price tag. I was going to sell at £3 before the Al-Fayed family bought the shares held by Lonrho. I decided to wait to see what they would do. I read the newspapers. But everyone knew I was going to sell. And I do not mind who buys them. It doesn't matter to me as long as I get my price.'

Less than one week after Lonrho unloaded their stake in HoF, they came back into the market looking to acquire more shares. They were talking the right price, so Marwan sold. He made himself a cool £3 million profit. Nothing could have been less mysterious.

'Why mysterious?' He truly is bothered by the handle. 'You know, I travel about 1000 flying hours a year. But I fly commercial because I like to sit with people, to talk with people. Does that sound mysterious? And all that talk about conspiracy. Why conspire? All the tips you need to know are in the newspapers. They're all there. All you have to do is read the newspapers and you can find out everything. But you must make your own decisions. I never listen to forecasters. I'll tell you why. I was in Chicago and there was a programme on television where they took ten forecasters and a monkey. They all picked shares. Six months later they showed the results. The monkey won.'

7

Tiny Rowland

Tiny isn't tiny. He's actually very tall. Which is of course why he's called Tiny. His real name is Roland – although he signs 'Tiny' on all things official, including letters to heads of state and on the bottom of the annual Chief Executive's report for his company, Lonrho.

He is a man with a definite presence.

His clothes are perfectly tailored. His bright blue eyes stare directly at you when he speaks. His handshake is strong. He collects art modestly – mostly African and German Expressionist. He has a number of cars – Rolls-Royces and Mercedes. He is a man who, for whatever reason, doesn't sell his possessions. Instead, clothes and cars accumulate with the years. He has a mischievous sense of humour, but is at the same time very puritanical. He doesn't like to hear reports of drunkenness, debauchery or sexual revelling. In 1968 he married a woman he had known for years in Rhodesia. They live quietly together with their young children. He has the habit of insisting that anyone dining with him order elaborate meals while he settles for a small plate of asparagus tips. Those who know always make certain that he orders first.

He is also a man who claims to have arrived at total independence.

'I am independent financially and socially.'

Financially independent means, 'I have more than enough money to do whatever I want to.' His salary is reported to be around £265,000 a year, although his total annual income, thanks to shareholdings and other investments, is upwards of £7 million.

Socially independent means, 'I have no friends. Every time I meet someone, an accountant, say, who makes £100,000 a year, I know he'll try to borrow some money from me.'

That independence is at the same time both his choice and his privilege. 'I'm a totally paid-up member of the Inland Revenue of the United Kingdom. I don't use tax havens. I don't go to dinner parties or cocktail parties. I have a happy family life. I've never been divorced and I don't plan on it happening. I don't belong to any clubs, so it's not likely I could ever be asked to resign from any. I enjoy meeting people but I don't keep a diary of appointments. I do whatever seems most important to do first. Some people talk to me about five-year plans, but with me five days is more like it. As long as I feel I want to work for Lonrho, I'll come to work. The day it bores me, I'll stop. I think in some ways I'm like a weed. You could plant me anywhere and after a few inches of rain I'd seed and prosper.'

*   *   *

In 1961, Lonrho was the London and Rhodesian Mining and Land Co., a lacklustre outfit that had been around for decades.

Enter Tiny Rowland.

He was born in India in 1917. His father was German and his mother was English. The family name was Furhop. Rowland's father was a successful trader, with offices throughout India, the bulk of his business with Germany. Because Rowland sidesteps questions about his past, myths invariably fill the gaps. Some have him working as a railway porter. Others have him making £5,000 a day in 1946.

In 1981 investigative journalist Charles Raw, writing in

the *Sunday Times*, revealed that, following World War I, the Furhops returned to live in Germany. Rowland's father was an outspoken anti-Nazi, which cost him his business and eventually forced part of the family to leave Germany for the safety of England. Rowland attended Churchers College in Hampshire but left after about a year. By 1937, according to Raw, Rowland took a job in his uncle's shipping agency. Also according to Raw, in 1939 Rowland spent two weeks in a Berlin jail because of his associations with well-known anti-Nazis. That same year he changed his name from Furhop and later found himself conscripted into the British army. Rowland explained his German roots, which restricted him from combat, and instead he served with the Royal Army Medical Corps in Norway and Scotland.

During the internment panic in 1940, Rowland's father was put into a camp, despite being an outspoken opponent of the Hitler regime. When Rowland was refused leave to visit his father, he went AWOL and was subsequently arrested by Military Police. After spending 27 days in a military jail, Rowland was eventually permitted to join his parents. His mother died before the end of the war, and his father remained interned. When the war finished his father remained in England, having patented a carpet-making machine. He died in the early 1970s at the age of 93.

Rowland went into business for himself, buying and selling factories. But he was bitter about the way the authorities had treated him and his parents. So in 1947 he left for Rhodesia where he bought a pair of farms and saw himself settling into the life of a gentleman planter.

Over the next 14 years his company, Shepton Estates, went into gold and copper mining, a car dealership and several acquisitions on behalf of Rio Tinto Zinc. That's when London and Rhodesian came along. They acquired some of Shepton's assets and also Rowland as a joint managing director.

It was 1961. London and Rhodesian employed 350

people, boasted assets of £2.15 million, turned over £4 million and had a pre-tax profit of £160,000.

Two years later the company name was changed to Lonrho.

By 1965, the year the Rhodesian government declared independence, Lonrho's assets were £13.2 million, their turnover £32 million, and their pre-tax profits £1.8 million.

Rowland had expanded the company's asset base quickly by taking Lonrho into new businesses – breweries, ranches and newspapers – and into new spheres of influence – the newly independent nations of Uganda, Kenya and Tanzania.

These days there are few doubts that Rowland and Lonrho are one and the same, even though Rowland continually plays that down.

'It's not at all like that. There are lots of chaps who work here. This is a comfortable, loose organization. Did you notice that there are no closed doors in the hallway? That's the way we work. If anybody wants to see me, they simply have to come see me. I'm really just an amateur surrounded by professionals. I've farmed, mined, retailed, manufactured and wholesaled. Maybe you could say what I do is buying and selling and that I have a feel for what I believe to be a good deal.'

Rowland insists that Lonrho is not a one-man band, although he now owns over 17 per cent of the company. 'But I've never sold a share.' He is Managing Director and Chief Executive. For many years the Chairman was Lord Duncan-Sandys, but he stepped down in 1984, succeeded by Edward Du Cann, MP, after Du Cann's failure to retain the chairmanship of the Conservative Party's 1922 Committee. The point being, Rowland does not surround himself with lightweights. It's a good bet that, while all the men on his board are, in their own right, capable of making decisions, they probably wouldn't dare make a really serious decision without Rowland's nod. What they do with great élan, however, is create a respectable establishment aura. They also help run interference for Rowland. To see him you can't really just walk down the hallway and step through the open office doors. You've first got to make an appointment with the Lonrho board member who is the company's spokesman. When this interview was finally arranged – it took half a year – and when Rowland made that remark about open office doors and always being so accessible, he was quickly asked, 'How come it took six months to get to see you?' He shot a stern glance towards that board member/spokesman, who only just managed to cover himself with the obviously lame remark, 'Well Tiny, you've been travelling a lot. . . .'

Rowland can say as often as he wants to that Lonrho isn't his show alone, but most people in the City think it is and the people who work with him act like it is. Yet when you ask him what Lonrho would be like without Tiny Rowland, you get a laugh and a show of modesty. 'Share prices would probably go up 50 per cent once they [the City] realized that such an unacceptable character was no longer here. But I have no intention of leaving for the next 25 years.'

His use of the word 'unacceptable' is well chosen because that was the handle Prime Minister Heath tagged on Lonrho. 'Edward Heath once called this company the unacceptable face of capitalism. It's the only notable thing he ever said. It's a boring phrase which is forever being repeated. But we've outgrown it. Although I don't think it was ever true. Of course, being called the acceptable face of capitalism would be equally insulting.'

* * *

If he has a hobby, it's politics.

Through business interests around the world, and especially in Africa and the Middle East, Rowland has over many years built up long-standing and trusted relationships with several national leaders.

Lonrho's resilience to nationalizations is proof of that. The company's assets in parts of Africa have twice been nationalized – once in Tanzania and once in Zaire. Both times those assets have been returned.

'It's an occupational risk. But through those nationalizations we have never lost our friendships with those governments. We have never lost the sympathies of the people there. Developing countries need western technology, skills that we have. You must be philosophical about such things. You must take the long view on a worldwide basis. Lonrho has a history and a tradition as a builder. The net result is, after both those nationalizations, we were asked back. We resumed those old friendships and they were perhaps even stronger as a result. That's very satisfying. It's a tribute to the company. Sure it costs us money in the meantime but, well, we must live with the world as it is.'

Rowland loves to play his part in the game of diplomacy whenever he's given the opportunity. It's a mildly well-known fact that he had a small hand in what eventually became the Camp David Agreement between Israel and Egypt. Rowland had contacts with the Sadat government, one of them being Ashraf Marwan, then Secretary to the Egyptian President. At the same time, Lord Marcus Sieff of Marks and Spencer had access to Shimon Perez and Moshe Dayan in Israel. Because it could be kept outside regular channels, 'interested parties' felt these relationships could be used in the cause of peace. Rowland and Sieff were asked to test the waters, to make informal overtures that would pave the way for official contacts.

'Sadat had to be conditioned first,' Rowland explains. 'No one in America had access to Sadat the way I did.'

A few years before, an even more revealing episode took place. And this one is not generally known.

Rowland nearly saved British Petroleum from being nationalized in Libya.

In 1971 there had been a dispute between the Gaddafi

regime in Libya and the British government over suspended contracts and the nationalization of certain businesses, including two British banks in Tripoli. At the request of the Foreign Office, that autumn Rowland was asked to use his commercial friendships to help arrange some sort of settlement. The three interested parties were: Major Abdel Salam Jalud, Deputy Chairman of the Revolutionary Command Council of Libya; Ashraf Marwan, representing President Sadat of Egypt; and Anthony Parsons, then Under Secretary at the FO. Within two months Rowland had forged an agreement that provided for a deposit of £25 million by the British government in a London bank against which payments could be made upon presentation of certificates of UK manufacturers for goods ordered by the Libyan government. In return the Libyans agreed to buy from Britain a £27 million Marconi air defence radar system.

Parsons assured Rowland that the cabinet would consider the agreement on 16 November. It didn't happen. Nor did it happen on the 23rd. Nor did it happen on the 30th. To keep the confidence of both Marwan and Jalud, Rowland flew to Cairo on 1 December. He had with him Parsons' assurance that the agreement would indeed be discussed by the cabinet on 7 December.

At the same time, and seemingly unrelated, British treaties were due to expire with Bahrain, Qatar and the seven Trucial States. One day too early, British forces abandoned the Tunb Islands in the Gulf. Within a few hours Iranian troops landed and claimed them. That England had allowed Iran to occupy those islands while still technically their protector was regarded as a breach of trust by, among others, Colonel Gaddafi. He warned that if the British refused to take action against Iran, he would make reprisals against British interests in Libya. That clearly meant BP.

Rowland arrived in Cairo on 1 December to hear that news from Marwan. When Jalud arrived later that same day, Rowland took the initiative by asking for a cooling-off period. He obtained assurances from Jalud that nothing would be done pending ratification of the negotiated agreement by the British cabinet on 7 December. Through Marwan's efforts, Sadat agreed to support the cooling-off period and to back the acceptance of the agreement both as a compromise and as a gesture of British sincerity. Rowland was then entrusted with an urgent personal message from Sadat to the Prime Minister restating the Arab position. Rowland returned to London and rang Parsons at 9:30 a.m. on 3 December. Parsons agreed by phone that everything would be done to obtain a quick decision, although it would have to wait until Tuesday 7 December. Rowland related this to Cairo.

On that morning, Parsons rang Rowland to say that the cabinet would not discuss the matter. He implied that the government was not used to any form of deadline and that there were more important topics on the agenda. Rowland, realizing that he had no choice but to pass this news on to Cairo, sent a message at noon. That afternoon Gaddafi grabbed BP.

Three days later, back in Cairo to discuss Lonrho business, Rowland saw the opportunity to confront Gaddafi personally. A letter was drafted with Sadat's approval, the text of which the Egyptian government hoped Gaddafi would issue to Rowland. The letter asked Rowland to intercede with the British government in gaining some form of censure of the Iranian government in exchange for promises from the Libyans to suspend the BP take-over. On Sunday 12 December, Rowland, Marwan and two other high Egyptian officials flew to Tripoli. That night they met with Gaddafi, who after three hours did sign the letter. Gaddafi then verbally confirmed that, as long as the UK would also in some way censure the Iranians, the BP nationalization could be reversed.

Returning to London for 24 hours on 13 December, Rowland found the FO was not prepared to make even the slightest conciliatory gesture towards the Libyans, no matter how much the denationalization of BP might mean. In January, Rowland learned that the Libyans were about to negotiate a deal with the Russians for crude oil. He sought an appointment with the Prime Minister. He believed that a top-line mission sent to Libya with the blessings of Downing Street could convince Gaddafi he had the respect of the British government and that would reopen the possibility of a settlement with BP. But high-ranking FO officials doubted the Libyans' sincerity – in spite of the fact that Rowland assured them the Egyptians were willing to intervene with Gaddafi on Britain's behalf to ensure that the delegation would be received. Nothing came of it. Then Duncan-Sandys, with the blessings of the Foreign Secretary, Sir Alec Douglas-Home, agreed to go to Libya. On 19 January he met with Gaddafi, hoping that the Libyans might agree to arbitration of the BP problem. Gaddafi said no. Duncan-Sandys returned to London to convince Sir Alec that Britain's best hope lay in disentangling the BP claim from the original commercial agreement organized by Rowland. Helping to buy some time for the British, Marwan got Jalud to defer his visit to Russia to negotiate the oil deal. But on 20 February, as no word had come from London, Jalud and Marwan flew to Moscow.

Jalud returned from his meetings with Brezhnev and Kosygin, an agreement in hand for the disposal of 10 million tons of crude annually. Half would go to Russia, 2 million tons each would go to Roumania and Bulgaria, with the Egyptians taking 1 million. It was obvious that, after refining, the resultant products could then be sold internationally without BP ever being able to trace their source. Jalud also gained a firm offer of military equipment from the Soviets.

Rowland refused to give up. He proposed to the FO that the British government should purchase BP's oil and sell onward to BP at the same price. In return, Libya should agree to sign contracts in the UK for some £400 million of equipment. Britain would export military equipment to Libya, which would then buy from Britain the Marconi radar system and air defence missiles. Based on certain assurances from the FO that the plan had merit, Rowland appealed to Marwan who spoke with Gaddafi. Marwan reported back confidently that a deal could be arranged. That's when Jalud summoned the British Ambassador. It seemed a simple thing. Jalud wished to confirm with the Ambassador that the British government was indeed aware of the possibility of a deal which would, in effect, solve the BP problem and start melting the frozen relations between the two nations. Rowland claims the Ambassador had been kept informed from London. Jalud claims the Ambassador denied all knowledge of the deal, and in fact refuted it. BP was forced to write off the entire book value of their Libyan operations – £38 million.

*　　*　　*

He tells people that Lonrho is run strictly along the lines of Harvard Business School's theory of decentralized management. It had to be that way because Lonrho is a conglomerate of some 800 companies spread throughout 82 countries, employing nearly 160,000 people. The group's annual turnover is fast approaching £4 billion. Each of the companies is run locally. Rowland and the handful of people who work at Lonrho's London office don't bother much with activities such as board meetings. Instead they concern themselves only with what used to be called 'the big picture'.

The main area of Lonrho's interest is still Africa, where among other things they are the largest single food producers. There are tea estates in Malawi, Toyota distributorships and livestock in Kenya, gold mines in Ghana, sugar plantations in Swaziland, cosmetics manufacturing in Nigeria, civil engineering activities in Zambia, airplane retailing in South Africa and farm equipment distribution in Uganda. Adding in the rest of the world, there are hotels, casinos, freight forwarding, postage stamp printing, finance, plumbing, stainless steel sink manufacturing, bed linen retailing, property management, insurance broking and newspapers, including London's *Observer*.

'Some companies prefer to limit their areas of interest to specific fields where they already have expertise. I take a different approach. I can always buy someone with the necessary experience to run a business. When you've got the right man you've got the experience. On the other hand, there are certain areas I generally try to avoid. I stay away from manufacturing in the UK or in Europe. As far as I'm concerned, in Europe and even in parts of the US, we're living in yesterday's world. I see today's world and tomorrow's world in the Pacific Ocean. All developing nations are tomorrow's world.'

His dedication to Africa is deeply rooted in the fact that he knows Africa and the Africans know him. For many years Rowland was considered to have more influence on that continent than almost anyone in the world, businessman or politician. Lonrho's interests there account for a shade under 25 per cent of its worldwide assets, yet more than half of Lonrho's pre-tax profits.

'Africa is our life's blood. I don't see it as a risk area. It's more of a risk to manufacture in England. Do you think a tightrope walker in the circus is taking a risk? It may look that way, but he knows exactly what he's doing. There is no risk for tightrope walkers. I feel totally at ease in Africa. We have always had a fair deal in Africa. Our problems there have only been temporary. We cannot, however, say the same for the City of London.'

*　　*　　*

Lonrho is the most investigated company in the history of British business. 'We've had years of investigations. Believe me, it's sheer prejudice. It wouldn't happen if I were a member of the club, the establishment. But for me it would be a waste of time, going to all those boring dinner parties. All those investigations. They've been looking for the spot. Too bad because I could help them. I know the spot.'

In 1961, a man named Angus Ogilvy was sent to Rhodesia on behalf of his boss Harley Drayton. Among Drayton's holdings was a heavy share of London and Rhodesian Mining and Land, and Drayton wanted Ogilvy to see if something could be done to revive the company's fortunes. A deal was struck with Rowland, who turned some of his Shepton Estate assets over to London and Rhodesian in exchange for 1.5 million L & R shares and an option to acquire a further 2 million. Rowland met with his first taste of criticism when questions were raised as to the actual values of those Shepton Estate assets transferred to Lonrho.

In 1971, the South African government opened an investigation into a small mining company owned by Lonrho, claiming fraud. Lonrho's merchant bankers, S. G. Warburg, resigned. A year later the South Africans dropped their charges, publicly apologized and even paid off some Lonrho officials. But the damage had been done. Lonrho's share prices tumbled.

That brought on the next crisis.

Lonrho appointed an auditing firm to investigate its financial position. By February 1972 they advised a reconstitution of the Lonrho board, including the appointment of a new chairman along with new directors. But when the 1972 annual report was submitted to the board for approval, certain members of the board openly questioned their confidence in Rowland. A coup was launched. Leading the rebels was Sir Basil Smallpiece, the former Chairman of Cunard who was put on the Lonrho board at the insistence of the Bank of England. Rowland forced a referendum. And the shareholders voted overwhelmingly in his favour. Smallpiece and the others went into a hasty exile.

The Department of Trade ordered a report. It took

three years to complete. During that time a sort of publicity lull took place. Rowland used it to expand in the Middle East, convincing the Kuwaitis to take a large shareholding in Lonrho and seats on the board. Little did he suspect at the time that he was already contributing pages to the next DTI report on Lonrho.

Rowland was hurt by the Smallpiece revolt, and that may account for those open doors on the sixth floor of Lonrho's Cheapside offices. It's a strange thought, but somewhere in the back of his mind he might want those doors open merely to reassure himself that none of his own are again plotting against him.

The 'boardroom coup' report was finally published in July 1976. In many ways it was critical of Rowland. Among other things, the report detailed off-shore payments, heavy expenses, conflicts of interest over a copper mine in Rhodesia and suggestions that Lonrho had failed to observe the 1965 sanctions ordered against Rhodesia. Given advance notice of the findings, Rowland bombarded the inspectors, his former bankers and those rebel directors with the most vitriolic responses. He took the offensive, preparing dossiers on British companies he knew to have broken the sanctions. It created enough of a smoke screen that he could face the problems of his own making, notably that the Kuwaitis on his board wanted a more important say in the running of Lonrho. In the end it was the Kuwaitis who left the board, although they retained their holding.

The Department of Public Prosecutions recommended that no action be taken. But the sanction-breaking story reappeared, as if to haunt him, in May 1978 when Scotland Yard showed up asking for certain papers relative to the issue. Rowland fought back again, this time taking on David Owen who was Foreign Secretary.

'The problem with Tiny Rowland over sanction breaking', Owen recalls, 'was that he claimed to have documentation which he believed showed the British government had been involved and explicitly accepted that sanction breaking would continue back in 1967–1968. I had established an independent inquiry, and I wanted to put the papers to them. But he was not prepared to let them free. He seemed to believe that you could negotiate with the British government. He would give the documentation in return for us letting him off the prosecution. But there was absolutely no way I could have dreamt of doing it even if I wanted to. There then grew a misunderstanding where I think, through talking to officials in my department, he got the impression that a deal had been made. In fact, no such deal had ever been made. But looking back at it, I understand why he got rather uptight about it. In his sort of world, deals are made which are not always expressed openly.'

Having seen Rowland operate close up, Owen feels one of the most interesting aspects of the man is the respect in which he's held by the African leaders. 'He hasn't got a trace of racial prejudice about him. That's one of his great virtues. He does deals and fixes things and organizes things exactly the same in Africa as if he were operating in London. And that's rather flattering. It's one of the reasons he's a success. He is also a loyal friend to people who help him when he's been in difficulties. That's the root of his friendship with Kenneth Kaunda who helped him when he was nearly ousted from Lonrho. I don't know the exact story, but I think you'll find that Kenneth Kaunda said if you kick out Tiny Rowland then you don't do much more business in Zambia. Ever since, he had a great affection and understanding for Kenneth Kaunda. So when Kenneth Kaunda was on his uppers, when the Rhodesian sanctions were biting pretty hard, Rowland did everything in his power to sustain him and support him. In terms of his diplomacy, in some ways, Rowland was a nuisance. On the other hand, you couldn't help but admire the character.'

As far as Owen is concerned, 'He's a great buccaneer. And like many buccaneers, they take short cuts. He's impatient with bureaucracy. I don't think a lot of his critics in England have ever understood the genuine affection that quite a lot of African countries have for him. He's certainly not an establishment figure, which is why the establishment dislike him of course. He's much too rough a diamond for them. But I say, if you had to quickly find out what was happening in Africa at this particular moment, you would get more information out of half an hour with Tiny Rowland than you would with the Foreign Secretary.'

That storm quieted down only to find the biggest one of all brewing on the horizon.

In February 1977 Tiny Rowland approached Sir Hugh Fraser and bought a 25 per cent stake in an industrial holding company called Scottish and Universal Investments – SUITS, for short. Rowland became Chairman of the company, which had been formed by Sir Hugh's father out of Fraser family trusts and held a 10.29 per cent stake in the House of Fraser stores.

Over that summer, Lonrho bought a small block of 60,000 House of Fraser shares, then added to it 23.55 million shares purchased from a California stores' group. Lonrho's 19.43 per cent holding put both Rowland and Lord Duncan-Sandys on the Fraser board.

Firmly in place, Rowland then led Lonrho into a bid for SUITS, and that led them both straight into the face of a Monopolies and Mergers Commission inquiry. The moment the MMC nodded okay, Lonrho acquired SUITS and topped up its House of Fraser holding to 29.9 per cent.

Enter now Roland Smith, Professor by trade, and friend to House of Fraser's merchant banking advisers, S. G. Warburg. (Don't forget that once upon a time S. G. Warburg were also Lonrho's merchant bankers but they opted out when the going got rough. So you can imagine how much love there was between Rowland and Roland, Warburg and friends.) In August 1980, Smith was named part-time Deputy Chairman (after all, he had to be a Professor at least some of the time), while Rowland was removed as non-executive deputy chairman. Warburg also brought on board Ernest Sharp as a non-executive director. Sharp, however, wasn't a Professor. He was just a former director of Grand Metropolitan.

By January 1982 the stage had been set and all the players were ready. Lonrho launched an attack on Sir Hugh Fraser and after splitting the board saw him removed as Chairman. Lonrho then bid for the House of Fraser. But Professor Smith replaced Fraser as Chairman and the MMC stepped in yet again. This time they ruled the bid would go against the public interest. And this time too Rowland vowed to fight on.

Having given his word that Lonrho would not increase its holding beyond the 29.9 per cent, Rowland tacked into the wind with a plan to de-merge Harrods from the House of Fraser. His reasoning was simple. With 130 stores in the group, Harrods accounts for over 50 per cent of the group's profit. Therefore, go with the profitable one and get rid of the rest. Smith came back with the response that Harrods' profits were necessary to upgrade the rest of the group so that all the stores would one day be profitable.

House of Fraser board meetings during 1982 got nasty. The Lonrho camp wanted rid of Smith, and the Smith camp wanted rid of Lonrho. An extraordinary general meeting of Fraser shareholders was held on 6 May. A resolution against de-merger and a vote of confidence for the Professor was passed with a narrow majority of 1.8 million votes. Rowland managed to force another EGM and vote on 30 June. This time a resolution was proposed approving de-merger. And this time the de-merger plan was effectively approved by a 53 per cent majority of the shareholders. Except the cards were stacked. The motion required a 75 per cent majority to win.

Even though the Smith camp lost but really won, cries of foul were heard all the way to the DTI. Someone thought it was pretty suspicious that four new share-holders, all buying abroad, had appeared on the scene between the two votes and swung the majority to Lonrho's point of view. The DTI decided to appoint an inspector and hold an inquiry. But just four hours before that announcement was made, Lonrho's Kuwaiti shareholders unloaded 2 million of their shares. A spokesman said they simply felt the time was right to sell. But Rowland noted they hadn't made a single sale from their 39 million shareholding for over three years. He suspected a leak from the opposite camp and asked for the sale to be subject to a Stock Exchange inquiry.

In the middle of all this, Rowland found himself embroiled in a family feud. In 1981 Lonrho had purchased the *Observer*. Four years before, Rowland had failed to buy *The Times*. Some years before that he wondered if he should buy the Daily Mirror Group. He could have had it for under £50 million because this was long before anyone discovered the Reuters' goldmine. The group was eventually sold to Robert Maxwell for £113 million. Anyway, when Rowland wondered about the Mirror Group, the advice he was given by someone close to him was, 'Buy it if you can afford it.' Rowland's response was, 'Afford it? Afford it? If I had thought for a moment in my whole career, "Can I afford it?" I'd have never done anything.'

In April 1984 *Observer* Editor-in-Chief, Donald Trelford, had been to Matabeleland, witnessed the aftermath of atrocities, and quite correctly assumed his responsibility to tell the world. Unfortunately, his boss had another view. Matabeleland happens to be in the heart of Zimbabwe where Lonrho employs 16,000 people and earns an estimated £15 million in profits. Rowland also maintains a firm relationship with President Robert Mugabe. Had the *Sunday Times* run the story, it might have gone no further. But for Rowland's *Observer* to publish such a story . . . it reeked of someone peeing in the soup.

Of course, if you believe that a free press is the guardian of a free society, then there can be no argument whatsoever. Trelford was not only right to publish the story, he was morally obliged to do so.

But Rowland bounced off the wall. Trelford accused him of succumbing to his crudest commercial instincts. Rowland said he'd get his way or sell the paper.

The fact of the matter is that Rowland found himself in a very awkward position with President Mugabe and especially the Zimbabwe Minister of Information, Nathan Shamuyarira. It was Shamuyarira who had arranged Trelford's interview with Mugabe. Trelford's story left Shamuyarira exposed. By pouring scorn on the story, Rowland was trying to distance himself from the story, which would in turn serve to protect Shamuyarira. Unfortunately it worked against Rowland. The story of the proprietor at war with his editor created far more publicity than the Matabeleland story otherwise would have. Master bites dog, the headlines read.

Trelford bravely stood his ground.

Then Rowland played his ace in the hole. Robert Maxwell was very much in the market for a Fleet Street paper. The next thing anyone knew, there were Rowland and Maxwell having breakfast together in the poshest suite at Claridges. (One wonders who picked up the bill.) Photographers snapped the two of them at the front door, shaking hands, forcing big smiles, looking as though they were the best of friends and couldn't wait to have breakfast again really soon.

Maxwell actually believed he had a shot at buying the *Observer*. He had even asked to reserve the *Observer*'s boardroom for noon that day to make his announcement. And maybe for a brief moment, Rowland contemplated selling it to him. But the message to Trelford was clear. Either do it my way or face the dreaded Bouncing Czech.

Trelford wrote a Dear Tiny: 'Should we not agree to differ on this matter and to respect our right to disagree? For my part I accept that you acted as you did, not out of crude concern for your commercial interests, as I originally suggested, but out of genuine personal conviction that the truth about Zimbabwe is more complex than I presented it.' And he offered to resign.

Rowland answered with a Dear Donald: 'I am extremely happy to receive your letter, as it gives me the opportunity to say, certainly not. I support your editorship and I refuse to accept your resignation. . . . It seems to me an absolute demonstration of your integrity and care for the paper that, although there is no need for you to offer your resignation, you have done so. . . . I am very glad our misunderstandings are behind us.'

When the *Sunday Times* rang Rowland, he told them he was writing off the whole affair as 'just a lover's tiff'.

If only he could have said the same for John Griffiths, CMG, QC.

Griffiths was the silk appointed by the DTI to carry out an investigation under Section 172 of the Companies Act of 1948. He called over 175 witnesses, filled more than 400 pages with facts and theories, and in the end could not prove that Rowland and others had acted in concert for the de-merger of Harrods from the House of Fraser.

Immediately following publication of Griffiths' report, Lonrho brought out one of their own. A Not-the-Griffiths-Report report.

It's the same format. It's the same layout. It's the same style. It's not as thick as the DTI report. But then the Lonrho editors forgot to number the 234 pages.

'A reading of the Inspector's report shows the following,' Rowland claimed when he brought out his rebuttal. 'The inquiry should never have been set up. There was nothing worth investigating. It was set up after receipt by the Department of Trade and Industry of one-sided reports from Fraser. The inquiry spent a year substantially investigating gossip and trivia. The report contains needless comments, damaging to a number of individuals who have no appeal. Mr Griffiths was the wrong man to conduct this inquiry. If the Inspectorial system has any merit, it is not in application to this kind of case.'

The battle for Harrods resumed. But now rumours flew that other parties were interested in joining the fray. Sears Holdings and House of Seagrams were both said to be interested in bidding for House of Fraser. Alfred Taubman, who had bought Sotheby's, was another possibility. But it took the Al-Fayed family to make a move.

An old established Egyptian family with interests in shipping, oil, banking and property (they own the Ritz Hotel in Paris, among others), Rowland had once purchased from them shares in the civil engineering group Richard Costain. The Al-Fayeds even had a place on the Lonrho board for a time in the '70s. They eventually sold their stake in Lonrho to the Kuwaitis. Named in the Griffiths' report was Adriana Funaro, an Al-Fayed sister-in-law, who bought House of Fraser shares that were involved with the voting for the de-merger. Her shares were finally sold to Ashraf Marwan, who also supported the de-merger.

In late September, at the annual general meeting of the House of Fraser, Lonrho failed to get two more of their directors elected to the board, although Rowland was re-elected. Exactly one month later, the Al-Fayeds made a formal approach for Lonrho's stake. A deal was struck at £3 per share for 46.1 million shares. On Friday 2 November, the Al-Fayeds delivered a cheque to Lonrho for £138.3 million.

The City was stunned.

Rowland was defeated. He was giving up. He had had enough. Professor Smith had won.

At least until the following Friday when Lonrho came back into the market and picked up a stake that made them the House of Fraser's second largest single shareholders.

With a verdict due from the Monopolies and Mergers Commission on Lonrho's take-over plans, the Al-Fayeds announced in March that they were going to buy the entire group. It would mean the group would finally see the back of Lonrho. Professor Smith would have himself a new contract with the Al-Fayeds. He would have been out of work with Lonrho. And the House of Fraser board supported the plan. Share prices shot up from near £3 to over £4. That's when Lonrho made the startling move of selling 9.7 million of their shares to the Al-Fayeds. The deal netted Lonrho about £10 million in profit, and pushed the Al-Fayeds past the 51.1 per cent mark, giving them control of the House of Fraser. Rowland, having kept a mere 500,000 shares for Lonrho, announced at the time that he expected the Al-Fayed bid to be referred to the Monopolies and Mergers Commission, which would drive the shareprices down again, at which time Lonrho would be a buyer. He lobbied Trade and Industry Secretary Norman Tebbit, as did the Al-Fayeds. Questions were raised as to the source of funding that the Al-Fayeds were using to buy Harrods. Was it their money or did some of it come from the Sultan of Brunei? Did some of it come from Dubai? Did some of it come from Kuwait? Rowland felt that the victimization of Lonrho at the hands of various commissions and investigations should necessitate a clear response to the questions raised. The government clearly had a responsibility to assure equal treatment for all parties involved. The announcement was delayed one day, and then released to a totally shocked City. Lonrho was given permission to go beyond their previously restricted 29.9 per cent limit, but the Al-Fayed bid would not be referred to a take-over panel.

The government was handing Harrods to the Egyptian brothers on a silver platter.

And slapping Tiny Rowland in the face.

Professor Smith was the winner.

But Norman Tebbit's decision – not long after the pettiness shown to Mssrs. Cogan and Swid when they tried to take over Sotheby's – might have finally made a mockery of the entire trade and industry investigatory philosophy. If Tiny Rowland was the loser, he might not be the only one. The system might have lost as well. The difference is that Rowland will live long enough to play again another day.

8

Paul Raymond

There's an ashtray in the lobby of Paul Raymond's office, above the theatre that used to be The Windmill and is now La Vie en Rose, and on one particular day that ashtray was filled with six cigarette butts – all of them ringed with bright red lipstick.

Instantly one's brain is filled with visions of some nubile lass, down from the provinces, just off the train at Victoria with no place to come but here . . . Okay, I'll do it but, I mean, do I actually have to take off all my clothes . . . She waits in the lobby, chain smoking, until HE appears, sporting a wide-brimmed hat and large lapels, literally dripping in gold chains while he smokes a huge cigar. Come into my office my dear, he says, and just slip out of that sweet little dress because, after all, we have to see what it is you've got to offer . . . and yes, certainly I can make you a star . . . hah, hah . . . now if you'd care for a little champagne while we discuss your career . . .

Reality is made of less romantic stuff.

No wide-brimmed hat. No large lapels. No gold chain collection. He smokes cigarettes. And there is no casting couch. In fact, at a distance of three feet, the bad boy of British business is actually less sinister looking than your average High Street bank manager.

*　　*　　*

He left school at the age of 15 – that would have been in 1940 – worked in markets and a shirt factory, and somewhere along the way he learned to play the drums. Then he flogged nail varnish and hairnets at funfairs – slightly reminiscent of those snake oil salesmen of yesteryear. But he gave that up to do a mind-reading act that he bought for £25 from a couple of palm readers at Clacton Pier. His father was a haulage contractor in Liverpool, although the old man disappeared when the family moved to Glossop. One grandfather was a cop in Liverpool. His mother always wanted him to have a proper job, you know, like an insurance salesman. But show business had bitten him. So for a while, after the snake oil, he was a part-time drummer and a full-time mind reader. He might have preferred it the other way around, but he had to earn a living. It was only after doing his mind-reading act for the millionth time that he began to understand how real money might be made by booking acts, instead of being one.

The huckster turned mind reader became an impresario.

The day he managed to talk two ladies in his show to take off some of their clothes, *Vaudeville Express* became *Festival of Nudes* and the impresario became Paul Raymond.

'That is my real name,' he says, 'although I wasn't born with that name.' Just to keep the record straight, he was born with the name Geoffrey Anthony Quinn. 'I suppose I changed it originally before I did the mind-reading act. I was a drummer in a band. And in those days, much like today, people in show business often changed their names. I was Gene Raymond, after Gene Krupa, one of the greatest drummers in the world. I wasn't as good as him, but you know, when you're young you go through all of that. Then there was Geoff Carlson, an appalling name. Then Geoff Raymond. And then came Paul Raymond. I've been Paul Raymond since my variety act days. Everyone knew me as that and it came to confusion when I started going abroad with a passport in the name of Geoffrey Anthony Quinn. There would be a phone call for Paul Raymond and I would be registered as Geoffrey Quinn. Or they'd know me as Paul Raymond and someone would ask for Mr Quinn and they'd say they never heard of him. In the end it was either go back to my original name or officially change it. It was easier to stay Paul Raymond.'

Not that it bothers him, no longer being Geoffrey Anthony Quinn. He doesn't miss it any more than he misses being a mind reader. 'Not at all. I don't miss not being on a stage. And I never do my mind-reading act, not even at parties. In fact, I'm very pleased. Had I been all that good I might still be doing my mind-reading act for a living.'

He earns his living these days as Chairman, Chief Executive Officer and owner of the Paul Raymond Organization Ltd – a series of companies he built from the ground up on the theory that men will pay money to look at ladies who aren't wearing clothes.

Raised a Catholic – 'No, I do not see any contradiction between being a Catholic, which I still am, and also being in the business I am' – he has, like Hugh Hefner of *Playboy* and Bob Guccione of *Penthouse*, long since managed to diversify, although his power base remains the naked lady industry. And while he doesn't care to discuss his personal wealth, which is obviously considerable, his business empire is estimated to be worth £30–£50 million. 'That's about right. It's close enough.'

The empire was conceived in the '50s, when he was booking shows around the variety hall circuit. 'How it all started really, was in the touring days, after my act, when I was producing shows in the UK. Towards the end, I had about 10 shows which each toured for about 40 weeks a year. This is the time when the music hall was dying yet all my shows did very very well.'

Some of his bigger successes from those days are now nothing more than memories and hand bills in simple frames scattered around his offices. *The Follies Parisiennes*, twice nightly featuring 'The only moving nudes'. And, *Nude, Neat and Naughty*. And, *Paris after Dark*. And *Piccadilly Peepshow*. For their day, they were pretty provocative. At times they were also filled with some rather elaborate stunts. For instance, *Les Nues de Paris* featured ladies undressed, standing in the middle of a cage where a lion tamer and a live lion did their thing. 'It wasn't pure burlesque because in burlesque there were strippers and the burlesque comics. You could say mine was an English version of American burlesque, for the want of a better word. They were revues, variety acts, and production numbers with the girls.'

There were no stars in any of these shows, although Shirley Bassey had a seventh billing in one and in another he employed Larry Grayson. 'In 1955 Larry Grayson played in one of my shows at £25 a week. He wanted a rise for £27.50 the next year and I said no. He left.'

He learned the business from the bottom up. How to stage shows. All the tricks you need to know about promoting shows. The ins and outs of being an impresario. And some of those lessons came expensive. 'One of the best lessons I ever had happened in the mid-'50s when I took a show to a nightclub in Vienna. It was a disaster. Yet I think I probably learned more from that time than anything else I have ever done. You see, one of the most difficult things to do is to get laughs. But if you're doing an international trade, it's very difficult to talk. The French don't understand, the Germans don't, and in the States it's a different sense of humour than it is here. So you do it visually. That's the best way to get laughs. But I wasn't too sure about that then and for the show in Vienna we booked two guys to speak a few words. They were Jewish comics. Two guys I had known for a long time. One did a clown act with a bit of Yiddish thrown in. The other could only speak a bit of Yiddish. It was close to German and I really thought everyone would understand so we could get laughs. I didn't know it but in 1954 they were anti-Jewish there. Believe me, the show was a disaster. I'm not saying only because of that, but it helped. However, what I did manage to do was learn a lot about the nightclub scene where before all I knew was the variety hall scene. I think I learned from that experience how to run the Raymond Revuebar.'

It was probably the Raymond Revuebar that took him from small-time impresario into the big time. 'The actual turning point? Well, I guess it all depends on what you call big time. There was no one deal. But certainly one would have to say the touring shows were important because they gave me the money to start the Raymond Revuebar. Or you could say that it was the Raymond Revuebar which then made that money into a lot more. And that money allowed me to expand.'

He opened a private club in 1958 with somewhere between £10,000 and £15,000 – he says he honestly can't remember the exact figure. He raised the money himself, although he nearly had a partner. There was a fellow he knew named Harry Kaufman who was a theatrical agent and also a very successful shoe manufacturer. The deal was to be Raymond 60 per cent, and Kaufman 40 per cent. But, on the day the contracts were to be signed, Kaufman suggested Raymond had got the figures the wrong way round. Raymond ripped up the contract and took on the world all by himself.

He called the club the Raymond Revuebar. 'It had to be a membership club because in the old days you couldn't do that type of show unless it was a club.' Ten years later a change in the Theatres Act meant the Lord Chamberlain no longer had a say in what was done on the English stage. And that meant Raymond could now run his Revuebar like a theatre. It was a major step. Foreign visitors didn't have to wait three days for their 'membership' to become good. He could sell tickets at the box office. That increased his revenue. His audience widened. Also, as a club he used to change his show every few months, trying to get the same people coming back. But as a theatre he could change the show less often, say every six months, then every year. That helped cut down on expenses. Profits became important.

These days he changes parts of the Revuebar show whenever he feels like it. He insists that it is a much more expensive show to do today than it ever was. Cast and crew wages have gone up, and so has his production budget. Sets are more elaborate. Lighting is more complex. 'But I'm not prepared to tell you how much we need per night to get out.' It is, however, a money-maker. The Revuebar averages 500 tickets per night – which represents two-and-a-half times the 220-seat house. That's 3000 a week. Admission is £9.50 – which gives an average take at the door of something like £28,500 per week. Drinks are extra, but, at 65p for a lager or £1 for a glass of wine, they're way below the Soho norm. 'Five hundred tickets a night? You think that's a lot? I wouldn't have thought so. Yes it is a lot for a theatre that size. But when you're talking about the London Palladium, you're talking about 2000 persons a night.' Still, for a tiny house it generates good cash flow – £28,500 per week converts to nearly £1.5 million per year.

The interesting thing is, he's hardly changed the original formula. It remains what it has always been – erotica mixed with humour. 'The show is acceptable but I wouldn't necessarily call it respectable. If it was respectable people wouldn't come. The audience has changed from the early days. Then we had the older men who would look around, up and down the street, and dart in. Now they walk straight in. We get a much younger crowd than we did, and a lot more women. The show is much sexier, but I am an entertainer, not a pornographer. I have nothing coarse like those Sunday pub scenes with everyone shouting "Get 'em off" at the stripper.'

It goes without saying that, like much of London theatre, the Revuebar is a tourist attraction – for the Japanese and the Germans, and also for the lads down from Manchester on the razzle. There's nothing wrong with that and he never pretends that it's anything else. He knows exactly what audience he's catering for. And he's made his fortune by understanding that, for many tourists, London is The Tower, Big Ben and the Revuebar. It's a fair bet that if Flo Ziegfeld had been born in Liverpool, he would have been Paul Raymond.

Not that the Revuebar was a success from the start. Within a few days of the opening, the cops raided the joint. They took down the names and addresses of the 165 people in the audience. But within two years the police harassment had pretty much subsided, and Kenneth Allsop, writing in the *Spectator*, observed that among the Revuebar's 70,000 members were 'enough businessmen and captains of industry to drain dry the Stock Exchange and the Savoy Grill.'

Raymond, by the way, has had other run-ins with the police over his shows. Most of the time the charges proved fruitless, especially in the case where one police sergeant found it necessary to see a nude show no less than five times before he tried to close it. 'If I thought I was doing something wrong, I would not do it. People who talk about corruption always say it is not they who have been corrupted but someone else.' He has won most of his battles, although one notable loss was the time he was fined a total of £10,000 for running a disorderly house. 'That was way back in the beginning. Running a disorderly house is a charge that isn't used much these days, but it certainly was then. It's from a law dating back to 1820-odd, and can be used on anybody who either has a stage show or a club that the police are rather against. It has nothing to do with prostitution or anything. It's something the cops can use when people get drunk and disorderly or shouting obscene things. But it doesn't mean to say it's that as well. Because that wasn't the case regarding the Raymond Revuebar. In the early days, when we were backing up against the law the whole time, they went for us all the time because we were new and what we were doing had never been seen before. Running a disorderly house was the law they dug up.'

With money coming in from the Revuebar, he quickly began to expand. He bought the Windmill Theatre and the Whitehall Theatre and flooded the West End with shows – either as Paul Raymond Productions or shows merely booked into his theatres. In 1969, at the Whitehall, he opened a show called *Pyjama Tops*, which featured lots of ladies minus pyjama bottoms. That show was in profit within nine weeks, ran for a total of six years and grossed over £2 million. There was *Come into my Bed*, and *Let's Get Laid* and, of course, *Oh! Calcutta*. They all made big money. His assessment of what the public wanted to see was proving right. Occasionally though he missed, like he did with *Royalty Follies*, which cost £350,000 to stage and lost him a cool half-million.

The Windmill is now *La Vie en Rose*, the Whitehall used to be the Theatre of War, but the Revuebar is still the Revuebar. 'We call it erotic entertainment. It's a theatre with a seat situation and you can take your drinks to your seat. We don't serve at the seats. La Vie en Rose is a different approach. There is food and drink. The audience is served at tables and chairs. It's a cabaret performance with some ladies who are semi-nude. It's probably more on the line of shows you'd see in Paris, like the Moulin Rouge.'

He sells drinks, but, unlike most Soho spots, he says liquor isn't the most important element. 'You've got to get the bums in the seats first, otherwise you can't sell drinks. If you've only got 20 persons in the house, they're not going to drink much. The show is therefore the first thing. If they don't want to see the show, forget about it. We don't do all that good in the bar at the Raymond Revuebar. A lot of people think that guys who want to see these types of shows get pissed all the time. They don't. It does all right. But again, the show is the most important element.'

As a theatre owner and theatrical producer, Raymond found himself in something of a minor crunch a few years ago when the West End looked as if it might be dying.

Anyone for Denis closed at the Whitehall (it wasn't his production, he was just renting them the stage) and there didn't seem to be much around to take its place. 'Broadway was very very very good about four years ago when London was not so good. It's reversed around now. But don't kid yourself that the West End is in good shape. The big shows – *Cats, Evita, 42nd Street* – they'll do well anywhere in the world. But I don't have to tell you that most shows are very lucky to get their capital outlay back, much less make a profit. I would say roughly that out of every ten shows that go on, maybe one or two at the outside will make any real money.'

Trying to make some real money was why he invented the Theatre of War. 'I was sitting at home one Sunday afternoon, thinking what I should do at the Whitehall and came up with this idea. I spent nine months buying Second World War stuff. I made contacts with people who were experts, and they had contacts who knew about planes and tanks and that sort of thing. It cost me a lot of actual money today because some of this stuff in 1946 you could get for free.'

He hyped it as, 'The greatest presentation of Second World War items in the UK. I think it had a great educational and historic value. At that time it was difficult to get a stage show in. It was May 1983.' Less than two years later, a zoning commission ruled that this wasn't a theatre and Raymond announced that the entire collection would be sold.

A veteran of the RAF ('I played the drums in the band for a time, then was put on a telephone switchboard. I liked that job because I was on shift work and you could always give someone a couple of bob to do your shift. You could only be there three days a week'), he says he spent around £1.7 million transforming the Whitehall and buying the equipment for the Theatre of War. But his name never appeared on the marquee. And that was very much on purpose.

'I didn't put my name to the Theatre of War because

people would think there were naked ladies sitting on the side of the aircraft. That's what has happened to my name now. But I don't complain. As a matter of fact I am more than pleased because all I have to do now, if it has anything to do with sex, is to put my name to it and they will know exactly what it is all about. Did you notice that I don't put my name to La Vie en Rose either? It isn't sexy enough for my name. Not because I don't want to. I'd love to. But I would confuse the whole thing. The punter who wants to see my type of shows or read my type of magazines would be a little disappointed. And people who wanted to come to La Vie en Rose and who saw my name on it might think, it's a bit too strong for the wife to see. Strong within the law of course. No, I don't complain about that at all because for 30-odd years I've been trying to build up a name.'

At about the same time he bought the Whitehall, he took his first dive into the world of magazines. 'It was 1964. I started a magazine called *King*. We started the same week and the same month as *Penthouse*. The first month we sold 75,000, which was very big for those days. *Penthouse* sold 40,000. The second month we sold 65,000 and they sold 55,000. Third month we sold 40,000 and they sold 65,000. *King* was originally to be the magazine of the Raymond Revuebar. But my editors and I didn't see eye to eye, so I gave it to them. I came out of the publishing side and swore I'd never go into it again.'

He took his losses, about £30,000 worth, but didn't keep his promise. Ten years later he tried again.

'A guy came to interview me for a magazine called *Men Only*. We got along very very well. He was then the editor, and he told me it was going downhill. Eventually he asked me if I was interested.'

That magazine was selling 35,000 copies when he paid £10,000 for the title. Within a month, by calling it *Paul*

Raymond's Men Only, the circulation was up to 85,000.
Now he's got a stable of magazines: *Men Only*, *Club*,
Escort, *Razzle*, and the *Model Directory* are monthly.
There's a quarterly called *The Best of* ——. Plus there is a
Club and a magazine called *Club International*, which are
edited in Britain but aimed specifically at the States –
they're considerably stronger magazines than their name-
sakes in the UK. He's also done some franchising of his
magazines, like in Brazil; although last year he ran into
some problems there. 'The Brazilians stopped paying in
advance at the beginning of the summer of 1984. We had
been producing a magazine for them for two years that
was a mixture of the English magazine and the American
version. The States was too strong for Brazil and the
British version too weak. Well, when we franchise we
want so much money up front before we ship the goods.
And in Brazil I don't have to tell you that with inflation,
and difficulty in getting money out, anyone dealing with
countries like that must be very very careful. It may well
be finished now. I don't know. But like all things, even
supplying shirts, if you don't get paid you no longer
supply the shirts.'

While he says he doesn't control every word of
editorial or every cartoon that goes into his magazines –
he is more concerned with the business side of them – he
definitely doesn't neglect the editorial side. 'One, in my
view, must let the editor run his magazine otherwise he
can't work, providing he works to guidelines of what the
magazine is all about. So the editor should have most of
the control. At one time I okayed the centrefold and read
all the copy. I don't have the time to do it now. The
covers are okayed by me, and I look through at proof
stage and if there is anything I think really should come
out, then I suggest that it come out. It's better to suggest
than to insist.' Here he shrugs, 'Which is the same
thing.'

From magazines and theatres, he branched out into
real estate – probably a natural extension of his interest in

owning theatres. And these days that's where he thinks his investing future lies. These days Paul Raymond happens to be a major landowner in Soho and a bullish buyer. 'I am certainly a very large real estate owner in Soho, but I'm sure that people like Trust House Forte have much more. It's mostly commercial real estate, although there is some residential. Two residential properties, in fact. And I've invested in real estate here because in my view Soho is going to become very big in not many years' time. I think it's going to be like Covent Garden. It has to happen here. It can't go any place else. The West End can only come into Soho. It can't go to Whitehall. It has to come this way. Five years' time, I would have thought. Values here in the last five years have gone up, out of all proportion.'

They continue to climb, in spite of the fact that since 1982 landlords could no longer get the astronomically high rents they used to demand from the sex shops and cinemas. That commerce, a part of Soho life that most residents would like to see controlled and continued – as opposed to abolished – is indeed being controlled now. A total clean-up of Soho would change it from being Soho and no one seems to want that. Least of all Raymond. So when the Westminster City Council enacted licensing laws and a quota system on sex shops and sex cinemas, he was one of the very first to say, 'Quite rightly. Sex shops should be controlled. It can't go on the way it was before with doors filled with people, scruffy people at the door, the places were filthy. I don't think anyone in his right mind ought to complain about a sex shop. If you want to go buy sex toys, so go buy sex toys. But let's have them run in a nice way. They were opening up all over the place until the new law came in. Now they want to know who the owner is and who's behind it. Which is quite right.'

After all, he's got an investment to protect, which in some ways explains why this has become a very favourite subject. 'Take displays in windows. I don't think it's right that, if a man and a woman are walking down the street with their little boy or girl, they should have to see all these displays. If you want to do it inside, okay. Then of course, worse than that is these clip joints, the so-called topless bars where live sex . . . I mean, if they were doing live sex, okay. At least you're not being clipped. If that's what you want to see, at least you're paying for it. But people, more so from abroad than from out of town, won't see any show at all. They get clipped for £80–£100 for near-beer or a so-called glass of champagne, which is not champagne. And some girl sits there with her top off and says, have one more drink, and it's £30 for her to sit down. I think that's a disgrace and is very bad for Soho. Clipping is one of the worst things here. And it gives the police a lot of trouble too. What happens is that people go and complain, but if they come from abroad they're not going to come back to go to court. So there's nothing much anyone can do.'

It wouldn't happen, of course, if the powers-that-be took it upon themselves to carefully gentrify Soho. To keep the sexual overtones, but to add better shopping and better restaurants and better housing. To block off certain streets as pedestrian streets. That's what he'd like to see. It would be great, he says, for Soho. He doesn't need to add that it also couldn't help but to multiply the value of all that property by three or four. 'My total investment in Soho? Somewhere around £10–£12 million, I suppose.'

With that kind of money at stake, he's not only in favour of gentrification, he's doing his damnedest to make it happen. 'I've already started. First, I've changed the Windmill to La Vie en Rose. People said it would never succeed in Soho. It's taken a long time to get off the ground. I spent £1.3 million on it and the first year lost £250,000. But it's working now. Then, I think the Trocadero site, which is not doing all that well, helps the place. I am not involved with that site, but I like the idea. I'd like to see more retail shops in Soho. I'm not saying that Gucci and Armani should come to Soho, but there should be good shopping. And more restaurants. And then the licensing laws do terrible damage. This has been going on for years and over 20 years ago people said it should be changed and oddly enough it was the trade themselves who blocked it. They were saying we'd have to have more staff in the pubs and be open all day. But times have changed again and people want somewhere to go and sit and have a drink. I'd love to stay open till 3 a.m. but the people who live around here say, oh no, too much noise, we don't want places open after 12 o'clock. Even the Soho Society, which has done a bit of good to be fair, is also against places being open late at night. Now, if you're going to close Soho at 11 there will be no Soho. That's the end of it as an entertainment centre.'

There is another factor about Soho and investment there – too important perhaps to overlook or even to take lightly – and that's the mob element. Anyone bringing a business into Soho in competition with the local mob, especially the Maltese, could be inviting trouble. Raymond's operation is probably big enough now that he doesn't have to worry. Although, according to him, 'I've been here 28 years and when I first started people said to me, you've got no chance, they won't let you live there, they'll control you. But it never happened. I pay my rates and if there is any trouble I'll call the police. You don't have to be tough with your fists. You've got to be tough with your head.'

Of course for years there have been rumours that the reason Raymond has never had any real problems with the mob is because he's part of the mob, or controlled by the mob. And he thinks that's pretty funny. 'A lot of people think we have Mafia connections, which we haven't. But a lot of people seem to think I have. I suppose they think it's because I'm in the business that I am, and in Soho, and I've never been involved in any fights or anyone wrecking the place. Only a few months ago, someone who knew me years ago was told, leave Paul Raymond alone because he has Mafia finance behind him. They've been watching too many films. They see the Al Capone image and it's a natural thing if you're in the nightclub business – except I'm not running a nightclub . . . but they expect you to have a big Al Capone hat on, and big broad shoulders and a couple of blondes and, that's what they expect. I think they're rather amazed when they find out it isn't so.'

While he admits to having a certain knack in certain fields, not everything he touches turns to gold. When video hit the scene, he bought a wholesaler called Carnaby Video. It seemed like a good idea at the time. But he closed it within six months. 'It was a disaster. I shouldn't have bought it in the first place. But it was the time when video was fairly new and lots of people were going into it and this was one of the main video wholesale firms. At that time, films came out from MGM and other studios and many of them started doing their own distribution of their own films. There was a lot of video shops, but there was a lot of the wrong type of person at that time going into the video game, like with all things that are new. No, my view on video today is, sure, if you're making a film it's got to come out in that way. But once the novelty's worn off, especially with cable coming out, unless it's a very good film you want to see, you're not going to sit at home and watch some old film. So I closed that out. I took a loss of about £250,000. I guess you could say I haven't got much faith in video. Even less now that I might have had a few years ago.'

But he does have some faith in films – new films, that is. He has partially financed two, while having fully financed two others – films like *Erotica*, *Let's Get Laid*, and *Hardcore*, which wasn't really hardcore. 'Film financing? Yes, we made some money, not enough to retire. But each film I was involved with was a success.'

Slightly surprising, because it is not in any way involved with some section of the media or real estate, is a growing interest in leasing finance. 'I thought it was something that would be a good investment for the company and make money. We lease goods, you know, like computers, to companies and councils throughout the UK. It's a pretty substantial operation. But I couldn't give you the turnover.'

According to records at Companies House, Whitehall Finance Ltd was incorporated in late 1978. Raymond, as part of Paul Raymond Ltd, holds all the shares. Turnover for 1982, the company's most recent reporting year, was £634,276. There was an operating profit of £34,676, although the accounts show a loss after tax. But then leasing finance isn't much more than a sideline interest. The future, he continues to believe, is in real estate. 'I think about expansion and I think about property more than anything else. But that's at the present time. But not theatres. Buying other theatres is the last thing I want to do now. If you spoke to me 10 years ago I would say, yes, I'd like to buy another theatre. Now, no. I'm interested in commercial property in Soho.'

At the same time, he's interested in slowing down a bit. In the past couple of years he's brought both of his children into the business – a son and a daughter – and they are, of sorts, his plan for the future of the dynasty. 'I hope they learn enough to some day take control.' In total, he employs nearly 300 people, counting the casts and crews of the shows. Otherwise there are about 65 in the organization running management and the magazines. 'We don't over-employ staff. I don't believe you should have staff unless they've got work to do. I'd like to think I delegate well. I'd like to think I'm a good manager. I don't think my staff will agree with me. But I think I am. Although the final decisions always come from me. I am not, however, a workaholic. What I'd like to do is come in at half past two and leave at half past six. I'd like to, but I haven't been able to. I'm here every day but the work that I used to do, the normal day-to-day running of the organization, I don't do. I've been able to delegate that. But the policy of the organisation is mine.'

So too is his success.

Of course, if he had become Britain's greatest snake oil salesman, or another Gene Krupa, or if he had mastered his mind-reading act to the point of Command Performances, there are some very obvious ways that success would be recognized. But as the man who has given the world the Revuebar – one wonders if he ever dreams about OBEs and knighthood. A royal warrant? Sir Paul? 'Absolutely impossible.' He roars with laughter. 'No, I can say that categorically, never! I could donate £10 million to charity and there isn't a chance of that. But then again, it's always a good thing to know what your limitations are.'

9

James Hanson
and
Gordon White

Lord Hanson and Sir Gordon are definitely not your average Batman and Robin act.

Not at all.

In fact, James Hanson and Gordon White are – at least in business – so interchangeable that Hanson could run the US operation and White could run the UK operation, and no one would ever know the difference.

'I guess I'm the more entrepreneurial of the two,' White admits. 'Most of my time is simply spent thinking. No one thinks any more. Everyone is too busy spewing out paper. But decisions can't be made by committee. Someone has to make them.'

So White is the thinker and Hanson is the administrator. And together, as a team, they are super-opportunistic. That means, if someone presents them with a pound note for 50p, they feel an obligation to do something about it.

*   *   *

James Hanson was once a part-time entrepreneur and a full-time playboy. His most famous engagement was to a then-unknown Audrey Hepburn.

Gordon White shared his interest in small-time business and big-time ladies, although he refuses to name drop. White had been best friends with James' brother Billy. But, when Billy died young, White says he inherited James. 'We just sort of drifted into a friendship. We think alike. Sometimes it's even weird how alike we can be. There are times when we'll come into a meeting and find that we're both wearing the same shirt and tie.'

Hanson's family had been in the transport business for more than a hundred years. Horse-drawn carts across the Pennines. He was running the Wiles Group, a Yorkshire fertilizer manufacturer and hirer of sacks, with interests in the trucking business. White tells people he was in publishing. But it was really more like the official programmes at sporting events.

They thought about doing some business together, had seen humorous greetings cards in the States, and figured that the same idea would work in Britain. They started the Hanson and White Greeting Card Company. It's still in business today, although they don't own it any more. They gave it up, only to find a few years later that they could no longer use the Hanson and White name. James suggested they buy back their names, but Gordon said it wasn't worth the trouble. No egos here. In 1964 their business was dubbed Hanson Trust.

Today White is 60 – two years younger than Hanson. He is also 6'5½", which makes him several inches taller than Hanson. During the late '60s, Hanson and White had pretty high profiles – a sabre-bearing pair, taking companies over, geared for a fight. In lots of ways it made them cult figures in British business.

They have not necessarily slowed down with age.

Hanson is Chairman of Hanson Trust PLC, based in London. White is Chairman of Hanson Industries Inc., based in New York and wholly owned by Hanson Trust. Hanson is on White's board – and spends a lot of time in the States. His wife is American. He used to live in America. And the people around him love to say he thinks like an American. White, however, is not on Hanson's main board. It was his choice. It is also probably very indicative of just how secure he and Hanson are in their partnership.

As defined by James Hanson, their company is in the business of industrial management, of buying businesses or developing businesses to make them more successful. Hanson Trust is run by some 25 people. Hanson Industries is run by less. About 20 in all. But Hanson Trust is Butterley Bricks, Ever Ready Batteries, Allders Department Stores and the duty free shops at Heathrow and Gatwick airports. It is Northern Amalgamated Industries (rubber), Lindustries (heating control systems), SLD (diesel driven pumps), Barbour Campbell (textiles), UDS (textiles), and Hanson Engineering (stainless steel brewing equipment). Hanson Industries is Endicott Johnson (shoes), Carisbrook (textiles), Interstate United (food catering), Ames (shovels), and Hygrade (hot dogs at baseball games).

The philosophy at both is hands-off management.

'I know everyone preaches that and no one ever practises it,' says White, 'but we really do. I've never visited a plant or a headquarters. I've never gone to look at what I'm buying. I don't know why I'd even want to. I don't believe in royal visits. The guy who makes the money for the company is the guy who runs it. When we take over an operation, we're not interested in firing corporate people, we just send them back to the division where the money is made. Corporate headquarters, that's us, well we're there to lend them money and constantly review budgets. And to incentivize divisional management. The lower the budget, the quicker the incentives kick in. So what we do is to make certain that the divisional managers work with budgets that are fair.'

In reality they have an enormous hand in management. They hold the purse strings. Once a budget is approved, no one anywhere in the group can spend more than £750 without the Chairman's personal okay. Of course there would be nothing to stop someone at headquarters ringing Ever Ready to complain, we don't like brown batteries, we want blue ones. But both Hanson and White say they wouldn't want to do that. Hanson says he'd hope to be employing somebody who is good at managing businesses and let them worry about brown batteries or blue batteries. As far as he's concerned, the job of Hanson Trust is to control the finances of the group, to devise methods of motivating the people who are actually making the profit and to look to the future in terms of new ideas. He says that to pick up the phone at HQ and ring a shop steward would mitigate the level of authority and responsibility that they want to ensure is in the hands of the man actually running the business. And that's very strictly adhered to. Real chain of command stuff. They never try to undercut or dilute local authority. They're much more concerned with saying, here's a whole business, we entrust that to you, get on with it and make money. They say, you too have every opportunity of being successful. They also say, the only thing we won't do is provide the opportunity to blame us for a failure.

Hanson and White look at companies from a detached viewpoint, making their conclusions entirely on the return of capital employed. They are particularly fond of fairly mature, basic-industry companies that have been poorly managed. While they cringe at the thought of being called asset strippers, they do tend to shed excess baggage from any of their purchases. In many cases it helps pay for the purchase. Once they take control of a company, they like to change top-level management, the ones who have probably been misdirecting the company. Then they give those good middle managers their head and see them properly directed. Growth becomes a head office activity. The mature cash flow provides them with enough money to buy something else.

To motivate, they rely heavily on incentives. In America, cash is used more often than it is in Britain. But

Hanson still believes that money is the ultimate motivator. He pays them a competitive salary, then goes about devising schemes that will enable managers in exceptional circumstances to receive bonuses up to the equivalent of their annual pay. In other words, he'll pay them twice as much as he's already paying them if they're able to materially improve both the return on capital employed and the profit over their budget.

And here he points out that budgeting at Hanson Trust comes from the bottom up rather than from the top down.

Many companies budget from the top down. The financial experts at headquarters expect a particular division to make a profit of X next year. So they impose budgets on that division to make their guess work. Hanson says he wouldn't be so bold. He wants the fellow running the specific company to come up with the figures. Hanson then stretches it by devising incentive schemes which encourage that divisional manager to be ambitious in his goals. The incentive schemes are redevised every year, based on the performance of the preceding year. That way, he says, it's always a moving feast. That way, budgets and incentives are always adapting to circumstances.

What you discover when you dig a little deeper is that every divisional manager also understands that Hanson holds the sword of Damocles. Divisions that don't bring in at least 25 per cent return on capital are got rid of. They're sold or simply closed.

*   *   *

The UDS Group was a business developed over a long period by the Lyons family. It was Richard Shops and John Collier and stores like Allders. In 1982, if you had been interested enough, you could have bought UDS shares for 60–75p. UDS under the Lyons family had ceased to be much of an excitement around the City.

Stockbrokers were saying, 'The value of the assets employed has exceeded the rate at which profit growth has accrued.' Translated into English it means they didn't have a lot of faith in the future of the business.

But a few people saw things differently. Gerald Ronson was one of them. Still smarting from his unsuccessful bid to take over Associated Communications Corporation, by the autumn of 1982 he was thinking he could do a lot with the UDS Group because it would meld easily into his Heron interests. He did his homework and came up with the figure of £1 per share. That valued the group at £191 million. He put a group of investors together – they called themselves the Bassishaw Consortium – and in January 1983 they launched a cash bid.

Ronson and Bassishaw were going for the knock-out punch in the first round. But UDS had Sir Robert Clark in their corner. Chairman of Hill Samuel, a Director of the Bank of England, and a most articulate man, he is by anyone's standards a mean opponent. No glass jaw here. To ward off Ronson, UDS began to negotiate with Ralph Halpern of the Burton Stores Group, hoping to sell him the Richard Shops and John Collier. By the beginning of February a deal was done for £78 million. That's when Ronson tried to stop the UDS–Burton deal with votes from shares committed to Bassishaw after the take-over bid had been declared. That gave Clark enough time to announce a profit estimate that valued the shares at 140p, not counting the Richard Shops and John Collier. Based on that, the share prices started moving. They rose over the £1 mark and, in effect, nullified Ronson's bid. It forced Ronson to come back with a bid of 114p. Another good punch. And that forced Clark and UDS to negotiate with Ronson.

It was 16 February 1983.

At Hanson Trust they had been watching all of this with the greatest of interest. They knew the players and they knew the style of the game. And on that morning in February, Hanson had a feeling that Ronson was going to make a raid on the UDS shares the very next day.

It was indeed Ronson's plan. Word had got out.

So, late that afternoon, Hanson spoke with Clark. UDS would welcome a White Knight to keep them out of Ronson's reach. Hanson saw his chance, and told Clark, '125p'. In exchange for the UDS board's recommendation, Hanson offered five Hanson Trust shares for every eight UDS shares.

Hanson's timing was perfect. His glove landed squarely on Ronson's nose.

It took Ronson nearly a month to come back with a cash offer of 130p. And when he did, he added, 'It's my final offer.'

Now Hanson was in control. He went to 145p. And he won.

The price tag was £260 million in cash and shares. But then Hanson sold Richard Shops and John Collier for £106 million, plus a few other smaller businesses for somewhere around £70 million, and wound up with Allders Department Stores and the duty free shops, a credit-selling business and some properties valued at about £180 million. His total outlay was under £90 million. And he made that back very quickly with the cash flow from the businesses he kept.

*   *   *

Hanson Trust is known on this side of the Atlantic as a predator. They're in the business of take-overs. When they bang on your door it usually means they're looking for a fight.

The favourite trick of the predator used to be the dawn raid.

A romantic concept – a gang of thugs in dark suits with fedoras pulled low over their eyes jumping out of limos and into the Stock Exchange with machine guns a blazing . . . Hardly! It's so unsexy that even accountants could pull it off. Someone merely walked around the

Stock Exchange at 9 or 9:30 in the morning and announced to the sleepy masses, 'We'll take as many shares in that company at this price as can be delivered to us.' Because the price was at a premium to the opening quote, there would be a surge forward and anyone looking to sell would see a golden opportunity. They'd wind up with 10 or 15 or 20 per cent over the morning's price. However, it's been a couple of years since such theatrics worked. First, the institutions and private individuals holding large blocks of the raided shares quickly understood that, almost invariably, the dawn raid was the first volley of shots. That the raiders would have to come in again with a higher bid. They started playing it cool. Second, new rules were imposed by the Stock Exchange limiting the amount of shares you could buy under such circumstances without making that offer available to all the shareholders everywhere. The way they saw it, because the little old lady in Torquay doesn't get to hear about what's going on in the market at 9:30, dawn raids aren't fair to her. Before she knows it, the raiders have run off with x per cent of her company without her ever knowing that an offer is available for the stock she holds. In the end the dawn raid died a natural death.

But that hasn't meant the end of the hostile take-over.
UDS was mild.

Once upon a time there was a company called London Brick.

A lacklustre operation, but with a 45 per cent market share in the British brick business, they were the sole major producer of fletton bricks – a particular type of clay brick that comes onto the market cheaper than non-fletton bricks. A couple of years ago, London Brick attempted to take over the last independent non-fletton brick maker in the UK, Ibstock Johnson. Because any sort of acquisition involving more than 25 per cent of an industry sector is subject to a review by the Monopolies and Mergers Commission, there was a hearing. The ruling that came down determined that the fletton brick business and the non-fletton brick business were non-competing. London Brick's stronghold on fletton did not prevent it from going into the non-fletton side of the business. As it was, London Brick backed away from the take-over because the price got too high.

But the Monopolies and Mergers Commission ruling opened the door to London Brick for another assault on the non-fletton side of the business.

And that had ramifications for Hanson. He owned a company called Butterley Brick, a non-fletton producer that would merge quite neatly with London Brick. A possible take-over was in the back of his mind until December 1963 when London Brick announced their take-over attempt of two smaller brick businesses. It was suddenly obvious to Hanson that, if London Brick could pull off those take-overs, Butterley might be threatened.

White queen's bishop takes black king's knight.

London Brick announced their plans at 9:30 a.m. By 5 that same evening, Hanson had rallied his troops and launched an assault on London Brick.

He offered £170 million.

Black queen takes white king's pawn. Check.

Two years before, Hanson could have bought London Brick for 30p a share. Now he had to pay 89p for a block of 7 million shares. That alone drove the price up to 104p. Hanson's bid was worth 120p per share. The London Brick board dug in and Hanson had a fight on his hands. It didn't matter at all to them that he was the reigning champ, having successfully manoeuvred five major take-over fights in the previous five years. Nor did it matter that Jeremy Rowe at London Brick was something of a novice at all this, although he had merchant banker Marcus Agius of Lazard Freres in his corner. Rowe and Agius decided that if Hanson wanted the company he'd have to pay plenty for it. Nothing personal. But let's face it, vengeance is sweet. If you're going to get swallowed by a whale, Jonah, the least you can do is tumble down its throat hoping it'll wind up with one helluva stomach ache.

To help give the whale that stomach ache, Rowe and Agius mounted their defences by telling the world that London Brick's estimated 1983 profits were up 70 per cent. They forecast 1984 profits up 38 per cent with a doubled dividend. They tried to make Hanson play an away game where the scoreboard read London Brick net assets were worth at least 215p per share. It forced Hanson to raise his 120p bid not once, but twice.

And that was unprecedented. No one had ever done that to Hanson.

He raised his offer to 150p per share . . . received a mediocre response . . . then came back with 165p, added a convertible loan stock alternative of 175p, and deftly increased his stake in London Brick to 29.9 per cent. The fact that Hanson could inadvertently underpin the London Brick share price at 175p was the risk he had to take to rally the institutional investors. But Hanson knew from experience that it was always much easier to get the additional 21 per cent worth of acceptances out of the remaining 70 per cent of the uncommitted shares than to get 40 per cent if there were 90 per cent of the shares left uncommitted.

Rowe and Agius refused to give up. The deadline was set for Tuesday, 28 February 1984 at 3:30 p.m. And, with 20 minutes left to go, Hanson was still 1.5 million shares short of 50.1 per cent.

Rowe and Agius actually came that close to winning.

'It generated a lot of emotion,' remembers Marcus Agius. 'Although it was quite straightforward. There were two or three things they did which were very impressive. Firstly, they moved very quickly. I'm sure Hanson had been looking at the company, but I don't believe they were about to make an offer. But the same day that London Brick announced its offer, they got themselves sufficiently geared up to respond by making their offer. Very impressive.'

That Hanson had to increase his offer twice, he says, 'caused a certain amount of fluttering as everyone was concerned that Hanson may have got his sums wrong and, horror of horrors, he might actually lose. But he was very courageous. At just the right moment, during the closing stages of the bid, he went into the market and picked up a total of 29.9 per cent of the company. I'm sure that was critical in the final analysis as he just squeeked over the 50 per cent mark. It was very close. Most exciting.'

The place where it happens is the notice board at the Stock Exchange. Hanson had to nail his declaration to the board, announcing that he owned more than 50 per cent of the company by 3:30. Had it gone up at 3:31 he would have missed the boat. As it happened, a large block of institutionally held shares swung the game to Hanson. He wound up with 58.6 per cent for which he paid £247 million, more than double his original bid. The notice went up with just about 15 minutes left. But Agius says he had seen the writing on the wall a few hours before. 'By then it was, as far as I'm concerned, a foregone conclusion. The share prices had shot ahead and it was quite obvious that it was just a matter of typing up the results and putting it on the board. Someone had told someone had told someone. The share price took off around 1:30 or 2 o'clock and I knew from then it was all over. He pitched it absolutely right. If he had gone 5p less he wouldn't have got it. Had he gone 5p more he would have overpaid.'

Yet the single factor that impressed Agius most of all was that Hanson himself controlled the battle. 'It was quite clear to me that the whole thing was being orchestrated by Hanson personally. Very very tight control. [N. M.] Rothschilds [Hanson's merchant bankers for this battle] was used pretty much as a post office. It was significant that press inquiries were directed only to Hanson's man. Rothschilds weren't allowed to talk to the press. That's most unusual. Hanson spent much of that time in America. Their press announcements went out at 7 o'clock in the evening because it was obvious that the discussion of the content of the press announcement was never started until 1 o'clock London time, which is 8 a.m. in New York. Even earlier in California. Feeling it from this end, it was quite clear that the whole thing was being done directly by him.'

It was by all accounts a bitterly fought take-over. But Hanson expects that. After all, he says, by the very nature of a bid the predator is saying, we can do better than the present management. If you approach a company to make an acquisition, the board of that company must wonder, how do we know that the price being offered is the right price. Because that board is supposed to think that their first loyalty is to their shareholders – and board members, don't forget, often tend to be heavyweight shareholders – the best thing they can do is say, we don't welcome this offer and want to see how far the company looking to take us over is willing to go. Everyone knows the first approach is never the last – or very rarely the last. Bid situations in the UK – unless it's a real rescue, or a white knight escapade where the besieged company invites somebody else in with whom they can do a friendly deal – well, a bid is something to be fought.

In the States there are different rules because it's a different game.

'A hostile take-over in the United States is not always a good idea,' says White. 'The cost of slugging it out legally, to me, doesn't usually make sense. It inhibits you from doing anything else. Although I admit that getting involved in a hostile take-over and what they now call "greenmail" is probably the only sure bet in the world.'

Although, if you look at White's record in the US – and Hanson Industries Inc. now accounts for more than 50 per cent of the group's worldwide turnover – you might think another sure bet is the leveraged buy-out.

✻   ✻   ✻

It was 1973.

Gordon White was closing in on the half-century mark – a time when most successful businessmen think of reinforcing their roots. But White felt it was time to do just the opposite. 'The Labour government had come to power and they threatened to squeeze the rich so hard that the pips would squeek. I just wanted to get out of the country, so James and I figured it was the right time to expand into the States. In those days there were exchange control regulations so we had to start up with what little money we could get. That was $3000.'

Today, Hanson Industries is listed among the 200 biggest companies in the States, and the 19th largest foreign investor. That happens to strike both James Hanson and Gordon White as pretty funny, because the company has never actually invested a nickel in the States. They owe everything there to leveraged buy-outs.

'I sometimes think I invented the leveraged buy-out,' White claims. 'It's a favourite move in the States that is not used much in the UK because the banks here don't think the way American banks do. When I got to the States, the first thing I wanted to buy was a fishing company called Seacoast. But I had no money. So I said fine, I'd pay them $32 million over a period of time. I simply used the assets of Seacoast to secure the notes I gave to the family who owned it.'

He did the same thing when he bought 25 per cent of Gable Industries. And as long as it kept working, White kept buying. Paying his way with what James Hanson liked to call 'Gordon White Promissory Notes'. He picked up no less than nine textile companies with $75 million worth of assets with a leveraged purchase of $35 million. He followed that with the purchase of Interstate United, although that was a public company and he had to tender for it. Once he got it, he stripped off some of the assets that were losing money – he sold a Michigan convention centre to the Shriners and divested himself of the Brass Rail Restaurants, among others – and what was left was a series of companies, including one in the food service business that sells hot dogs at baseball games. It also caters 1.8 million meals a week thoughout the States.

Last year White managed to buy US Industries, a whole series of companies representing some $1.2 billion worth of sales from building materials, furniture, clothing and a range of industrial products. And that acquisition was as close as White and Hanson have ever come to hostile activities in the States.

USI was originally supposed to be a management buy-out. White heard about it and stepped in with an offer of $23 a share for a total of $531 million. The management team then proposed a leveraged buy-out at $24. But they couldn't get the financial support. With their enormous weight and skill behind them, Hanson and White moved in and mopped up.

US Industries was an especially good deal, says White, because it was a whole series of companies where the risk was well spread. 'I'd rather have 700 companies making $1 million each than three companies making $250 million. The trick is to try to make sure that you're insulated in case a major division has a bad year. When I go to buy, I'm not interested in what I can make with the company as much as I am in knowing what I can lose if it all goes wrong. The upside will take care of itself. Look at USI. Interest payments on $530 million are $62 million. Last year, USI's pre-tax profit was $67 million. At worst it will wash through. But the chances are we will substantially improve earnings. Just the oil interests could bring $20–$25 million.'

Instead of going into USI, he says, he could have bought Norton Simon for $700 million, including Avis, the cosmetics side, and three or four other major holdings. 'I turned it down because the divisions were out of proportion. Any one of them going wrong would have tilted the balance. I'm not interested in a major one-product business, such as Boeing. It's too many eggs in one basket. Look at Warner when Atari got into trouble.

That will not happen to us. We avoid making those kinds of mistakes, although I'm sure there have been other mistakes that I've made in not buying a company. When I turn down a purchase it's because I feel that if they went wrong they'd bust us.'

What he wants to see when he goes shopping is usually no further away than the company reports. 'The first thing I do is look back to see what a company has spent and also at its depreciation. If they've spent in excess of their depreciation, I might be interested. That's because I figure I'll be getting value for money. I never look at figures like the P/E. They're bullshit. It's not possible to judge a company that way. P/Es are nothing more than the number of years it would take to get your money back if the company paid all of its earnings out as dividends with tax put to one side. Except it never happens that way.'

They finance what they do in America with dollars either out of cash flow or through the banks there, matching dollar for dollar assets and liabilities. Hanson says they are now long in both dollars and sterling, having built up a very solid equity base. As most of their American businesses aren't exporters there is no real worry about foreign exchange exposure. In fact, many of their American businesses have over the past year or so been taking advantage of the strong dollar to stockpile raw materials. In the UK, very few of their businesses are exporters. When they do export, they invoice in sterling.

The Hanson–White success story in the US is not one that many British firms have ever equalled. And credit for it really has to go to White's understanding of the American scene. 'Being successful in the States is not easy for a foreign company. Just look at the enormous number of failures. But we took our lessons from King George III. You can't run your American interests from London. He made that mistake in 1776. It simply doesn't work.'

There are, he says, lots of reasons why. 'Business moves much faster in the States. The mentality is very different. The US is a much tougher business environment than the UK. You can't even compare the two. In the UK you can featherbed inefficiency and high prices forever. The thing about America is its freshness. If you want to see someone in America, they'll see you. If you've got something to sell, they'll listen. That's what's wrong with Europe. England is well known for having invented many new products, but it takes the US or Japan to make them commercially viable.'

He stops to think for a moment, then makes one last point. 'You can't forget that the US is much more a lawyer-built society than Europe. Lawyers run everything. To survive in the States you have to know the ins and outs of the law. If you don't, the Americans will soon have you in knickers and necklace.'

10

Gerald Ronson

Gerald Ronson is what The Godfather would have been if Don Corleone was British of Eastern European extraction and honest.

The man voted Businessman of the Year for 1984 is a tall, muscular guy who batters the King's English with an East London accent that is totally inappropriate because he doesn't come from the East End. He is the sort of man who can tell you exactly how many times he's been to the United States – 55 trips in the past five years. He is also a man with a proven knack for making money. It is a talent, like standing on your head, making a perfect soufflé or speaking Russian. Some people just know how to do such things.

When you ask him he tells you he is a contented, respectful, upstanding, happily married man who is totally in control. He says the most important thing in the world to him is his family. After that it's business. Then comes his charity work. Then come his boats. Simplicity might be the last refuge of the jaded. Except in Ronson's case, he never bothered getting jaded. He just stayed simple and made billions.

'I have a reputation of being tough. I wouldn't say I have a reputation of being hard. If tough means no nonsense, if tough means I won't tolerate a lot of stupidity or a lot of b/s going on around me, then absolutely. But hard, I wouldn't like to think of myself as being a hard man. I think you have to differentiate between being tough and being hard. Two different things.'

He quit Clark's College in Cricklewood before he was 15 so that he could go to work in his father's furniture business. Today he is one of the wealthiest men in Britain. 'I would not be what I am today if it was not for the training I got from my father when I went into the furniture manufacturing business, which is like 32 years ago. I started by sweeping the sawdust off the floor in the mill. That's a fact. I went through every single department in the furniture factory, which employed about 300 people. What I learned from him was the work ethic, your name is your reputation, a sense of responsibility, discipline and how to deal with people. He was very much out of the old school. He was a man who believed in working six-and-a-half days a week, getting into the factory before everyone else and going home after everyone else. It was that development of my character which gave me a good grounding for when I came out of the furniture business in 1957.'

He was 18 in 1957, had three years' business experience, and now wanted to go out on his own. With £150,000–£200,000 of the family's money, Ronson plunged into the house-building business. That led him into commercial development. And that led him, in a roundabout way, into the oil business.

It really began for him when he started buying up petrol stations. Hardly a way to wander into English upper-crust society. Even his pals said, 'Petrol stations? Look what Gerry Ronson is doing with his father's money.' But he didn't care what his friends said because he was in real estate, and petrol stations were prime sites that would bring in some sort of income until he chose to develop them. Then oil prices went from $3 a barrel to £36 a barrel. He originated the self-service petrol station, which successfully created a hefty cash flow and allowed him to expand further into property, insurance, motor distribution and consumer products.

'If you look at how we built our business, it's been built brick by brick and with the reputation the company has. A lot of people think they can do it in five or ten years. But you've got to be a long-distance runner if you want to build up a serious business. You've got to have the right people, the right infrastructure, the right credibility, the right reputation. It's the persistence, and being able to put all these things together that make the business overall. It takes a lifetime.'

Making his own fortune didn't take him that long, however. He says he could have retired when he was 24. 'I remember saying to myself when I was 15, when I become a millionaire I'm going to retire. Then I said to myself, by the time I'm 30 if I make £10 million I'm going to retire. Which, looking back, I realize how ridiculous it was to say it in the first place. Some people refer to me as a workaholic. I'm not a workaholic. I enjoy what I'm doing. If I didn't enjoy it I wouldn't do it. That doesn't mean I'm stupid and enjoy everything I'm doing because there are days I don't enjoy it and there are days I find it frustrating and there are days I find it aggravating. But everything in life is a challenge and I enjoy my business. Just like some people enjoy golf or swimming or tennis or whatever their hobbies are. My hobby is my business and my business I enjoy as much, if not more than doing those other things. If that wasn't the case, I wouldn't be at my business six-and-a-half days a week, I would be doing those other things.'

When he does take time off, he has a boat. A big boat. The kind that always gets referred to as a yacht. He builds them himself. No, he doesn't put on the overalls and get out the hammer and saw. He only fools around with the designs so that the boat will be to his personal specifications. Then he orders it built. He names it after his wife. He staffs it with crew and keeps it in the south of France. He plays with the boat until he gets tired with it and then he puts it on the market. He sells it. To date he's done it eight or nine times. And each time he sells a boat, he makes a profit.

It keeps him in boatswain's whistles.

* * *

The company is called Heron.

The name comes from Henry Ronson, Gerald's late father.

It is a private company. Ronson's salary is £460,000 per year, but that's all he gets. Heron pays no dividends. The shares are owned by Gerald Ronson, several family trusts and three charitable foundations, all controlled by Gerald Ronson.

'I don't discuss my charities in terms of telling the outside world. It's not anybody's business. But I'm a great believer that if the Lord blesses you in terms of being able to make a lot of money, you've got a responsibility to do something with it. And more importantly, you've got a responsibility to show your children that those seeds have to be replanted.'

Structurally, under the charitable foundations is a two-tier board.

The Heron International Board is four people. Ronson is Chairman and CEO. His three closest lieutenants are there as directors for finance, for property and for legal and commercial matters. Beneath that is the Heron Corporation Board, with those four plus the managing directors of the trading companies. About 14 in all. Heron Corp. is about 120 companies, although there are only 30 main active trading divisions falling under four basic headings – property investment, house building, general trading, which is consumer products, and insurance.

In the UK, Ronson is the largest independent petrol retailer; office buildings and developments such as St David's Centre in Cardiff; auto retailing and distributorships including H. R. Owen Rolls-Royce, Massey Ferguson products plus the sole concessionaires for

Suzuki motor products and Lancia cars; audio, TV and video equipment; the National Insurance and Guarantee Corporation; Baileys of Westbury, Ltd. for haulage, parcel delivery and warehousing; Herondrive for fleet sales and leasing; and Heron Homes for house building. In the United States, he is the Pima Savings and Loan Association of Tucson, Arizona; Western American Financial Corporation and Western American Insurance Agency (both of Phoenix, Arizona); Media Home Entertainment for video distribution and film financing; plus Heron Properties and a 50 per cent stake in the California developer Hall Properties. For 1985, 50 per cent of the group's earnings will come from the US, where Ronson figures he's got somewhere around $2.5 billion of assets, which are expanding at the rate of 30–35 per cent per year.

'I have built up a team of what I would regard as 50 key senior managers. Although we employ something like 5000 people worldwide, I would say there are basically 50 people who are the key players. I think I delegate well, but I am also a very good detail person. I like to know what's going on in my businesses. Just look at our board meetings. I mean, we could sit here at Marylebone Road [across the street from Madame Tussaud's wax museum in London] and have all our board meetings here. But we alternate the board meetings to the major businesses. There's nothing like walking through a warehouse, a plant, a major site, a business or whatever, walking around insurance company offices, you get a feel for the business. Our approach is very much a hands-on approach. We believe that leadership should be in the front, there should be direct lines of communication.'

He travels 200,000 miles a year 'to visit the troops.' He Concordes to New York and then rides the Heron plane around the States. 'It's the same old persistence and dedication. It all sounds very boring. But that's what it's all about. You visit the troops. The people have got to feel that the business not only has a figure head, but that person is visible, that person is there. Because if I don't make the effort, if they don't see that I care, I can't expect them to care.'

There is, he assures anyone who asks, a chain of command. But when you own the game and can make up the rules as you go along, that sort of thing probably doesn't matter as much as he says it does. 'I don't have a problem with the people around me. If I want to go direct to anybody, they won't object to it. They would object to it if I delegate somebody else to do it. Then they would take umbrage. But because they know my style of business, which is open – I'm not a politician in terms of how I operate within my corporation and you can interpret that whichever way you wish – but I believe things should go in straight lines.'

In other words, and just in case there has ever been any doubt, Gerald Ronson is the boss. He is Heron and Heron is him. Although here too he tries to play that down. After all, he does have to live with the people he employs. 'As far as the business is concerned, there are 30 operating companies around the world. It's all run by first-class managing directors and a very capable management team. A lot of these people have been with me 10–15–20 years. You never hear about people leaving Heron, because they don't leave. But every ship has to have a captain on the bridge. Every team, there has to be a team leader. I'm the team leader of my team. Yes, I'm the architect of the business.'

He stresses though that strategy and planning is these days much more of a team decision than it was 10–15 years ago. 'We work on four-year rolling corporate plans, which is current financial year plus three. I don't believe you can look out much further than that. Some major corporations look 10–15 years. But in my opinion there is no way in the world we live in today you can look 10–15 years up the road. You're very clever if you can guess it right three years up the road. In some businesses, three months up the road. But we've worked for the last 15 years on a four-year plan. You get more sophisticated as time goes on. More experienced with the input and the way the plans are structured. Our plans are very complex in terms of assets, cash flow and development of specific businesses. We update our four-year plan in the last quarter of our calendar year. All my managing directors of every division participate in the input, because obviously this is the way to involve the whole team. You've got to have people around you who are thinking forward all of the time, because if they're not thinking forward they're going backwards.'

Because he wants to maintain extremely tight controls on the corporate finances, he gets a full weekly management package, and full monthly figures on every single company in the group. 'Our financial directors are watching daily the movement of cash and treasury. Our turnover will be say $1 billion for 1985. So, yes, it is very important to keep tight controls. Especially when you're in eight different currencies. You've got to be watching this.'

To protect his foreign exchange exposure he matches and swaps but never opens positions in currency. 'We don't gamble. We make sure we know where our exposure is and our exposure is a controlled exposure. I'm not a gambler. I'm not in the business of gambling. Gambling is for the needy and greedy. There are risks in my business but there are risks in everything. You analyse the risks. You take a view based on experience and judgement. As a business gets bigger your approach is much more conservative, much more careful. Now, if you'd have spoken to me 15 years ago I might have said I'm going bonko or something. But that's not how we run this business now. We haven't run this business like that for maybe the last seven years.'

It was the middle-1970s when the penny dropped. It was the time of the property crash. 'The banks had over-extended themselves by loaning to people who were not responsible or professional property developers. Half the secondary banking system went bust. Even the major banking system needed the encouragement and support of the Bank of England. You just couldn't sell a property for its real value. When you see institutions today buying on a 4–5 per cent yield, you couldn't have given away those properties on an 8–9 per cent yield. There was no confidence in property.'

A lot of people he knew were suddenly broke. He says Heron was lucky and came through it basically unscathed. 'We realized that it could have happened to us. You know, there but for the grace of God go I. Thank God we had a very successful petrol business, among others, which generated the cash flow to take us through that hump.' He says he was lucky and learned a great deal. 'It was worth 25 years of business experience. Now I'm probably one of the most conservative businessmen you'll meet.'

* * *

Gerald Ronson is a heavyweight.

He plays in the big leagues and he plays for big stakes.

He says his handshake is his bond. 'When you shake hands with Gerald Ronson, the deal is done.' And that's when he comes up with the story of the deal he once negotiated with the British head of an American oil company. Ronson was selling some sites, and the two came to an agreed price. The next day, Ronson received a call from another company willing to pay more for the sites. Ronson refused to sell at that higher price and stuck with his original deal. 'They thought I was stark raving mad.'

But that's the way he says he likes to do business – on both sides of the Atlantic – which, he adds, is not always the case with everyone else. 'In certain places in America, especially the Southwest where we operate in Arizona, because of the structure of the community your word is still important. Everybody knows everybody else. All the players know who the other players are in the marketplace. If you give your word, or if you do a deal, your reputation is very important. You get into a different ball game in California, or even in New York. I'm generalizing because there are certain businesses where people know who the players are, such as in the diamond business. If the people know one another, a word counts for something. But generally you need to read the fine print very carefully on every contract you look at in America. There are always armies of lawyers on both sides and it's a whole different ball game than the European attitude where reputation and integrity, I think, has different values and meanings. It really depends on where you're coming from.'

Heron is a cash-rich company, which means Ronson can buy anything he wants to.

Almost.

'You don't have to jump on every bus coming along up the street. A proportion of our acquisitions have not come out of a great scientific development plan, they've come out of opportunistic deals. And any entrepreneur who says he's never done any opportunistic deals is either kidding himself or not telling you the truth.'

Because he's sitting on a pile of cash, the market knows he's a serious player. So opportunities come his way. But Ronson labels himself a runner of businesses and not the kind of entrepreneur who buys businesses, strips and sells them. 'That's not our style. We build up business and we build up the management. That is how I have all these businesses. Therefore, when people know you're out there as a major player, and that you're in a position to sign a cheque for a big number, then who do they pick the phone up to call? They don't pick the phone up to the faceless crowd. And in the UK there are only half a dozen people who are in a position to write out a cheque and can make a decision like we can make a decision. In fact, I'm not even sure there are half a dozen out there.'

Who are they? He shakes his head. He won't list them. 'You know who they are.'

Obviously everyone knows he's one of them because Ronson is a favourite of the crystal ball gazers. Whenever a company looks ripe for a bid, somebody invariably whispers with a knowing nod, 'Gerald Ronson.' It's as good a guess as any. And it happens all the time. For instance, his name was for so long linked to a possible take-over bid for Burmah Oil that he alone might have been the only businessman in England who doubted Gerald Ronson's intentions towards Burmah.

'I think that can be a figment of people's imagination because we own a reasonable stake in that company. But having said that, I would not assume that Burmah is the one. I can think of other companies that we've got stakes in that nobody talks about. But then I read about a lot of companies I'm supposed to have stakes in that I don't have stakes in. Every Sunday I open the newspaper and I laugh because I see last week I bid for Burmah with a Saudi consortium, and the week before I was bidding for some other company. I mean, what's the guessing game this weekend? I'm surprised how irresponsible some Sunday papers can be that they don't do their homework properly.'

On the other hand, he does his homework. 'Yes, we do our homework. We are very conservative people because we are spending our own money. Our reputation is on the line. If we borrow money from banks, we give them information, we give them facts and figures, and they've got to be right.'

The way he comes into the market to buy or sell has to be right too. He may quite happily make money on a lost take-over bid but he won't get involved with games like 'greenmail'. Actually Ronson cringes at the thought of being put in that category. 'I'm not in the greenmail business. If I wanted to take advantage of Heron's charisma in terms of Heron buying shares in companies, then we could make a lot of money playing those sorts of tricks. But that is not where our reputation is. We are serious business people running a serious business, not playing out there in the market to make opportunity killings in the stock market on either side of the ocean. In America, it's a different ball game. In America, very respectable people play that game and it's not looked down upon or frowned upon the same way it is in the City of London. But in the City of London, if you want the right reputation – and I believe I know the reputation we want and we have – then that's not the game you play. That's not the game Heron will play.'

Nor does Heron go in for the 'back door' approach to take-overs. Ronson says they don't use shell companies in strange places to do their bidding for them, hoping to keep their intentions quiet as long as they can. Life can get expensive for guys like Ronson when lots of people find out what he's up to. But that's one of the things he just has to live with because, for Ronson, playing the game is not enough. Somewhere deep in his psyche there is the compelling need to play by the rules. 'It's very difficult to stay quiet about anything. You may be fortunate to pick up a block of shares over a period of time. But we don't hide behind back doors. Within the rules of what you can do, we do. We don't get involved in all those funny shareholdings, etc. That's not our style.'

Gerald Ronson is a heavyweight.

But he's not an undefeated champ.

In 1982 he got into a skirmish with Robert Holmes à Court for the Associated Communications Corp., Lew Grade's former empire. Holmes à Court had opened the poker game for the £120 million company with a bid close to £35 million. Ronson raised him 30 per cent with a £46.6 million bid. Holmes à Court matched it, and Ronson raised to £49 million. Then Holmes à Court came back with £60 million and Ronson folded. He lost the bid. But ACC was burdened with lawsuits, and riddled with a £38 million overdraft and another £67 million worth of debt. Once the smoke cleared it looked as though Ronson may not have lost as badly as some people thought he did. He even told *Forbes Magazine*,

'Sometimes when someone is too greedy he gets left holding the bag.'

A year later he bid for UDS (The United Drapery Stores group of manufacturers and retail outlets like Richard Shops, John Collier, Allders Department Stores and the duty free shops at Heathrow and Gatwick airports). This time James Hanson beat him.

'Hanson bid for the company and was the successful acquirer, and it's been a very good deal for Hanson. I'm very pleased that it has been a good deal for the Hanson company because we were major shareholders in Hanson Trust. But having said that, I know they didn't do their homework anything like we did. Again, the reputation of Heron. If we're bidding X for that, other people figure that must be right because Heron does its homework. They didn't have any qualms about going in and overbidding us. Of course they're in a position to, I won't say overbid or pay more, but they use paper. And if you have paper that yields 3 per cent that's a lot different than using pound notes that cost 10 per cent to borrow.'

To bid for UDS, Ronson put together the consortium called Bassishaw. It was half-owned by Heron, half-owned by institutional investors. 'I'm sure that we knew more about UDS when we were ready to bid for it, than the management running the company. In fact, I know we did.'

Using only one broker – it keeps his plans quieter that way – Bassishaw built up a whole load of shares. 'I think we had 4.9 per cent or 5.1 per cent. We had an agreement with certain partners of ours that they would tender their shares with us. So I think at one stage we had 10 per cent of the company. I'm pleased to say half of those shares we bought at very low figures when the company's results were very bad, which was maybe 12–18 months prior to when we bid for the company. But it's much harder to bid for a major company all cash, believe it or not, than it is to just do a straightforward paper exchange where I'm swapping my shares for your shares. That's a great game to play, until the wheels stop spinning and the last fellow in line holding the stick looks up and says, what happened? That's not the business I'm in. I'm in the business where I have to make real money with real cash, a positive return with proper cash flow and just keep it very simple and very old-fashioned.

He started at £1 per share. He says he had a pretty good idea what he was prepared to pay for the company. But he was almost certainly not expecting as tough a fight as he got. He was quickly forced up to £1.14 by a feisty UDS board. 'There was a time when we went to a certain figure. There was also a time by the way when we actually agreed a deal with the board which they reneged on. People are very good at hiding behind boards of directors. It's not a game I've ever played. I can give you a big long list of people who have agreed deals with me over the years and have reneged on them. They say, well, I've taken it to my board and although I've recommended it, the board won't go along with it. Well, when a Chairman and CEO recommends the bid, the only reason the board doesn't go along with it is because in between somebody else came along and offered more money.'

Ronson was eventually forced to raise his bid to £1.30, which is where he announced, 'This is my final offer.' When Hanson Trust walked away with UDS, the pundits turned around and said Ronson's mistake was the 'final offer' remark. You aren't supposed to do such things in a take-over battle because it means you've reached the end of the line. Once you say this is the end, that's the end. It's like throwing in the towel. It opens the field to the next guy. It's admitting defeat, unless of course you're simply not prepared to pay a penny more for the company because you don't think it's worth a penny more.

Asking him point blank if his 'my final offer' was a mistake, the answer you get from him is, 'You've got to interpret these things as you want to.'

*   *   *

He'd like to make a major acquisition in England.

'This is where I live, which to me is very important. I am a man of roots. I'm a family man. This is where I've been brought up. This is where my commitments are to my community. This is where my commitments are to the people who have been with me for many years. That to me is very important. I don't want to live anywhere else other than where I'm living now.'

As he sees the US as the last true bastion of capitalism and potential, if he doesn't make that major acquisition in England, he will in the US – although, with 50 per cent of the group's profits already coming from the States, he says a major acquisition there would create an imbalance in his corporate structure. 'That's not an unpleasant imbalance, so don't misunderstand what I'm saying. But I would like to make a major acquisition. We have not been successful in the last major bid we made in the UK, that was UDS, but that's because we have a discipline that we will not pay more for something than we think it's worth. At the moment, with the stock market where it is, and we have to buy for cash, not for funny paper, we have to focus our mind on buying real value.'

That means he's not in the business of paying for goodwill. 'There is a price for goodwill, but when you're buying a business for cash and when you're spending your own money, it helps focus your mind very clearly. The more hard assets that you're buying for your dollar or your pound is where it's all at. Goodwill at a stroke you write off your balance sheet. But if you've got hard assets, if a business doesn't always turn out the way you expect the business to turn out, then you have something tangible. If you have a lot of hot air, then there's nothing tangible unless you're in the balloon racing business. Remember that when you look at our balance sheet you're looking at hard net worth. There's nothing in the balance sheet for goodwill.'

Last year Heron was the first company ever to do a

revolving Euro-note facility. Ronson broke new ground to raise money because he operates most comfortably from a position of being highly liquid. 'We're not raising money because we need the money to pay our debt. What we've done is restructure our debt in terms of extending the period out; but at the same time giving ourselves an enormous amount of liquidity in terms of our lines of credit. Cash gives me the ability to purchase when the right opportunity comes along. So does leverage, yes. But with leverage you take a bigger risk. Leverage and cash are two different things. Having the cash enables me to go out there and do it. Leverage, well, you're leveraging your assets and then you have to go out and get the cash. You're in a much stronger position to do deals if you have money when you don't need it.'

Why not, he's asked, simply go public. 'Because I like Heron being a private company. It's a luxury we can afford.' Forever? 'If we take the short term, in the next four or five years I see Heron being twice the size it is today. Where do I see it 10–15 years out? I hope I can maintain the same momentum.'

But in 15 years' time he'll be just past 60. And by then he's always said he hopes to have found someone to take the reins. 'At 60 years of age I wouldn't want to be running around quite as much as I'm running around today, that's for sure. Looking five years out, I would like to be in a position, instead of being Chairman and Chief Executive, of just being Chairman and having a Chief Executive who is following in the footsteps. Not a yes man. But someone following in the footsteps of the development of the corporation. I would like to step back more in terms of looking at where we're going internationally, in terms of corporate planning, and bring on my team. In actual terms of where the business will be ten years down the road – well, if we're going on at the same momentum that we've been going at for the last 30-odd years, and we know what's there for the next five years, we will keep on growing. We could shortcut that by floating off parts of our group and going on the paper chase, building up much faster and accelerating the group, but there are no plans for a public flotation or any plans to go that route.'

Although now he adds, 'Things could change. The important thing in business is to be flexible.'

And lucky.

Ronson is one fellow who is well convinced that luck has a lot to do with it. 'Luck is very important. You've seen some of the cleverest people in the world screw up situations. Why? Over-confident. Wrong time. Wrong place. Luck plays a very important part in what you do. I've seen the most stupid people make fortunes. Especially on the other side of the ocean, where I've seen people with vast wealth that don't particularly have any great ability. But they were in the right place at the right time. They struck a hole in the ground and found oil, or found gold. Or they were sitting on a piece of land their grandfather left them which was umpteen thousand acres.'

He's even fast to admit that he's been lucky. 'I haven't sat down and worked out what percentage, but 50 per cent good luck, you will come out a winner. I think, looking back, yes, I've been lucky. I wouldn't say today that we're putting 50 per cent luck into the equation for our decision making. But that luck factor plays a very important part. You've got to get the deal right, you've got to get a lot of the pieces together, but that luck is the difference between success and failure.'

Being successful usually means you can minimize the luck element by controlling the game. And, after all, he is a man who says he is totally in control. He doesn't, for instance, calculate a deal by putting his finger up in the air, figuring he's half-right, and hoping his luck will carry him through. In fact, he says, he doesn't rely on his luck in anything. He relies on the judgement of the deal. The luck element comes into play when the deal works out better than he ever imagined.

Case in point. Heron is the only foreign company in the United States to own a savings and loan association. That's the American equivalent of a building society. Ronson went to Tucson, Arizona, to buy that savings bank, at a time when most people in the UK had never heard of Tucson. The Howard Hughes estate came up for sale – 12,500 acres of the most valuable land in Tucson – with a price tag of $75 million. But it had to be cash. And anybody in the world could have bought that piece of land if they had the cash. Ronson would never have heard about it or looked at it had he not already been in Tucson with his savings bank. Realizing immediately that this was the finest land in southern Arizona – it's the 20 square miles between the airport and the city centre – Ronson jumped on it. He could see that if the city is going to expand, it has to go towards and onto his land. It can't go the other way because there's a mountain. So, in spite of interest rates running at 17 per cent, it was an opportunity he didn't want to miss. He put together a few partners, and bought the land – having pre-sold $40 million worth at the closing. He has since sold another $80 million. Not wanting to flood the market, he and his partners only release so much of the land every year. They can afford to sit on it because they're also looking at the appreciation. In the end, he supposes this deal is going to make, by his own conservative guess, $150 million net.

Is that luck? Or is that just Gerald Ronson doing his thing? He says it's luck. In truth, it's probably one and the same.

'I call it good luck that I first came to Tucson, Arizona. If you had said to me five years ago, Tucson, Arizona, I would have looked at you and said I never heard of Tucson. It's cowboy country. But how did this Englishman from Marylebone Road find himself in Tucson, Arizona? Elements of luck. Now you may give me a strong argument that there's no luck there because I did my homework and I looked at the metrics and this and that. Yes. If you were talking to somebody with a Harvard MBA, he could give you that argument. But I bet he wouldn't have had the nose. He wouldn't have got on his bike to go to Tucson. He would have gone to California or Houston or Dallas. Elements of luck put you in a position.'

It also helps to have $75 million cash in your pocket.

11

Asil Nadir

He was once the wonderboy of the City.

He was Polly Peck . . . and Polly Peck was the hottest stock of the century. The shares were trading at about 5½p – capitalized at around £300,000 – when suddenly they shot to £35.

'The speculators did that. Not me. You have to understand that share speculation does a lot of harm at times. Others speculate and we get the blame. The shares should have never gone up to £35 at that time. If you look at the P/E ratio it didn't make sense.'

But then the shares came slipping down. They fell to around £22 before being split 10 for 1. And now the word around the City was that he had no staying power, that it was a fluke, that his organization didn't have the infrastructure of a business pretending to be so important, that he was probably some sort of Turkish Cypriot spy here to steal the secrets of capitalism.

'In this country there are people who believe that it's a sin to be successful. I don't know if it's jealousy, but the attitudes are not constructive. I go to a country where the produce is not worth anything because it's wasted. I pay them a proper price. Because I'm efficient and integrated, I earn a higher margin than someone sitting here just distributing food. Tell me why I should be criticized for that. I ought to be complimented because I've gone to a developing country, created employment, and put up plants. Our corporate partners have done a lot of business. Our relationship with Thorn-EMI hasn't done any harm to Britain. I could have done a deal with some Japanese concern. But we're faithful to England. We are here. We live here. We have a certain debt and I think we are repaying it aptly. I don't mind constructive criticism, but this is not constructive. If Polly Peck wasn't about, direct and indirect employment of 20,000–30,000 jobs wouldn't be here. In 18 months' time it could be possibly over 40,000. And for this you get criticized!'

Asil Nadir has found out the hard way that life isn't easy in the First Division.

*   *   *

The north side of Cyprus is the Turkish side. And that's where he was born 42 years ago. 'My father was a very innovative businessman in Cyprus. He was the first man to do public transport there. He brought double-decker buses from the UK. He also started rental libraries, although it wasn't a very good business because my father believed in education and used to rent out the books at cost.'

When he finished his studies in 1965 – he got himself a degree in economics from the University of Istanbul – Nadir moved to England. 'My family had to leave Cyprus because all our businesses were taken away during the crisis. We thought we could get a better start here.' For the next two years he divided his time between the UK and Turkey, trying to find himself, trying to decide what to do. Then in 1967 he started a company called Wearwell. 'The rag trade is, I think, one of the few industries you can enter without too much capital.'

But it wasn't until 1978 that he started to hit the big time. 'We had a request from the Turkish Cypriot government. Citrus was their main export but they were having massive problems. They weren't able to compete internationally because they had no marketing expertise and lacked the right kind of packing facilities. They called me and said, can you help.'

There has always been speculation around the City why Nadir got that call. After all, why would someone concerned with fruit in Cyprus ring a garment manufacturer in the East End of London? The reason is simple – he was connected. It's hardly surprising because he grew up there, because he comes from one of the right families, and because he was already successful in the west. Even the sometimes cynical *Financial Times* calls him 'the best known Turkish Cypriot businessman in Britain'. So when his pals in the government looked for one of their own to talk to, the field was pretty narrow. 'In all these countries you find that they actually think the centre of the world is the centre of some tiny village. They come to decisions or organize themselves only within their own sphere. They thought because I knew the outside world I would be the right man to give them some expertise. But if they hadn't phoned me, I would have visited them myself. It was an idea whose time had come.'

He set up a feasibility study, the result being a project to build a fruit-packaging factory in Cyprus. But here's where the story gets a little complicated. Wearwell was designing in the UK, manufacturing partially in the UK and partially in Cyprus – higher labour intensive work was done there – and exporting 70 per cent of their goods to the Middle East. They went public in 1972, and that made Nadir a millionaire. By 1980 Wearwell was winner of the Queen's Award for Export Achievement (they won it again two years later), and were capitalized at £12–£13 million. So his first thought was to build the packing plant on the back of a Wearwell rights issue for £1.5 million. But his advisers argued that foreign investment should not be done in Wearwell because shareholders had invested in a UK garment manufacturer and they might not take kindly to such a risk. Nadir looked around and spotted Polly Peck, a textile firm that made money in the '60s but had run into trouble during the '70s. It was ripe for a take-over. He bought a 56 per cent stake, with 34 per cent of that stake going through Restro, a Jersey company of which he is beneficial owner. The cost of the Polly Peck shares at the time was minimal, about 5½p. But he made it clear to Wearwell shareholders that the purchase of Polly Peck was conditional on their approval of a rights issue to invest in the packaging plant, which would be called Uni-pac I.

'When I spoke to my friends in Cyprus about packaging, I had to explain that I didn't just mean packing something in a carton. I tried to make them understand it's got to be to the standards of the western world. It must get the items to the consumer in perfect shape. You know, if you examine all these countries, they're not using the right technology, they're not using the right expertise to produce their cartons. They're using recycled paper. They penny pinch. If a carton should cost 40 pence, they only want to pay 30 pence. They save 10p per carton, ignoring that within the carton the value of the produce is say, £5. It becomes an educational process. You actually have to teach them.'

He tried to teach them, while learning himself along the way. And before too long he wondered, if the problem exists in Cyprus, then maybe it exists in other countries too. He went to Turkey and found that it did. 'Turkey has massive resources: 1¼ million tons of citrus, going to 2 million tons in the next three years; 3½–4 million tons of grapes; 2 million tons of tomatoes. We found they were excellent up to the growing stage. But from there, they didn't know what to do. Spain exports something like 66 per cent of their crop. Turkey was exporting 20 per cent. Like most of the developing countries, their economy is inward-looking. They don't always think beyond their own borders. Yet, with the deficits and inflation, they have to find so many more dollars just to survive. Unless they start looking outward they are not going to survive. They need technology. Their capital markets are in such a mess. Today in Turkey there are interest rates of 70–80 per cent. You've got inflation there of 40 per cent. They haven't got a chance to survive unless you take to them inexpensive capital and technology. In return, you mobilize those massive resources.'

These days, that's exactly what he does. Solve the problem in one country, find another country with the same problem, and implant the same solution. But to some people it looks as if those big profits only come at the expense of big risks. Not everyone wants to put their money into areas sometimes described as politically shaky even if the dangling carrot is 40–50 per cent returns. 'There are political risks only if you don't know the country. What happens with many multinationals is that they get a bad surprise from some division. That wouldn't happen with us. We believe in communication with the grass roots. Whether it's financial or general information, we have people based in those countries who mix with the people. We're always trying to get a better feel as to how the country is doing. Of course political stability is important. But any fluctuation or any movement towards instability starts as a rumble among the people. That's where you have to listen. The rulers are the last to know. When they find out it's too late.'

Perhaps. But what would happen to his investments in, say, Cyprus, if tomorrow the Greeks came across the border? 'You're asking the question because you don't know the country. Everything in life is a balance of power. You have the western bloc, you have the eastern bloc. I must say, by the way, that we're not a political entity. Please understand that. My business has nothing to do with politics. But doing business in a place like Cyprus only looks like a political risk if you don't know the country and don't understand this concept of the balance of power. You have the smaller Turkish community in northern Cyprus and you have a bigger Greek community in the south. You have Greece, with 8 or 9 million population. And then you have Turkey. So although the balance is to the advantage of the Greeks in Cyprus, you then have to add in the size of Greece, economically and militarily, and the same for Turkey. When you balance the whole thing, although you think it's politically insecure, the risk element is one we can accept. Today I feel there would never be any trouble in Cyprus unless the Turks want it. And we know that the Turks don't want it. The whole problem in Cyprus was that a minority wanted the same rights as the majority, to live without the fear of being annihilated. Today I reckon there is less of a risk in Cyprus than the radical left-wing unions taking over in England.'

*   *   *

Polly Peck started out as a penny share refugee from the '60s. Nadir combined it with emerging businesses, green fields ventures, and the price began to rise. Almost from the off, Uni-pac was making phenomenal money. Profits quickly headed from a couple of million pounds towards £10 million. Uni-pac II was born. Nadir's Sunzest label went on oranges and lemons. Markets were opened. Shares had been on a 1x–2x earnings until those first profits came in. That's when people started thinking the P/E should be higher. There was buying. That buying drove the prices even higher, until they soared away. Having gone from 5½p to 9p and then 35p – they stayed there for a while – the next stop was around £8. Then they went £10–£12, stopped for a pause at £20 and finally raced up to £35. Everyone was talking about Nadir and Polly Peck . . . the agricultural industry is severely under-developed you know, and Cyprus had previously been importing packaging, so this Nadir chap comes along, you understand that he's got an in with all the politicians there, hum, yes, and so he comes along with this start-up business . . .

Enter here the Greeks bearing rumours.

It was early 1983. The Greek Cypriot government began to realize that, apart from the Turkish Cypriot government, Nadir and Polly Peck were the major industrial investors on the northern side of the island. It goes without saying that the Greek Cypriots have a stake in ensuring that the Turkish Cypriots never become economically viable, so they put out the word. A Greek merchant banker became the mouthpiece. He spread the alarm just when Polly Peck shares were particularly vulnerable. Big-risk area, he said. Big risk taker this Nadir. Could be a big loser very fast. Those scare stories bred more scare stories. Nadir and his huge margins. Nadir and his profits tied to nothing more than currency fluctuations. Nadir and his political connections. Or even better, the secrets that could be unlocked if the Restro Investments books were made public. Restro holds a heavy block of Polly Peck shares. But, according to the *Observer*, Restro is just a subsidiary of a Manx company called Hillgate. And, while Hillgate is owned by Nadir, Restro has several other shareholders besides Nadir. Among them are shares registered to nominees at various banks, including one in the Cayman Islands. The *Observer* said shares are held by Ashraf Marwan, another Egyptian businessman named Hani Abd el Salam, a Panamanian company called Shadow Valley Inc., a Liberian-registered company called Mosel Investment Corporation, and something known as Kipeco Finance SA. Restro doesn't concern anyone, Nadir argued. It's a private company. The press can insinuate anything they want as far as he's concerned because it really doesn't matter. 'I can assure you, nothing moves me. We know the goal. What we have to do. We know what we're doing is right. They're the wrong ones and we don't have to be proved right.' No, he insists, it doesn't matter to him at all.

But the *coup de grâce* was the story that Polly Peck's seven-year tax holiday in Famagusta was non-existent. That it was just a Nadir pipe dream. That all his fancy profits were pre-tax and destined to disappear into the Turkish Cypriot treasury. As it turned out, the story was totally false. The tax holiday was very much a reality. But people got nervous. Share prices had gone too far, too fast. They were overcooked. Just as Polly Peck was about to absorb Wearwell, the share prices fell. The Greek Cypriots' timing was immaculate. Nadir's bankers decided it was wiser to wait until the prices stabilized. The planted stories effectively caused a 13-month delay.

What little good news there might have been easily turned sour. In one case, perhaps even negligently so. A British journalist went out to Turkey to have a look at the mineral water bottling plant Polly Peck was building in Niksar. He didn't find it as complete as he thought he would, and he told the world. Nadir tried to argue that the journalist had got it wrong, that he wasn't looking in the right place. The journalist stood his ground. Nadir filed a whopping libel suit. But it was too late.

It happened in just about a fortnight. Buoyed up and keyed up by tremendous hopes – by balance sheets that showed over 40 per cent return on turnover – Humpty Dumpty had a great fall.

And, at least for a couple of mornings, Greek Cypriot merchant bankers everywhere dined out on scrambled eggs.

* * *

Asil Nadir readily admits that the risks he's taking in Cyprus and Turkey would not be the same if he was British.

'There is a tremendous mistrust with the west. They look at these countries and think they're risk areas, that it's unsafe to trade there. And so the attitude out there is that the western world always wants to take advantage. We've seen a lot of bad examples. In the pharmaceutical industry, for instance, left-over products are pushed into those countries. Business ethics – without specifically pinpointing any western companies – are non-existent. They start by taking the developing countries for granted.

The quality of goods shipped out there is usually substandard. I think they try to sell there because they can't find a market for certain products in the west.'

He says the pharmaceutical industry in particular has such a poor reputation in some parts of the world that he's discovered a huge open window – and he intends to crawl through it. Last year he paid £600,000 for ICP Pharmaceuticals Ltd, a small operation that needed investment, new machinery and expanded facilities. He set them up with a plant in northern Cyprus, and is getting them licensed there to produce a full range of products, from painkillers to insecticides. His plan is to sink another £1 million-plus into it, making it his base for exports to Turkey. The plant won't be in full swing until some time in 1986, but over the next two years he says he'd like to see turnover in the £10 million range. 'Pharmaceutical sales in Turkey alone represent a potential of over $300 million. Why shouldn't I be able to get a part of that market?'

He's got the same approach towards advanced technology in the developing countries. 'Why shouldn't they, in Turkey today, have the same quality of video or television as other consumers in the west? Our relations with Thorn-EMI all started when we saw the huge purchasing power in Turkey for electronics. We felt that Thorn's products are better than the Japanese products. Currents in some countries can fluctuate incredibly from 220v down to 160v. Thorn's products respond to this drop of current without having to buy an adapter. When we looked at the market, we saw the Japanese were selling only a few thousand sets per annum there. Ask them and they'll tell you that their studies show there is a very big market but they just can't seem to sell there. To have the right product and to have a huge market and not sell, there must be something wrong. In their case it was a lack of understanding of the area.'

The marriage of Polly Peck and Thorn-EMI is not a joint venture as much as a 'corporate agreement'. It's a concept that Nadir has been steadily developing. Each project is a Polly Peck investment but with technical know-how and quality control coming from the 'partners'. For the Polly Peck–Thorn deal, Nadir is financing the overall £25 million investment out of cash flow, and has built a 350,000 square foot plant in Manisa, Turkey. Thorn-EMI keeps a team on site and benefits by virtue of royalties on the kits.

It's the same sort of deal Polly Peck has with Metal Box. That should be in full swing some time in 1985 with a plant going up in southern Turkey. Again, the implant theory. It worked in Cyprus so it will work in Turkey. 'If you look at Turkey and their citrus crop, there are many possibilities. It's not only a question of growing and marketing fresh produce, there is also food concentrate, and fruit juices. You see, the more you proceed down the line, the more your income per ton starts multiplying. Metal Box will help us in food processing, from canning to bottling to packaging. Distribution and marketing could possibly be done through the resources of the Albert Abela Corporation, a major customer of ours. They're a large international catering company with a wide network of branches and associated companies. It means we could use Turkey as a stepping stone for marketing in many other Middle Eastern countries.'

It's the same as their agreement with Racal. Also on the books for 1985, Polly Peck is trying to exploit the fact that all NATO partners have the right to participate in the production of certain NATO equipment. 'Our electronics division is split into two. Defence and Consumer. We've done extensive feasibility studies with Racal. The idea is to go into components which will allow Turkey to take advantage of some of its rights as a NATO partner. Until recently, Turkey has not been able to because of lack of technology and lack of production capacity. Now we are giving that to them.'

For the mineral water bottling plant in Niksar, Nadir teamed up with the West German firm Bekum Maschinenfabriken. They're the turnkey contractors, although this partnership was through Cornell Holdings, PLC. (Nadir bought a stake in that garment manufacturer in 1982, with the specific idea of tying it into a project. Cornell is 56 per cent owned by Polly Peck. 'It's our intention to get Cornell within the company as well. It's much neater. There are also some tax benefits. But mainly it's easier to administer, easier to operate'). He arranged for a £2.76 million rights issue in 1982; a further £6 million has been invested by Polly Peck but directly from Cyprus.

However, the most ambitious project to date is the Polly Peck–Daihatsu corporate romance. 'When you look at these developing countries and see that earning standards are not what they are in western countries, then you've got to look at less expensive means of transport. We thought about it and looked around and noticed the Daihatsu Motor Corporation of Japan. They have the world's smallest diesel engine in their car but it gets 100 kilometres per gallon. This compared to the next-best two cars, you know the Renault and the Fiat which is produced in Turkey and does 42–44 kpg. On top of that you have a 40 per cent advantage on the price of fuel against the other two because they're not diesel. It's the ideal car for the developing nations.'

With that in mind, Polly Peck got themselves the rights to sell Daihatsu in India, Pakistan, Iran, Iraq and North Africa. On the cards for late 1985 is a production deal which would have them actually building cars under licence in Turkey. They'll probably assemble them at a brand-new Volvo plant there that is working at only 20 per cent capacity.

'Spotting opportunities is not difficult when you know what to look for. It's like being a doctor. Once you've seen a hundred cases of the measles, you recognize it right away. Come on, to have a plant as large as that new Volvo factory, and to have a market as large as Turkey, but to work at only 20 per cent capacity, it's not right. Believe me, the opportunities stare you in the face. I suppose one has to have a certain degree of intelligence and knowledge of business, but the opportunities are massive.'

The secret of making money once you spot those opportunities is integration. Call it, if you will, the 'full trading circle method'. By starting with a natural resource product, like fruit, Nadir finances his other investments. The fruit is exported, which turns Turkish lira into hard currencies. Those hard currencies are then brought back into the country to create further investments, such as cars or video recorders. In turn, they're sold for Turkish lira which are then pumped back into products for export, and more hard currencies. The circle cushions the foreign exchange risk while also allowing Nadir to take his profits wherever he wants.

'We work mainly with dollars and pounds. Turkish currency is floating so you're all right as long as you don't hold it. We spend it as soon as we get it. Turkish lira are utilized for putting up plants or purchasing raw materials or buying agricultural products. Immediately we transform that money into goods, which in turn earn foreign currency. So our risk is minimal. As a matter of fact, it works to our benefit because, as the lira devalues, our purchasing power gets bigger. Prices don't move as quickly as devaluations where you have such large surpluses.'

With successes in Cyprus and Turkey on the board, it's hardly surprising that he's thinking about other parts of the world. The implant theory moves on. To Egypt: 'We're looking at Egypt, because it is a nation with a tremendous surplus of agricultural products.' To India and Pakistan: 'The agricultural problems there are exactly the same that we've seen in Turkey and Cyprus.' And to Somalia: 'It's a country that has a little wealth – four or five products from bananas to grapefruit to timber. The per capita income per annum is around $300. We have a team there now, looking into all sorts of possibilities. We do a lot of studies before we commit ourselves. It takes a lot of time and is very expensive. But we do our homework. You have to do your homework. You have to minimize all of your risks. Then, once we know what the real opportunities are, we pick a partner.'

* * *

The headline in the *Financial Times* read, 'Nadir Makes £2.5m on Strong and Fisher Sale'. The story explained how Nadir had sold his 24.9 per cent stake in that leather manufacturing group at twice what he paid for the shares. 100 per cent profit. Total time elapsed, nine months. The article then noted that those shares were acquired '. . . amid the strong market speculation which surrounds Mr Nadir's every move . . .'. It seems he bought them at 70p, and as soon as word got out that he was in (that very same day) they shot up as high as £2.30.

'He's a gunslinger,' one City broker calls him. And it's exactly that reputation which gives Polly Peck the look of a personalized business. Polly Peck is Asil Nadir and Asil Nadir is Polly Peck, and often the twain shall meet.

'It's not a personalized business.' He doesn't care for the reference at all. 'It's a team effort. I'm merely the face of the company because dealing with the City or the press is so time-consuming and I want to keep my management busy with the job we have to do. But the real problem is not that. It's that the British don't understand or know much about Turkey or Cyprus. They don't know much about the potential of those countries. Many people in the UK don't know that Turkey is self-sufficient in food, for example. They have a fairly negative view and are a bit nervous about those areas as an investment. They've not understood what we're trying to do. Did you know that we have 250 people working here in London. There is an identical structure in Turkey, in Cyprus, and different smaller teams in quite a few other countries. In 1978 the management team was about 30 people. Today it's no less than 400.'

Yet as he explains it, and even when he shows you videos to prove that he's doing what he says he's doing – to prove that the profits are there, that the infrastructure is there, that the business is indeed as important as the City once said it was – there is still some lingering doubt. The press has helped create an image and the Greek merchant bankers probably can't afford to let it die.

And deep down he knows that, probably better than anyone. 'When you look at the inaccuracies in the press it's unbelievable. In the end, we don't really need public relations. We feel that by doing what we're doing perfectly, given time, it will be understood. But one hopes that, given time, the quality of journalism will be better.' He shrugs. 'One hopes.'

12

Ian Posgate

They called him 'Goldfinger'.

But the nickname wasn't born out of affection.

For years, Ian Richard Posgate was the most unanimously disliked man who ever stalked Lloyds of London. He was frequently rude, often contemptuous, and even at the best of times difficult. Yet he was also undoubtedly the most flamboyant underwriter that Lloyds has ever seen. For a time he was the highest-paid man in the UK. These days he is down, and the vultures are circling overhead. Someday he may come back – although there are plenty of people at Lloyds who seriously hope not. If he ever does make it back, you can bet that he won't get angry, he'll simply get even. He is the stuff of legends. And a hundred years from now, if Lloyds of London still exists, 'Tales of Goldfinger' will be told – the way folks in Dodge still talk about Wyatt and Doc and the OK Corral.

*　　*　　*

The demise of Goldfinger began as a $300 million deal (then £170 million).

John A. Bogardus, Jr, Chairman of the Board of Alexander and Alexander Services, the second-largest insurance broker in the United States, had been shopping for a way into Lloyds of London. He found it at Alexander Howden, a flashy, entrepreneurial UK broker-

222

age house, which was the brainchild of Kenneth Grob. For $300 million, Bogardus bought Howden, their very complex network of more than 200 companies worldwide, and the wheeling–dealing skills of Posgate. But it quickly turned out that the $300 million merely got Bogardus into the game. Unknowingly, and/or clumsily, he stumbled into the biggest scandal the City has ever seen.

Lloyds of course is not an insurance company. It's a marketplace where brokers bring risks and where under-writers openly compete against each other to insure those risks. Operating on a trading floor known as 'The Room', there are some 400 stalls – like a large antique fair. The broker begins the process with a form called a 'slip', which gives the details of the insurance cover he's seeking. With the slip in hand, he literally walks around the room shopping for someone to underwrite the deal. As the insurance business is based on the concept of spreading risk, underwriters generally only take a small percentage. For example, one may sign on for 2 per cent. Another may go for just 0.5 per cent. The broker has done his job when he's filled 100 per cent. If there's a claim, the underwriter pays his agreed percentage. If there is no claim, he receives his agreed percentage of the premiums. Except, in practice, it isn't that simple. For many people, Lloyds is also an investment. Each underwriter represents a syndicate in which people have pooled their wealth to cover risks. These 'names' – and there are more than 20,000 of them – have committed the full extent of their personal fortune to cover claims. Going bust means losing everything – cash, homes, cars, silverware, paintings – at least, everything that hasn't been safely transferred to a husband or wife. To become a name you must be worth £100,000–£500,000, depending on where you are and where your fortune is. The further away, the higher the ante. A certain portion of this must be liquid. But, nicely enough, none of your liquid assets need ever leave your savings account – unless there is a claim. So your £100,000 can pick up 10 per cent down the block, while on the syndicate's books at Lloyds it might earn another 15 per cent in premium income. If the syndicate has a good year, there might be a share in the profits – perhaps another 15 per cent. That can put you 40 per cent ahead at the end of the year, and some of it is tax-free. Naturally, if the syndicate has a tough year, you might get a bill from them. It happens, but the gain is the rule and the total loss is the rarity. And even if the more conservative folks at Lloyds hate to admit it in public, being a name can at times be nearly as good as having a licence to print money.

Making money was what Ian Posgate wanted to do when he left Gonville and Caius at Cambridge without a degree after a year there in 1953. He came to Lloyds to learn the underwriting trade. But he never wore one of the correct school ties. He never had one of the correct regimental ties. And at Lloyds those things matter. Yet by the time the '70s came along, his undisputed genius for the insurance game and his stunning ability to make both money and enemies brought him super-star status. In 1965 he was underwriting for fewer than 30 names. By 1982 he was underwriting for 5000–6000. One estimate says that by 1980 almost 10 per cent of all the business conducted at Lloyds was coming through him. And in 1980 Lloyds did nearly £4 billion worth of business.

With nearly 25 per cent of Lloyds' names on the books of the four syndicates he controlled, Posgate always appeared to take big risks – war risks, satellites, kidnappings, hijackings – and he always appeared to win. Jealousy ran high. That helped breed more contempt. His lack of friends and his maverick reputation meant there were plenty of people stalking the bushes, waiting for their shot at him. Yet he made fortunes for people – including himself – and being a name on one of Posgate's syndicates was worth putting up with his temper.

'I don't know, if I was the best who ever was,' says Posgate. 'I think Roy Merritt was very good. I think I was the best there was in the '70s. But it's very difficult to say. It's like comparing one baseball player of one generation with one baseball player of some other generation. Roy Merritt was doing the same thing except I suppose the field was smaller and in those days you wore longer trousers.'

The Committee of Lloyds, acting like a board of directors, took their first shot at Goldfinger in 1970, officially censuring him for 'writing on the back of the Central Fund'. It was, and still is, a favourite trick of the high-flyers. It was, and still is, against the rules.

One of the main safeguards built into Lloyds is a multi-layered series of reserve funds to insure that a policy can always be paid, even if all the names in the syndicate go broke. Billions of pounds are set aside to insure the insurers. Since each syndicate is limited by the wealth of the names, overwriting means that policies are written for more than that amount and the underwriter is risking not only the total wealth of his names, but also the funds held by Lloyds in reserve. If the underwriter has guessed wrong, the names go bust and the reserve funds must cough up the difference. But if the underwriter wins, the names of his syndicate make more money than they otherwise could have hoped for.

'I was not popular in '70,' Posgate says. 'And the unpopularity remained. I would have suggested it was jealousy.' And no, he still maintains, he was not writing on the back of the fund. Anyway, he adds, 'I've always believed that Lloyds should be net underwriters, risk-taking underwriters. And I don't think there's any question, with the spread of my account, of writing on the back of the fund. As was proved, the idiots who wrote huge lines on computer leasing [a £222 million fiasco for Lloyds], who were safe syndicates, were far more likely to wind up on the central guarantee fund than in fact I was.'

Chairman of the Committee in those days was Paul Dixey, an elegant man whose father had also been a Committee chairman, and who was the third of four

Dixey generations at Lloyds. He makes no bones about saying that he thinks Ian Posgate is 'a ruthless bully who has consistently and deliberately broken the rules. He is a most unpopular man.' But then Dixey gives Posgate his due by admitting he was very successful, especially when times for other underwriters were bad. And, yes, 'that can breed envy and jealousy. He may be a man of courage, single-minded and completely self-reliant. He has a wonderful memory and a terrific head for figures. But I would say that he has a complete lack of moral scruples.'

Yet Dixey and the Committee stopped short of total banishment and agreed to let Posgate underwrite for a managing agent. They wanted him to have a babysitter.

Enter now the Alexander Howden Group.

Ken Grob had created a massive empire and he was just the man to see the possibilities of joining forces with Ian Posgate. All Grob had to do was be a minder. All Posgate had to do was make money. And it worked so well that at times during the '70s Posgate was able to post 40 per cent annual profits. 'To some extent,' Posgate says, 'Ken Grob was quite a good minder because he was a rogue and therefore he was adaptable. I made a lot of money for a lot of people including Mr Grob.'

As far as Ken Grob is concerned, Posgate was not as great an underwriter as he was a risk taker. 'He was a risk taker, that's for sure. But of course he had huge reinsurance facilities behind him. He was essentially a dealer. He'd say to a broker, look, I want your war risk account. And the chap would say, well you can have 5 per cent, and Pos would say, no, don't be silly, I want 100 per cent. They'd finally compromise with Pos probably writing 50 per cent. Or the broker would find that Pos would undercut his rates to his competitor. He was that sort of dealer. It was marginal stuff. But he had got a flair for the short-term risk. He loved war and kidnap and ransom, that type of thing. He wasn't the kind of underwriter to whom you'd take a really serious complicated risk, because he couldn't be bothered to read it. He always had 30 people waiting to see him. I don't want to denigrate him because I have the highest opinion of his ability in the market to stir things up and get the market business. As great underwriters go, no, he simply wasn't one. As a great risk taker, yes, he was.'

For a while, the Howden Group with Goldfinger had the world at their feet. There were big cars with fridges in the boot to keep the champagne cold during Royal Ascot. There were country estates in the UK and holiday mansions on the Riviera. They had cash in their pockets and art on their walls. Even Horatio Alger couldn't have invented Ian Posgate.

*   *   *

Jack Bogardus watched it all from the other side of the Atlantic. In his mid-50s, tall with light hair, his father had been a big deal in the US insurance industry, and he was determined to be just as big. With great determination Bogardus, Jr, worked his way up at Alexander and Alexander, manoeuvred a boardroom shuffle and took control. Then he did what most men do to prove that they're in control – he made decisions. Under the previous chairman there had been flirtations with Howden. But A&A always walked away. Now in 1979 Bogardus was willing to have another look. After all, Howden was a way into Lloyds, and along with Howden came Ian Posgate. A fortune was in the offing. So there were meetings in London, afternoons at Grob's villa in the south of France, and expensive lunches in New York. But Bogardus hesitated and told one member of his board, 'These guys are too rich for our blood.' He turned to the much less glossy Sedgwick Group, Britain's largest independent insurance broker. They courted for two years. They held hands. There might even have been some goodnight kisses. But one day the romance ended. Interestingly enough, near the end, Bogardus reportedly mentioned to someone that if the deal fell through he'd go back to Howden. The advice he got was, 'I wouldn't touch them with a barge pole.' Bogardus denies it. The source of the advice dined out on the story for a year. But then Bogardus also denies that at least one member of his own board also cautioned him against Howden. True or not, it instantly became a moot point. Two days after the Sedgwick deal fell through, Bogardus rang Grob to ask, 'Are you still for sale?' Six weeks later the deal was made. For whatever reason, Bogardus never ordered a pre-take-over audit. He simply handed over $300 million and, on 1 January 1982, Alexander Howden became the third 'Alexander' at A&A.

While this was going on, in December 1981, Posgate ran for a seat on the 16-man Committee of Lloyds. He lost. In January another seat came vacant. Posgate ran again. And this time, to the establishment's horror, he won by 27 votes. 'My election to the Committee infuriated Peter Green who was then Chairman. In retrospect it was probably a very bad thing. I wonder whether certain things would have happened if I was not on the Committee.'

Then came the Qantas scandal. Insurance for Australia's airline was up for renewal on 1 April. In March, to everyone's surprise, the account was taken away from a company called Bain Dawes, which had placed it for 30 years, and wound up at Howden's. When the slip went around the room, the top line was a whopping 15 per cent signed by marine specialist Ian Posgate. It caused a stir for three reasons: aviation insurance is usually written by aviation specialists; the largest piece of the action most underwriters take is well below 15 per cent; and the $5 million Posgate quoted for the business was way below the going rate. Aviation underwriters screamed 'foul', and Posgate couldn't find enough associates to pick up the remaining 85 per cent. The Qantas affair put Howden in an embarrassing light. To set the situation straight, they soon announced that Posgate had been replaced on the Qantas account by another underwriter who would take it for $5.5 million, with Howden paying the $500,000 difference. To some people the episode pointed up the flaws in a system where one firm could represent both the insured and the insurer.

In the midst of this, on 16 March, Posgate resigned from Howden's board. 'I was unhappy about being left out of the merger talks between Howden and Alexander and Alexander. Because it was quite wrong. And it was very dangerous.'

Before long, a steady trickle of Howden names were defecting to Posgate's own syndicates.

Unbeknownst to Bogardus or Grob, Ian Posgate appears to have been thinking about his swan song with Howden for some time. A bill had been introduced in Parliament that would separate the powers of brokers and underwriters. If it were passed, Posgate would be free of his minder and, in a sense, have carte blanche to take with him all of the names he was otherwise dividing between his own syndicates and Howden. Grob and every other broker in the market petitioned to defeat the Lloyds Bill. And they might have swung it had Posgate himself not gone down to Westminster to testify before the House. His argument was so damaging to the case against the bill that he alone might have been the reason it passed.

'If you like, I had two mistakes that I would do over and over again. I stood for the Committee and got on. And I fought the Committee of Lloyds and [then Committee Chairman] Peter Green on divestment. Green and all the major broking houses hated me for that. I would do it again. I think that in a hundred years' time the most important thing of this century, for Lloyds, is the recognition of conflicts of interest and the consequent divestment. And there is no question that, without me, divestment would not have taken place. I single-handedly got divestment through and I paid for it. I was the only person who gave evidence for divestment. But divestment moved Lloyds into the new century and towards facing up to conflicts of interest, which in fact have been faced in

America for some years but have not been faced in the City of London.'

However, Grob has never been sure just what Posgate's motives were. He doesn't seem to think it was an obvious raid on the Howden names. 'I've never understood that. It does seem obvious. Too obvious. But he didn't have that sort of mind. And he didn't need the Howden names. He had Posgate and Denby, and it was already becoming one of the biggest agencies in Lloyds. Had he just contained himself and not done anything silly he would have finished up today with an agency which would have a huge value on it.'

On 3 July, the House of Lords approved the legislation. On 4 July, Posgate shook the market by announcing that he would cease underwriting for the two Howden syndicates. 'I wanted out.'

The trickle of names from Howden to Posgate and Denby increased.

But, as the expression goes, the best was yet to come. Bogardus had finally ordered an audit of Howden. And the accounting firm of Deloittes Haskins & Sells reported 'discrepancies'.

The operative word now became 'reinsurance'.

Once an underwriter signs a slip, he's committed his syndicate to that percentage of the action. But he can, if he wants to, hedge his bet by reinsuring the percentage elsewhere. And reinsurance, explains Ken Grob, was something Posgate understood very well. 'He was a natural-born man to sit there in his box, with really no one telling him what to do. I mean, no one had any control over him at all. I forget the numbers now. But where he had, for example, a £90 million capacity after reinsurance in 1982, I think his final net figure was £120 million. He'd gone over his limits by a third. That didn't put him on the Central Fund, all it meant was that if individual names as a result of his overwriting had exceeded their individual limits, they'd have to put up pound for pound. If he had a really major loss, he had two things: huge reinsurance protection running something like £100 million on which he could call first of all; then he'd call on these 4000 or 5000 names. I used to say to the Committee, don't worry because there's no such thing as a risk which Posgate couldn't pay if the market was still there. I mean, one could envision a risk, obviously, which Posgate couldn't pay, but then nor would anyone else pay it. It would be a national catastrophe and the nation would have to fund it. Or the Americans would have to fund it, like California falling into the sea.'

What Deloittes believed to be happening was that Posgate's syndicates were reinsuring through the Howden-owned Sphere Drake company, and then – somehow – the monies were being filtered through various companies and trusts until they disappeared. One of those companies was registered in Panama as Southern International Re (SIR) – the 'Re' being the generally accepted abbreviation for reinsurance. And all of this might have been fine except this time the 're' stood for real estate. Making matters worse, SIR, it turned out, was owned by the 'Gang of Four' – Ken Grob, Howden directors Ron Comery and Jack Carpenter, and Howden finance chief Allan Page. That disclosure, while required, had not been made. Putting SIR under the microscope, Deloittes found certain monies going through SIR being used by the Gang of Four, and possibly Posgate, to purchase a bank in Geneva called the Banque du Rhone et de la Tamise. The Deloittes conclusion was that a lot of pennies were missing – like $55 million.

Now Bogardus had to make a tough decision. If fraud was involved, he'd have to call the cops. On the other hand, if this was simply a matter of accounting procedures, maybe he could get the money back without upsetting his shareholders in New York. He must have figured it was worth a try because on Friday night 13 August he and the Gang of Four sat down to do some big-league haggling.

Posgate was not invited.

Bogardus showed up at the meeting well armed. He even had the code names they were using to keep money in Liechtenstein trusts. Grob was Bloomers. Comery was Blissful. Page was Karoli. Carpenter was Skyair. In the end Posgate turned out to be Hereford.

The result was a secret agreement whereby Alexander and Alexander promised not to take civil action against the Gang of Four in exchange for more than $29 million in cash and assets. In the final draft the word 'civil' was used, although in the initial draft the words 'civil or criminal' appeared. The word 'criminal' was struck out at the insistence of Rod Hills, who was linked to the meeting from his home in California by an open telephone line. His advice carried a lot of weight with Bogardus, not merely because Hills was Chairman of A&A's audit committee, but also because Hills was a former chairman of the American Securities and Exchange Commission (SEC).

The agreement was signed in the early hours of Saturday 14 August. A contingent from A&A arrived at Posgate's home near Henley-upon-Thames later that day for lunch. 'I was on very good terms with them,' he remembers. 'I thought at the time I could work with Bogardus. With hindsight, I do not know. But other people got his ear. I do not attempt to get people's ear. Other people got his ear before me. And there we are.'

Nine days later, Jack Bogardus mysteriously announced that A&A was severing all ties with the Gang of Four and that Posgate would be chairman of Alexander Howden Underwritings. Four days after that, Bogardus admitted there was a $25 million shortfall in Howden's assets. Then came the first public claim that the Gang of Four had secretly controlled a company that did extensive rein-surance business with Howden. Public announcement was totally unexpected by the Gang of Four because in Clause Four of the secret agreement all the signatories, including Bogardus, had pledged to honour the confiden-tiality of the agreement. And in case of disputes, they had all agreed that arbitration would be the proper step. Now Bogardus seemed to be going back on his word.

Sir Peter Green and the Committee of Lloyds sat nervously on the sidelines. First, no one on the Committee was overly thrilled to see Posgate there. Some were second-generation Lloyds. Posgate was a 'parvenu'. But then Posgate always said that one of the main problems with Lloyds was that it suffers from 'the second generation'.

'It definitely has. It still does. The problem, and this applies to Miller [Peter, current Chairman and great nephew of Thomas], Chester [Henry, nephew of Guy], Merritt [Stephen, son of Roy] and Green [Sir Peter, son of Toby], is that the people who inherit, and have not in themselves created, spend most of their time protecting what their family created. And that of course creates inward looking and creates the problems that Lloyds have.'

Second, it was hardly their fault that someone like Posgate had been elected to the Committee. But, given time, they would find a way to even that score by throwing him off and banning him from Lloyds.

Third, and very importantly, some people at Lloyds, including Committee members, felt that the less the public and the authorities knew about the actual workings of Lloyds, the better. Many of them were well aware of the all-too-many entangling alliances that could come to light if the scandal spread.

Case in point: the possibly embarrassing explanations that would have to be made by Committee Chairman, Sir Peter Green. 'Gang of Four' member Allan Page had worked for Toby Green, Peter Green and Peter Cameron-Webb. As a senior partner in an auditing firm, Page acted as their adviser. That firm was also auditing Howden's books. One day Grob offered Page a job. Only later, when full disclosure of hidden assets became the rule at Lloyds, did one notice that some of Peter Green's offshore reinsurance interests had a familiar ring to them.

They were very similar to the ones in question at Howden. And similar again to the ones which were run by Peter Cameron-Webb and which would eventually drive him out of Lloyds. Nothing illegal of course. That would hardly befit a second-generation Chairman of Lloyds. Just familiar.

All this time Bogardus was still saying that there was room for Posgate in his organization. 'I get along fine with Mr Posgate. It often happens that the best people in any company are the most entrepreneurial and of course those are the most difficult to control.' He also said he didn't expect Posgate to steal away into the night with Howden's names. 'If Mr Posgate decides to leave, that is something that we will have to worry about when it happens.' But he too, had heard the rumours that Posgate was thinking about cutting out – although, as late as 30 August, Bogardus was telling the world, 'If we lived on rumours we would all be committing suicide hourly, especially in London.'

By 8 September, Lime Street was in turmoil. The Lloyds Committee had no choice but to ask their own auditors to look into the matter. And a lot of people at Lloyds were making phone calls to places like Panama, trying to divest themselves of certain interests before it became too late. Then, on 20 September, A&A filed what is known as a 'Current Report' of '8-K' with the SEC in Washington. There is some reason to believe that, during the meeting on 13–14 August with the Gang of Four, Bogardus had been urged to sign the secret agreement on the advice of Hills who assured him that he, as a former SEC chairman, knew what kinds of agreements the SEC would accept. But when Hills failed to get SEC approval for that agreement, or when the SEC on their own looked askance at it, he warned A&A to immediately cut bait. They had no choice but to file the 8-K. And that's when 'the shit hit the fan'.

Bogardus turned on Posgate. He was fired by Howden and A&A. He was suspended by Lloyds. The Department of Trade stepped in, and with them came the City of London fraud squad. A&A filed civil actions against the Gang of Four and Posgate. And then they filed for and were granted an Anton Pillar against Posgate. That's a draconian order allowing lawyers and accountants enormous powers of search and seizure without giving the victim any protection by the police. Posgate's home and offices were searched. So was the home of his assistant, Laura Davies. They literally turned everything upside-down, paying particular attention, Ms Davies said later, to her underwear. The lawyers and accountants took with them everything they personally deemed relevant. That was followed by invocation of the Mareva Act, a writ forbidding Posgate from disposing of any assets pending trial. His assets were frozen, although he was allowed a weekly pittance on which to live. Posgate also claimed he was being followed by private detectives. 'It was very insulting. The Anton Pillar. You know, looking through underwear and this sort of thing. Looking through female underwear and getting a delight. I think they were rather kinky, personally.'

It wasn't until 13 October that Posgate was able to rally his forces. He started proceedings against A&A, Alexander Howden and the Committee of Lloyds. The next day the Gang of Four announced through their lawyers – where an entire office had been devoted solely to their case and was being dubbed 'The War Room' – that they had answers to all of the questions being asked.

In 1983 the courts ruled in favour of the Gang of Four in their motion to force Bogardus back to arbitration. Both parties knew that a loss in arbitration could involve gigantic sums. So, at the initiative of A&A, with total legal fees on both sides quickly approaching the £1 million mark, they sat down to settle out of court. An agreement was reached in April 1984. In that settlement, A&A received some £300,000 worth of marketable securities, a Renoir painting, and a house in London. In exchange, among other things, Ken Grob got back the villa in the south of France. Carpenter and Page resigned from Lloyds, so it's unlikely that Lloyds will be able to discipline them – although Lloyds think they still can. They also believe they can take action against Grob and Comery. It remains to be seen.

The courts also ruled in favour of Posgate and against the Committee of Lloyds' suspension, saying that they could not deprive him of his livelihood. They unsuspended him as they were ordered to do, then simply suspended him a second time, renewable every six months. At the end of 1984 he was permanently suspended. When a guy is down, it's wise to keep him down or someday he may get up and remember. Earlier, a boardroom coup at his own agency, Posgate and Denby, deposed him, sending him into exile to a small office across the street. The cases he can muster against Lloyds and A&A and even Posgate and Denby won't begin to be heard in court until 1986. But he says, in the meantime, 'I'm super. And working.' In spite of the magnitude of this scandal, he says, 'I think Lloyds will come through all right. I wouldn't worry.' However, he is decidedly less sure about his own future. 'I have no idea.'

*　　*　　*

The A&A/Alexander Howden scandal was followed by others. The newspapers were filled with scandals – Minet . . . Sasse . . . Peter Cameron-Webb . . . Peter Dixon . . . Unimar. Lloyds was so rife with fraud and larceny that the Committee were forced to hire a full-time Chief Executive, an accountant named Ian Hay Davison. Under his guidance, and obviously under some pressure from the Bank of England, the ruling Committee passed a series of regulations that require everyone at Lloyds to thoroughly disclose their interests. At the same time, Sir Peter Green announced that he would not stand again for another year as Chairman of the Committee.

At least according to Davison, the scandals have had a

minimal effect. 'The concerns about the reputation lay mainly in the UK, mainly with the British establishment, who were concerned that there was corruption among certain of the agents in their relations with the names. Which is not, of course, an insurance matter; it's an internal matter in Lloyds and concerns the relationship of names and agents. I think the steps Lloyds has taken to correct those situations has been different from what people expected. They assumed that matters would be swept under the carpet and there would be the good old nudge and fudge compromise. You know, at the end of the day we'll meet the bill, sort of thing. Instead there's been much more of a root and branch reforming approach. Lloyds is clearly seen to be anxious to get its act cleaned up and get the crooks brought to book. In addition, the rule book is being changed and in particular accounting is being brought into line. The motto is, you know, sunshine dries away the mist. I would remind you that in July or August 1984 the accounts of all the syndicates were placed on public record. Two years before it would have been inconceivable.'

But then he's paid to say that kind of stuff. And when you try to pin him down to know if Lloyds is now squeeky clean, you get a less direct answer. Question: Weren't these scandals just the tip of the iceberg? Answer: 'There are no other cases, to my knowledge, of plunder other than those that have been reported in the papers.' Question: So Lloyds is now clean? Answer: 'Well, no, I didn't say that. I didn't say that. There are no other cases of plunder, that's to say large-scale depredations of the PCW type [the Peter Cameron-Webb affair]. The papers have found and reported on all the cases of plunder.' Although eventually he admits, 'There are, I believe, still widespread misunderstandings about the proper handling of conflicts of interest, the proper accounting for secret profits as between mains and agents. But these have not led to major depredations and they still fall to be corrected in the sense of disclosed, and in some cases the arrangements discontinued.'

*   *   *

There is a slightly personal PS to all of this. Throughout the affair, four journalists were competing for information. John Moore of the *Financial Times* was on top of everyone. Gareth David, then writing for *The Times* and now for the *Observer*, proved he had good sources but often complained that his editors didn't share his enthusiasm for the story. Margareta Pagano at the *Guardian* also managed to stay on top of the events. At the same time I was writing for *Barrons* – the sister publication of the *Wall Street Journal*, and the most influential business weekly in the States. When the first of my five-part series broke the news of the scandal in America, CBS television reported that A&A's share price fell 2 points.

Because *Barrons* carries such weight, Jack Bogardus returned my phone calls, although he was not as accessible to any of the others. His comments were always closely guarded, and answers that might have shed some light on the scandal and A&A's position were all too often handled with, 'I cannot discuss that on advice of counsel.'

In early October 1982, I obtained a copy of the 14 August secret agreement. And it looked to me as if it could raise serious questions about a possible attempt to cover up. Until *Barrons* published it, almost no one outside of the major players in the story had seen it. As soon as I had it, I made a copy and dispatched it to New York. I had already published four of my five stories on the scandal – and was very much the only one of the four writers suggesting at the time that A&A also had questions to answer. I was therefore not necessarily A&A's favourite person. Yet on 6 October, five days before going to press with the secret agreement, I was coincidentally invited to a breakfast meeting at the

Berkeley Hotel in Knightsbridge with Bill Farley, who was A&A's Finance Director and a member of the board, and Jim Donahue, the corporate press relations guy. The meeting was to be a secret, Donahue explained in advance, because Farley didn't want it known that A&A was speaking officially. In the trade, and in the movies, they call it 'background'. I have no way of knowing whether or not Jack Bogardus was aware of this meeting. I can only assume that no one, especially a board member, would have dared to come near me without Bogardus's blessings.

Donahue and Farley were about the same age – mid to late 30s – but very different types. Donahue was stocky, with a beard, the kind of guy who wore checked shirts with a corduroy jacket. Farley was tall, in good shape, fair, wearing an expensive suit, sort of a younger version of Jack Bogardus. We met in the lobby at the ungodly hour of 7 a.m. Donahue was sleepy. Farley had already been out for his morning jog. Over breakfast – Donahue and I had eggs, Farley stuck to fruit and yoghurt – I actually asked Farley if he'd leak me a copy of the secret agreement. He said that if it ever got out it would be disastrous. But he never said for whom. Donahue admitted that he had never seen a copy of it, so I volunteered, half-heartedly, to send him one. Farley immediately sneered, 'You haven't seen it either.' There was no sense in bragging because he'd find out soon enough. Anyway, the purpose of the meeting was to hear what they had to say. They had information they wanted to leak. As it was officially off the record, I feel that I cannot in good conscience repeat it now. On the surface it appeared to be a pretty juicy piece of information – and I promised to check it out. Finally, as breakfast ended, I asked Farley a direct question. I wanted to know if everyone on the board and everyone in the upper echelons of the corporate structure of A&A and Alexander Howden was solidly behind Jack Bogardus. He assured me that they were. He said they knew they were right, so

they were sticking with Bogardus through thick and thin.
Donahue agreed.

Within nine months Donahue found himself another
job, and Farley's resignation was announced by A&A
with the explanation that he wanted 'to pursue other
interests'.

And the information I was fed that morning proved to
be false.

A week to ten days after the secret agreement appeared
in |*Barrons*, Margareta Pagano rang me at home. We had
never met. I don't know where she got my phone number
as it was ex-directory. She wanted to know if at any time
I had been threatened with possible legal action by
A&A. She explained that there was a rumour around the
City that A&A's lawyers were so infuriated with me for
publishing the secret agreement, and fearing that I might
have other documents, they were going to ask for an
Anton Pillar on me. She said the rumour was that A&A
or their lawyers were going to raid my flat and seize
whatever documents and notes they could find to stop me
from publishing anything further.

I told her the truth – that at no time had I ever received
any such threats. She then wondered if anyone might have
put pressure on *Barrons* either to stop publishing the
story, or at least to go easier on A&A. I explained that
Barrons was hardly the type of publication to give in to
pressure, that they were the best street-fighters on the
block. However, I suggested she check for herself with
the Managing Editor, in New York. She did. There was
no pressure. Then came a second call, from someone in
the City with his ears to the ground, asking the same sort
of questions. I rang Gareth David who said he too had
heard the rumours. Eventually, so did John Moore.
Delighted with the possibility of becoming an instant
media star, I phoned John Donahue in New York and
wondered if he had yet completed the plans for the assault
on my flat. He said it was an absurd idea. I told him that
A&A's commandos were welcome to come barging

through the door and, yes, I did have more documents – although I assured him I had learned from spy movies always to make copies, which then get stored with a friend. You know, if anything happens to me Sam, mail these to the FBI! He said I was out of my mind. I wondered if he could please ask the raiding party to bring doughnuts. I promised to put on the kettle, and to turn the whole thing into a big party complete with TV film crews and every journalist I could muster. He said I was getting carried away because there was never any plan by anyone to attempt a seizure of my notes and documents – although he would have been glad to know where I was getting some of my information from . . . his own side! I thanked him, but insisted that if A&A ever changed their mind, not to forget the doughnuts. A few nights later, John Moore rang. His opening line was, 'I've joined the club.' I asked, 'What club?' And he said, 'A&A have now threatened me too.'

13

Clive Sinclair

Clive Marles Sinclair became Sir Clive a couple of years ago, his knighthood being a reward for high-flying in the hi-tech world of mass market technology.

He is a smallish man with a receding hairline and a bright red beard. Born in London in 1940, the son of a mechanical engineer, Sinclair's school career left a lot to be desired. 'I can only concentrate if I can do what I want.' So he left school at the age of 17 to make his way in the world as a journalist.

In October 1984, when the *Sunday Times* published their list of the nation's 100 wealthiest businessmen, Clive Sinclair was said to be worth an even £100 million. They ranked him Number 6, behind Gerald Ronson (No 2: £300m.) and Robert Maxwell (No 4: £151.49m.), but ahead of Terence Conran (No 8: £74.14m.), Tiny Rowland (No 10: £63.79m.), Asil Nadir (No 11: £59.87m.) and James Hanson (No 64: £9.68m.). However, unlike Nos 2, 4, 8, 10, 11 or 64, Sinclair's head office has an ex-directory phone number. Also unlike Nos 2, 4, 8, 10, 11 or 64, he looks less like a businessman and more like everyone's university calculus professor.

'I think you could say I was an inventive kid. I was always interested in calculating machines and electronic gadgets. My mother was most anxious that I become an academic.'

Instead he became an inventor who made it his business

to understand how the business of inventing worked.

'You can't really separate the inventor and the business-man. The idea of the lone inventor sitting in an attic somewhere is pretty impractical. By its very nature, invention itself is improbable. If you rush around with all your ideas in a brown paper bag, knocking on doors of big companies, those big companies are going to say, no. The way society arranges things makes it very difficult for all inventors. So the way you get around that problem, the way you turn your invention into something, is by being a sort of businessman. You go out there and you start a company and you get your own invention off the ground.'

He also became an inventor who made it his business to understand how the press worked.

After quitting school and before starting Sinclair Radionics, he got himself a job as a journalist, producing small books for the electronics hobbyist, writing most of them by himself, admitting that he learned far more about his subjects than anyone who ever read what he wrote. 'Being a technical journalist seemed a good idea, as it was an attractive and lucrative way of being employed. It got me about and gave me considerable freedom. It also gave me the opportunity of learning at someone else's expense.'

Like learning how to deal with the press.

'I think that perhaps some businessmen, not knowing journalists or where they come from, are a bit mystified by them and perhaps a bit afraid of them. They don't know what drives them or makes them do a story one way or the other. We do get a lot of good press, yes. But not always. I don't think the press is always fair with anybody. Quite often they'll slant stories because it makes a better story. But I suppose it's been quite a benefit having been on the other side of the fence.'

In spite of his experience on the other side of the fence, he is a difficult man to interview. He's laconic. He contemplates questions before coming up with short answers. Face to face, when you ask him something, he jots down notes, as if half his brain is doing the interview while the other half is suddenly coming up with the solution to a long sought after problem. He is just slightly distant and not the glibbest of men. Although he is pleasant enough.

He is rich and famous, but lives quietly. He reads poetry and jogs. He was married in 1962, but he and his wife split up a few years ago. They have three children.

While he has sold more than 5 million computers, he employs only 120 people, about 50 of them working on future projects, the others taking care of a business that sells computers in 70 countries and turns over nearly £100 million annually. If you ask him how well he manages people, he'll tell you that he's a poor manager. But he says he delegates well and has surrounded himself with people who manage better than he does. He is, however, all too modest. You don't just start with nothing and wind up with £100 million if you don't know what you're doing. Yet even here he shrugs, 'I don't see the money I earn as mine. It's just a tool, like a machine that is going to make something. There's nothing material I might want. Everything has been fulfilled. I'd be perfectly happy with less.'

In 1962 he founded a company called Sinclair Radionics to sell radio and amplifier kits for under £3 by mail order. Five years later he added hi-fis to his list. By then he had an annual turnover of £100,000.

And here is where he began exhibiting talent for knowing how to use the media. He knew his customers would come from hobby magazines. But instead of buying the usual small ad, as his competitors were doing, Sinclair went for half-page spreads. Nobody had ever done such a thing before. He says he didn't even have enough money to pay for those adverts at the time. But his feeling was that such a large plug would help instil confidence in his product.

These days his approach is a bit more sophisticated, but

the basic philosophy is the same. He likes to announce new innovations before they are actually available. That's what he did with the microdrives he designed for his Spectrum series. That's what he did when he decided to float off a part of the company in the City. That's what he did with his pocket TV. That's what he did with his electric car. That's what he always does. And even when the Office of Fair Trading said 'Shame on you' for long delivery delays, even then he managed to get a fairly reasonable press with good-sized pictures of him promising that everything will be all right soon.

'There is very good reason to announce the kinds of projects we're coming up with. That way people who can offer services to us come forward. A good example is my electric car. We announced it because that helps attract talent for work on the project. It gives a flavour to the company.'

It also helps keep his cash flow in line.

*   *   *

By 1973 Sinclair was the leading manufacturer in the UK pocket calculator market.

From there he went on to digital watches and the world's first pocket television set.

And from there he nearly went bust.

'We ran short of cash in about 1976. But no, we weren't going broke. We were a bankable proposition. We got investment in from the National Enterprise Board. As it turned out it wasn't a very satisfactory arrangement. But it seemed a good idea at the time. It didn't turn out well at all. Originally the chap running it backed us, quite rightly, on the strength of our flat-screen television programme. Unfortunately, he soon left the NEB and they brought in someone else and they took a totally different view. As it happens, a wrong one about which way the company should go. They also appointed a managing director who was really not satisfactory. I was

Chairman. And, well, by a combination of things, the net result was really disastrous.'

The NEB wanted him to go into the instrument business. Sinclair wanted to stick with consumer electronics. In 1979 there was a formal parting of the ways and Sinclair formed the company he owns and runs today, Sinclair Research. The first product he put onto the market was the Sinclair ZX 80 personal computer. The price was so low – under £100 in the UK and under $100 in the more competitive United States – that just about any home could afford one, whether they needed it or not. He sold 130,000 of them. The following year he came out with the even cheaper ZX 81. The price of that one hovered around £50/$50. And in the first 18 months that they were on the market he sold, worldwide, 1.1 million of them.

Since then there's been the Spectrum, a 16k basic language home computer with a full range of add-ons, followed by a 48k model, and followed yet again by the Spectrum Plus. They account for nearly 80 per cent of his turnover.

Then he came up with the QL (the Quantum Leap), Sinclair's first real stab at the world of business computers.

'As far as the man on the street was concerned, our computers didn't change the market, they created the market. Of course there were always hobbyists interested in home computers, but that wasn't true of the general public. The average guy doesn't think he needs one. What I think our computers have done, priced for the average guy, is to give him the chance to learn how a computer can work. Our initial sales were made to people who wanted to learn. Now, many of our sales are based heavily on the games market. Although we never intended the computer to be a toy.'

He justifies the relationship between computers and games by saying that lots of the games now aimed at the home computer market actually require intelligence to master and can be very demanding to play. As any adult with children knows, it's more than simply blip-blip amusement park video tennis. How dare 8-year-olds instinctively understand such things! Parents everywhere should curse Clive Sinclair for the humiliation suffered by the over-30 crowd because he's invented machines that play fly your own jumbo jet program, or Espionage Island or The Ship of Doom or something called Super Glooper: 'Help the Super Glooper complete the maze before the guards catch him. Help the frogs hop across a fast-flowing stream.' Why does he refuse to come up with something like, Only Parents Can Win: 'Help adults beat the daylights out of their kids at all these damn computer games!'?

Sinclair himself doesn't produce software; he buys it in, mainly from the United States, but there is a huge market that has mushroomed for games playable on Sinclair machines. It's so enormous, there are even monthly magazines put out by independent publishers solely for the Sinclair computer user. That doesn't mean Sinclair computers are merely super-sophisticated toys. He figures the game business is just a phase we have to live through. One of the steps along the road towards the computerization of the world's homes.

'The first step is computer literacy. That's really what the ZX 80 and ZX 81 were all about. The game stage is next. But it is only a stage. It's followed by functional applications. The machines being developed today are coming with those changes. The actual application of computers as an integral part of the home are a little way off. Before it happens in the home it has to happen in the office.'

Oddly enough, there are no desk-top computers in the Sinclair offices. He says he'll have one some day but he doesn't feel that there are any machines available right now that can do anything more than, say, store data. What he says he wants is a truly useful machine. And that, when it comes, will be the final stage in the home computer evolution.

'I'm talking about machines that you might call intelligent. The money-dispensing computer at the local corner bank is a stupid computer. It can only do what it's told to do. I see computers coming along that will be able to reason. For instance, in the personal computer for the home, we haven't really begun to teach. Or take the place of the doctor in diagnosing illness. At the moment it's not easy to get all the information necessary for medical diagnosis into a computer. But I don't think a computer diagnosis could possibly be as dangerous as some doctors I've seen.'

The idea is that, one day, a computer working in a logical fashion will be sophisticated enough to draw inferences from information. Life will not be black and white. There will be many degrees of grey. George Orwell might have finally won.

'Computers are not yet teaching. What people are learning to do with them is program. I think the day will definitely come when computers themselves become the teacher in their own right. I think a computer can much better teach children than teachers as we know them can. The ratio can be brought down to one per child. A computer is infinitely more patient than a human teacher. The possibilities are at their earliest stage right now, but I see no reason why a computer shouldn't do anything that a teacher does now.'

When and if this 'fifth generation' happens, it will represent a leap forward so spectacular that comparisons are difficult to make. A computer that thinks, and might even surpass man's intelligence, would be similar to Christopher Columbus in the year 1492 somehow reaching the moon. It will, not surprisingly, reap untold wealth for the man who makes it happen.

'Computers are the roots to the latest frontier. They've been around for 30 years or so, but the sudden explosion in technology has been changing computers at a drastic pace. Machines of immense power are now within our grasp. They will change society. No doubt about it. That kind of thing has been said before. This time we mean it.'

Sinclair does say that there's no need to worry yet about being owned by a computer because it's not something that is just around the corner. Although he thinks it could happen in the next decade or two. 'Machines will absolutely begin to exhibit intelligence. Might even happen around the turn of the century. And I don't necessarily see that as frightening a prospect as you might. The job that computers will be able to replace could create for us a golden age which in turn will give us more time to educate our children as original thinkers. I'm an optimist.'

So was Murphy!

❊   ❊   ❊

He insists that his main interests lie in innovation.

That he's not interested in what might be termed a conventional market.

'Older companies of any sort, and our's will be an older company some day, find it very hard to innovate, not because of any intrinsic reluctance, but because once they have an established manufacturing base they find it hard to change direction. Leyland can't just suddenly go out and make plastic cars, and throw away all its capital equipment. It might suddenly be the right thing to do, but it's wrong from the accountancy point of view.'

It's certainly the right thing to do from the competitive point of view. Sinclair is in a field that has for the past several years been much too overcrowded. For every success story – like Sinclair or Apple's Steven Jobs – the road is littered with casualties.

'All our competitors say, of course we can do the same. But they're talking about what they will do a year from now. They don't know what we'll do a year from now. We learned a lot from the problems we had with our calculators. Then we weren't working on a world scale. Now we realize that we can be challenged in any market we're in. We're no longer complacent. Of course, I think anybody in any field always thinks there are too many people in the field. But in home computers, yes, there are. There's bound to be some sort of shakeout still yet to come.'

What Sinclair does so well – at least to this point he's almost consistently managed to do it better than his competitors – is to identify what people want but still can't afford. Then he sets about building one that's affordable. In the end, the Sinclair version might not suit the buyer's needs right down to a 'T', but it's so far been close enough and so far been affordable.

With the QL he's tried to take on the big kids at IBM and their PC. It isn't the same computer, but the QL isn't a ZX 81 either. And while the IBM PC price tag is upwards of £2000, the QL has been costing merely 20 per cent of that. Unfortunately for Sinclair, the QL came onto the market very late, and followed closely on the heels of the problems he was having in the States with Timex.

Sinclair, in predictable form, announced the new QL and orders began coming in. But no QLs started going out. Complaints went to the Advertising Standards Authority, which agreed that Sinclair was not living up to his delivery promises. The Office of Fair Trading came along and exacted from Sinclair an assurance to comply. They said they had received some 80 complaints. And with characteristic frankness, Sinclair answered, 'We're in the business of innovating. We're not proud of our delays and we're not at all happy that we've let people down. But as bad as we got it, we're probably better than the competition.'

He didn't find that to be true when he and the Timex watch company were in love a few years ago in the United States.

Riding high on his successes of 1980 and 1981, Timex licensed the Sinclair name and technology for North America. They intended to make a fortune along with

him on the 16k version of the ZX Spectrum. But the
Timex Sinclair 1000 (an adaptation of the ZX 80) created
an excitement in the States that the Timex Sinclair 1500
(the ZX 81) couldn't quite follow. One computer writer
said the Model 1500 suddenly seemed 'out of sync' with
the North American market. The reason is simple – the
North American market is more competitive. VIC and
Texas Instruments had reputations in computers, whereas
Timex is thought of as a company that makes inexpensive
watches. With the Model 1000, buyers faced the problem
of the machine's memory. It wasn't in itself sufficient to
compete in the market. An additional memory unit was
necessary. But there were long delays and the competition
closed in. The Model 1500 made certain improvements,
but by the time the Model 2000 came along – to compete
directly with the Commodore 64 – it was thought of as
merely a grown-up version of the troublesome 1000 and
1500, and also ran smack into the face of a price war.
Discounting is the way almost everything is sold in the
US. Timex tried to fight back. They looked towards
direct mail firms that specialize in the school and library
markets. They tried to sell the computers along with
dictionaries and encyclopaedias. They banged on doors of
banks and real estate developers, thinking they could use
the computers as give-aways to important customers.
Sinclair made a few million pounds in licensing fees, but
the romance ended and the agreement was cancelled. He's
decided to tackle the US by handling the QL marketing
himself.

At least in the UK his marketing skills are fairly
evident.

He's taken the QL and joined with ICL to come up
with a 'One per Desk' system. He wants to incorporate
all of the usual office functions into one small terminal. It
sounds like a smarter bet than Sinclair's small screen TV.

'That's for occasional viewing.'

Like most Sinclair projects, the pocket-sized, two-inch,
flat-screen black and white TV has involved a great deal

of outside cooperation. And that may be one of his personal strengths. He's one inventor who seems immune to the it's-not-good-if-it's-not-invented-here syndrome. He goes to wherever the expertise is if he doesn't have it in-house. He contracts out almost all manufacturing. The single-chip circuits for his television were designed with the help of Ferranti Electronics, Ltd, a digitalization specialist. AB Electronics worked on the tuner. Its 15-hour lithium cell battery is a Polaroid idea. Thorn-EMI and Timex have handled the final assembly.

But, more so with the pocket TV than any of his other inventions, the basic question is, who would want one. It's not quite the same as a portable radio. Tough to balance one on your dashboard while fighting commuter traffic. He says, however, that sales are doing well.

Those who claim to know say that the pocket TV, like the ZX 80, is merely a first step. The trick was to develop a flat screen and a battery. That done, there will one day be a colour version. That should be followed by a much larger flat-screen TV – hang it on your wall like a painting – and, parallel, a cut-price DBS system. That's 'direct broadcasting by satellite', which, depending on who you ask, is either the future of television or simply a pipe dream. In the United States, where satellite transmissions are used by the television stations themselves for intra-transmission, home enthusiasts have satellite dishes on their roofs to pick up these broadcasts. There is also a television company in Atlanta that broadcasts commercially by satellite, although, with the advent of cable TV, there is some question about the feasibility of such a venture. The fun is sitting in your livingroom in Omaha, Nebraska, and being able to tune into the satellite transmission meant to be going from Los Angeles to Boston. Whether or not Sinclair ever gets into such things depends on the legality of it in Europe, and the market potential.

'I'm convinced there are enough new products waiting to be put on the market to last me the rest of my business life. I can see a whole range of ideas that I want to do.

They are always swimming around in my mind. But it's hard to describe the sort of judgement you make whether a venture is going to be a success. It's in the subconscious, really. It's a question of building up a mental image, a feel for the market.'

*   *   *

For the past two or three years, there has been a lot of talk around the City about Sinclair going public. He sold off a 10 per cent share of the company to some institutional buyers in 1982. He said at the time that he planned to use the money to finance an array of projects, including his stated intention to take over the defunct De Lorean factory in Northern Ireland. He told the world he was interested in building a petrol engine automobile there. The take-over never happened. Nor did the petrol engine automobile.

Nor will a large-chunk flotation of Sinclair Research. If he hasn't done it yet, look for the flotation to be rather small. First, he says, he doesn't want to relinquish control of the company to the institutions that would buy the shares. Second, he doesn't really need the money. The company is sound and the cash flow is good. Third, the flotation is nothing much more than his making good on a long-standing promise. When he sold that first 10 per cent chunk, he told the buying institutional investors that he would one day publicly float off a part of the company. The Stock Exchange has a minimum 25 per cent that they like to see – at least a quarter of a company's shares available to the market – and that may be too much for Sinclair's personal liking. The Unlisted Securities Market is the likely option. But there are some minor problems there too. All he really wants is to find an easy solution so that, by offering 3–5–7 per cent, he'll provide a market for the shares. Then he says he'll get back to the business at hand, which is, after all, coming up with new inventions.

'We depend for our early sales on people who have great tolerance to new ideas. With the computer, that would be the sort of person who, if you put it down in front of them, would just want to play with it straight away. We get the product to them, other people see it, it becomes more familiar and they lose their fear of it.'

The electric car is not a new idea. There have been electric cars on the drawing boards and even on the market for decades. Every golfer who rides his 18 holes does it in a battery-operated cart. What Sinclair seriously hoped to do was take those carts off the golf course, make them a lot sexier and much more economical, and put them on the street.

'I've been toying with the idea of doing an electric vehicle for years, and have done various little experimental vehicles to try out this idea or that. But it wasn't until a few years ago that there had been enough innovation in all kinds of fields to give us a package that clicked. For example, the steady progress in battery design hadn't seemed particularly impressive in any one year. But over the years it's rolled up to a considerable advance. The science of lightweight materials has advanced to the point where we could actually buy a body with the right strength/weight ratio. Other people's problem solving has made our project possible.'

He says he designed the car completely from scratch, and doesn't like the comparison with the golf cart. Perhaps a better comparison might be with a battery-operated go-cart. To many observers it came as a disappointment. When you ask him why he's gone into such a different field – cars require specific areas of technology that computers don't – he tells you he doesn't see it as all that different. 'My business is consumer products that are basically electrical, and the electric car falls into the category. There is a massive difference, in a way, between hi-fis and computers. I don't see any greater difference between computers and cars.'

The main obstacle he faced with the electric car was the

classic one. Even today's most improved batteries won't provide very great range without recharging, and then they won't recharge very often without burning out. Yet Sinclair believed there is a big market for a modest-range town car. And previous failed attempts in search of the same market didn't daunt him. 'You must of course be able to find the market spot and meet it. If you're GM, you clearly hope it won't happen. It's not really the role of the large companies to explore new realms because it invariably threatens their capital base.'

That assumes there really is a market for a souped-down version of a golf cart. The Sinclair C-5 vehicle has three wheels (golf carts have four), bicycle pedals just in case the battery fails, no roof (which makes one wonder how well suited it is for the British climate), room for just one person (which rules out Sunday afternoon family outings) and a mini-boot which is notably much too small for golf clubs.

Sure, the world laughed at Alexander Graham Bell and the Wright Brothers. But General Motors tried electric cars and they couldn't make them work economically enough. The Sinclairmobile may cost next to nothing to run, but then so do electric golf carts and at least they're comfortable.

14

Terence Conran

'We've just bought a house in the south of France,' he
said.

'Where?'

'Not far from Arles.'

'Do you know the Hotel Jules César in Arles?' he was
asked. 'They make the best pâtes aux cèpes in all of
France.'

He pondered that for a moment. 'Yes, we pass the hotel
on every trip down there. But I didn't know about the
pâtes aux cèpes.'

He does now.

And for Sir Terence Conran – who once ran a chain of
restaurants called The Soup Kitchen and whose current
wife Caroline writes and translates cookbooks (ex-wife
Shirley writes best-sellers like *Superwoman* and *Lace*) –
knowing where to find the best pâtes aux cèpes in France
is not something he's likely to forget.

In between trips to Arles, Conran runs an empire called
Habitat–Mothercare PLC. A retail operation that now
spans the globe, it all began with a store concept called
Habitat exactly 21 years ago. He is probably best known
as the first, if not the only, retailer in the UK who has
gone out of his way to try to create excitement in what must
be called the otherwise dull world of British retailing.

'The retail business in this country only started
changing about three or four years ago. In fact, to be

perfectly honest, it's really only been in the past 10 years that the rest of the world has seen changes in retailing. But this country has been particularly slow to change. Like Sunday trading laws. We're one of the great promoters of Sunday trading in the UK, and when that comes about it should bring with it enormous changes in the way retailers operate. But the main changes over the past three or four years in England have come about because retailers are starting to understand the importance of design. Until recently, it was only the manufacturer who worried about design. Now the retailer is becoming the catalyst, deciding for himself what he can offer to the public. That represents a major breakthrough.'

The idea is one that has been popular in supermarkets for years; it is known as 'private labelling'. Goods are packaged under, say, the Sainsbury or the Safeway label and inherent with the product comes the retailer's reputation for quality. Probably the best-known example in the UK is the St Michael label at Marks and Spencer. In fact, M&S take the private labelling concept to the extreme. Whereas Safeway will put a competitor's strawberry jam on a shelf right next to their own-label strawberry jam, M&S will not sell anything but goods bearing their own label.

It's a slightly different approach at Habitat. Conran likens his kind of private labelling to designer collections. Instead of doing what M&S do, that is, provide some decent-quality but otherwise bland goods that try to cater to the widest possible taste levels, Conran has imposed very specific design ideas about the goods being provided for sale in his market. Either he goes to specific manufacturers and asks them to produce something of Habitat's own design. Or he takes the manufacturer's designs and amends them to suit his markets. Unlike a Harrods or Selfridges, which by their nature must offer something for every taste level, Habitat really only caters to one taste level. There is a well-defined Habitat client. He and/or she is young, married, an upwardly mobile white-collar worker, probably living in their first home, without children. He and/or she can afford restaurants once or twice a week, sincerely wants to become urbanized, and does some entertaining at home. He and/or she cannot afford Picassos but is perfectly at ease with dhurri throw rugs, red and white striped saucepans, and ersatz hi-tech metal units for records and stereo.

Because Conran knows pretty much who his clients are, he knows pretty much what to design for them.

These days, with nearly 1000 Habitat–Mothercare stores around the world, when you ask him if he sees himself as a designer turned businessman or a businessman who is also still very much a designer, you get a slightly perplexed expression in return, with the explanation, 'You can't separate the two. The process of design is interrelated to business. I'm not only concerned with how our products are retailed, but also how they're made and how they're marketed. My greatest pleasure in life is not balance sheets but products. I make it my business to concern myself with how those products are designed. I concern myself with how they're advertised. I get involved with the design of the shops. Everything comes through me. I try to go to all our merchandising meetings. I try to have some say in about 95 per cent of all that's sold.

And here he insists it is not at all a question of ego. 'One of the most important things I have learned as a businessman is to delegate. To get people around you who you can work with. People you trust. People who become part of a team. In the early days it wasn't easy for me to realize I was also part of that team. That I too had to be a team member. That I had to take my position and let the others on the team take theirs. So, although I try to have a say in everything we do, my point of view is not the one that necessarily wins. There are times when the team tells me no and we do it their way.'

But the basic concept is his. Terence Conran was, after all, given the reward of knighthood for having been the man who conceived and built the foundations for what is now one of the most copied formats in retailing.

Born 54 years ago in Surrey, Conran was hailed as one of the hot-shot designers of the so-called 'swinging '60s'. 'Growing up in England before the war meant life was extremely austere. During the war we had rationing and there were no materials for building. So in design schools they taught that design actually had to have some social intent. And I think what we as students in those days saw at the time was that good design could make a big contribution to the quality of life.'

In the early 1950s Conran opted out for some time in Paris, and worked there at a restaurant. That's when he first discovered Les Halles (the Parisian markets), and years later he would return to Les Halles to buy kitchen utensils and equipment for his stores, hoping obviously to re-create that 'market' feeling in the Habitat kitchenware departments. However, during that first stay, among other things, he learned to make soup. When he came back to London, he and a friend decided their future lay in soup, so they opened a restaurant called The Soup Kitchen, just off London's Strand. Conran decorated the place in a bright, clean way and, although he didn't realize it at the time, the embryo for the 'Conran style' was fertilized.

He had been designing furniture during those years, selling mostly to the trade. But he wasn't yet the Terence Conran he would become. His partner in the Soup Kitchens eventually decided to take the restaurants off in a direction slightly different from the way Conran saw them going, so he sold out. He began to concentrate more on design, and little by little started to refine his vision of design coupled with retailing. If he first saw it around Les Halles, he certainly started to materialize it when he helped to create the market atmosphere by designing Mary Quant's Bazaar on the King's Road.

By 1963 it all came together in the first Habitat. 'I think the reason I went into the retailing business was because I believed that there was another way of selling furniture. The way I see it, the art of retailing is understanding that selling your product and creating an atmosphere to show off that product is exactly the same thing.'

The first Habitat store in London was generally categorized as merely being a child of the swinging '60s. London then was the King's Road and Carnaby Street, the Beatles, *The Knack* and *Hard Day's Night*. But then Conran isn't quite so sure that the swinging '60s were happening any place else. 'Frankly, looking back on it, I think the term 'swinging '60s' was merely a media catch-phrase for what was happening in a very small area of London. And only there. What was going on in those days wasn't happening everywhere. It began with a few designers opening their own shops. We had just emerged from the extremely dreary '50s where nothing at all happened and some of us wanted to put our stuff in front of the public. Music came first. Then design. A few Italian restaurants came to London and suddenly there was a renewed interest in food. But this 'happening', if that's what you want to call it, really only touched a few people until the media came along. They're always searching desperately for something to print, so they made it much bigger than it was. Take that first Habitat store as a good example. In reality, other retailers saw the first Habitat store and said, it's okay for Chelsea but it's not for Manchester.'

Not only has it turned out all right for Manchester, but he's taken his act on the road, throughout the UK. And onto the continent. And into North America. And into Japan. And also into a few off-beat places, like Martinique and Iceland.

He knew from the beginning that he had a winning formula, but he also realized that a winning formula in Britain might not be a winning formula in another country. He believed that to successfully retail in other places around the world, he would have to make various subtle changes to the Habitat concept. For instance, in some countries you just can't sell bed linen that isn't 100 per cent pure cotton because that's what the people there want. In other countries, they'll buy man-made fabrics, or perhaps they only want percale sheets. So what he's done is cater to the locals. The designs on the sheets in England and the designs on the sheets in France may be exactly the same, but the material is different. And the way he knows what his customers want in those foreign markets is by being an especially strong believer that you cannot make a success of a foreign operation without the influence of localized management. It must be the right approach because some of his foreign clients simply can't believe the stores are foreign. 'We've been in France and Belgium since 1973. And I think the highest compliment we've ever been paid there came from a real estate agent who told me that Habitat was a French company. I said no, it was English, but he insisted that I was wrong, that Habitat was French. I guess that means we're doing the right things in France.'

Even with localized management, he faced an unusual problem when he chose to go to Japan. There, vast cultural differences always play a role when western businesses are set up. In Conran's case, he minimized his risk by carefully studying the market and then waiting for the most opportune time to strike. As far as he was concerned, Habitat in Japan would only work if Japan was ready for Habitat. And these days it is. 'Some serious cultural changes are happening there. They're acquiring western taste. They are trying to become a western country. They're rejecting their own traditional culture. People there are wanting to live like Americans and Europeans. They're even trying to cook exactly like westerners, which is pretty funny because westerners are trying to cook like Orientals. So we know that the climate is ripe in Japan for Habitat.'

However, there are some physical differences he had to consider as well. 'Because the size of rooms in Japan is much smaller than in the west, everything there is neat and precise. To fit in with the size of the rooms, we've had to scale down our products. Especially seat-related products such as chairs. We've actually scaled them down by about 7 per cent. The Habitat style represents young European and US taste. Yet there is also a slight connection with the more formal Japanese traditional style. So maybe we're a transition.'

The most difficult area to conquer, however, has been the United States. Business there is littered with the carcasses of British companies gone in search of the vast riches that go to the winners in the land where the greenback is almighty. Conquer America and you've conquered the world. Yet too many firms come a cropper there. And that, as Conran sees it where retailers are concerned, is often for a couple of reasons. The size of the country is one. The thoroughly unique American attitude towards retailing there is the second.

Both are mistakes he is keen to avoid.

'A year ago or so I spent a week doing a whistle-stop tour of the States. I got to see a lot of America, and I can tell you that the best retailer I saw was absolutely terrific. There are lessons to be learned. It was Macy's in San Francisco. What they've managed so wonderfully to create is a store filled with excitement. That's because they've got the right management. I especially liked the management style, and believe me, you could see just by walking through the store that it was a close-knit team. What you usually find in retailing is that the marketing people and the retailing people never talk to each other. But they do at Macy's San Francisco. You can see it the moment you step inside.'

It's very much the feeling he had hoped to create when he opened the first of his stores in New York eight years ago. They're not called Habitat in the States because there is already a chain with that name, so instead they're called Conran's. And he admits to having had a difficult time setting up there. Although in the beginning, for those first few weeks, it looked dead easy. 'It was during the time when New York City real estate had ebbed, and the only building going up was Citicorp's. Well, first we managed to swing a long lease with a low rental. Then we got a fantastic amount of publicity. We honestly thought our business would just go through the roof. But New Yorkers didn't understand what we were doing. Until we came along, there was never anything quite like a home furnishing supermarket. You know, take-away furniture. Lots of people came to look, but it took about four years to get it off the ground.'

In fact, he says it was only two years ago that the American side of his business started showing profit. It took that long because retailing in the States is not like retailing in England. 'No, there were some new things we had to learn. For instance, America is vastly overshopped. It's more difficult to make money in the States than it is in the UK, for a variety of reasons. The country is so big that distribution can be difficult. There are also lots of climatic changes. Florida is different from Boston, so you have to have the right merchandise in the right place at the right time. Management is also more costly. Although one of the joys of retailing in the States is that it can go very fast. There are shopping malls everywhere in America. There are relatively very few in the UK. Then there's sales promotion. In the States, a higher percentage of turnover goes for promotion and advertising. Ads in the UK cover the entire country. In the States, again because of its size, there are no national newspapers so you have to take the time and expense to target your advertising.'

Just as importantly, he insists, the word *sale* in the US doesn't mean the same as it does in England. '*Sale* in the UK means that you've bought something badly and want to get rid of it, or you've got damaged goods to get rid of, or you've actually bought in goods to be marketed on sale. In the States, the word *sale* means this is the regular price. I'm afraid that Americans are incredibly gullible. Before we managed to figure that out, our competition in the States came from retailers who used to scream, *Sale*. To get even, we simply joined the bandwagon. We started promoting ourselves very heavily. Although in the end we've actually found very little real competition for what we're doing in the US. The department stores, for instance, don't sell furnishings with the same sort of conviction we do.'

The chain now has 11 Conran stores in the US, all of them clustered into the northeast corner of the country. The reason is because Conran seriously believes that it's wrong to attack the huge American market by thinking that it's all just one country.

'I don't look upon the States as one country or 52 states, but rather four very distinct regions. The Northeast, the Midwest, the Sunbelt and the West Coast. I think that's the way you have to see America. I think you're looking for trouble if you say, I'll just go across the States with a chain and cover the entire country like that. You have to adapt your product range to suit these four different areas. You find lighter colours in Los Angeles than you do in New York. California is obviously less metropolitan and that is reflected by requiring slightly different shades and styles. You've got to cater to the local tastes.'

With his figures there now in the black, he feels the time might now be right to start an expansion in the States. If he does that some time over the next few years, the area he'll aim at is the West Coast. 'Having established ourselves in the Northeast, we think our next opportunity is the West Coast. You know, California. To do that we'll actually set up a different management to adapt our product range. The secret to success in the States is that you must take advantage of regional management, marketing, product and store design. I honestly believe that, if you get it just right, there's a lot of money to be made. If you simply try to pick up what you're selling in the Northeast and drop it on the West Coast, you won't be as successful as possible.'

Establishing Conran's in California won't be an easy task. The competition is fierce. And over the next few years it will probably get even tougher as retailers fight for survival. 'I mentioned the "own brand" concept, you know, the designer label idea. It hasn't really happened in the US yet, but it's about to. It's beginning. Retailing groups are starting to employ their own designers. You have major retailers getting into collections, like Calvin Klein and Ralph Lauren, and then they get disillusioned because before long they see the same stuff discounted down the street. What will happen is that these big stores will start to develop their own products because it will be the only way they can survive.'

*   *   *

'Terence Conran's handwriting spreads to everything he touches,' says Robin Guild, one of Europe's most successful interior designers. Guild, who owns the London store Homeworks, also just happens to have been one of Conran's first retail accounts back in the days when Conran was designing and manufacturing furniture only for the trade. 'There is no doubt at all that his was the first business empire in this country built around style, taste and design. I'd say he's brought style to a certain level of the English public and drastically changed furniture retailing. He opened up a whole new world for that middle-income, professional management, white-collar type. He made stylish good taste affordable.'

Yet, however skilful he is as a designer, Conran's rise in the world of business was hardly meteoric. Nine years after he opened the first Habitat, his empire was a mere 15 stores. Then again, in those early years, Conran made a few less-than-satisfactory deals. One of them was buying into and nearly merging with Rymans, the stationery and office supply chain. It tied up a lot of his capital and a lot of his energy. It wasn't until 1972, by getting out of that deal, that he managed to raise enough capital to begin his expansion. Even in the States, it wasn't until last year that he started showing a profit.

Asking various analysts around the City what they think of Conran gets you the overall impression that Terence Conran is not a financial whiz-kid. But, of course, he's never pretended to be anything like that. He's never pretended that his skill is in creating the structure of the company. It's not. But he has every right to say that he is extremely talented when it comes to merchandising. He makes his shops look attractive and makes what's in them look attractive. He's certainly not a workaholic – again, he doesn't pretend to be. But he says he manages to fit everything in. It's only when you dig beneath the surface a little – past the public image of a guy who is accessible to television interviews and a guy whose photograph gets taken a lot, and a guy who openly admits that he lives with antique furniture as well as his own Habitat stuff – when you get past 'Terry Conran media star', you find Sir Terence Conran the retailer who is smart enough to have installed the right people around him. He's got an excellent financial man, and an excellent design team. There is a lot of talent in the background.

For example. The 'design is saleable' attitude spreads to all levels – like the department in charge of the Habitat catalogue. They've created it to look like a glossy magazine specifically so that they could sell it. These days, at least in England, those catalogues are sold in all of the Habitat stores as well as through selected newsagents. There are four a year and worldwide they sell over 1 million a year. It not only turns out to be good marketing, it also turns out that the revenues they generate with those catalogue sales come very close to paying all of the marketing department's catalogue costs.

*   *   *

It was January 1982 when Terence Conran pulled off a terrific coup. He and his financial team managed the reverse take-over of the Mothercare chain. Habitat sales were then about £78 million with profits at a mere £6.6 million coming from just 52 stores. Mothercare, however, was turning over £117 million and making a profit of £20.6 million with 429 stores in 11 countries. Based on the number of employees alone, Mothercare was three times the size of Habitat. It was also getting a better return on turnover than Habitat. In other words, if there were rules of politesse about such things, if chivalry prevailed – which it doesn't – it should have been Mothercare swallowing Habitat. 'As far as we were concerned, all you had to do was go into one of their stores to see why they needed us. Mothercare had lost its way. The shops had no direction. They didn't look good. The product line wasn't right.'

That helped make the big tuna a perfect victim for the smaller fish.

'Our idea was to turn Mothercare into a pre- and post-natal version of Habitat. I bought the chain because, in spite of their problems, they still had 35 per cent of the market. When I say in spite of everything, I mean that while they had good sites and good management, they had dull products and had lost the middle-class market. Did you know that there are 200 Mothercare shops in the States? No one does. Not even in America. It happens to be one of the best-kept secrets in America. The Mothercare shops there are spread right across the country. That's nothing we would have structured, but we're in the midst now of trying to fill in gaps. I figure that with our marketing and design talents we can improve products and widen the price range. We're in the process of bringing that middle-class market back.'

He managed to finance the Mothercare acquisition by taking Habitat public. Except Mothercare wasn't being talked about publicly when Habitat went to the market. And that raised some eyebrows in the City. Some analysts thought the reverse take-over was too risky a move so soon after going public. Others went so far as to warn their clients to be careful because Conran and Habitat were 'trendy'. And that's a term he's heard often. That's precisely what the banks told him when he tried to raise capital for expansion in the States. 'We've suffered too many times at the hands of the all-too-usual near-sightedness of the British banking community. None of the British banks wanted to know. "You're reasonably successful, they told us, but you are very trendy." They saw us as some sort of Carnaby Street jeans merchant, here today and gone tomorrow. It was all very disappointing after struggling very hard for years.'

Even today there are brokers in the City who say that Habitat–Mothercare shares are trendy. The group will probably do close to £500 million worth of business this year, yet some analysts look at the shares and warn that they have a certain fashion about them. It might not matter that both Habitat and Mothercare have a definite niche in the British market and neither of them has any real competition. The real question is, what will happen when all those young trendies get older, have more money to spend, and outgrow red and white striped saucepans?

Conran's answer is Heals.

Heals was a popular store in London's West End. It was, until last year, a sort of Habitat competitor. Now it is not. Conran bought it and made some changes. But his reason for buying it was not to wipe out the opposition. Instead he envisioned turning Heals into 'a mature man's Habitat. And it's a very exportable idea. We think that there are people who have outgrown the Habitat concept, so we're trying to create something for them.'

In between Mothercare and Heals, he picked up a 48 per cent stake in Richard Shops, opened a chain called Now for the teenage market, built up a strong base business for Conran Associates (which is a design consulting firm – they've done stores like Miss Selfridge), and joined forces with Paul Hamlyn at Octopus Publishing for a joint venture in the book business.

Being a retailer, he's always been able to depend on financing growth out of cash flow. When Mothercare and Richard Shops came along, he started using convertible unsecured loan stock. That gives the group the look of a high-leverage operation. But he's become a clever operator and in three or four years that loan will be converted into shares, which should prove to have been a cheaper way of growth than bank loans, as long as the company continues to do well.

'When you struggle hard and lose money, you're a hero. When you start making money you become a capitalist swine. Listen, I learned my business the hard way. I worked at it. Then again, twenty years ago the furthest I could plan was one year ahead. Now I find myself thinking four years ahead. It must mean old age.'

15

Robert Maxwell

Scene from the Life and Times of Chairman Bob: No 1.

A young man nervously drank a coffee in the waiting area in front of the Chairman's office. From the gold ring on the fourth finger of his left hand you could tell that he was married. From his rosy cheeks you could tell that the marriage had only happened recently. This probably wasn't his first job. But it could have been his second. And by the way he was whispering to himself, you could tell that he had a well-rehearsed speech for the Chairman.

'Now here's the way I see the situation, sir.' He had practised it the night before while his bride lay on her satin pillows and watched him with wonderment. 'That's right, I'm going to get into the Chairman's office and say to him, the way I see the situation, sir, is that improved cash flow will allow us to make further investments in related businesses.' He looked like an accountant, wore accountant-type shoes and an accountant-type suit. God only knows, he probably also had an accountant-type wife. 'Oh yes, dear, yes, that's very good,' she nodded to him as he continued. 'From my experience with such matters, sir, I can recommend a cost accounting method which would in turn assure that stock control. . . .' By God, he was going to give the Chairman a first impression of a young man on the way up. A team player. An organization man. A young man who was going to find his way onto the board before his 30th birthday . . .

The Chairman came out of his office and walked up to the young man. He extended his hand and said in a very strong voice, 'I'm Robert Maxwell.' He did not add, as is popularly believed, 'But my friends call me Bob.'

The young man jumped to his feet, nearly spilling his coffee, fumbling with the cup and saucer before putting it down to shake the Chairman's hand. 'Hello . . .'

'You're the new accountant for the printing works I presume.'

The new accountant at the printing works tried to recall his speech.

But the Chairman had met new accountants for the printing works before. Hundreds of them. Thousands of them. He had heard their well-practised speeches before, too. He knew exactly what to expect. And he had long ago learned how to cut short that sort of thing. The Chairman is a very large man, tall and bulky, and an expert at using his body weight, at using his air space. 'Now here's what I want,' he said, moving right in on the new accountant for the printing works. The Chairman towered over him and poked his finger into his chest. 'I want a system which will allow you to report to me. . . .' The Chairman's direct orders lasted two minutes. Then he asked the new accountant for the printing works, 'Is that understood?' The new accountant for the printing works was barely able to utter a feeble, 'Yes, sir.'

'Good,' the Chairman smiled victoriously. 'Thank you for coming to see me.' He shook the young man's hand, turned around and walked away.

*   *   *

He keeps people waiting 45 minutes.

You sit in the enormous outer office on the top floor with dozens of cubby-holes where other people are working, and an aproned woman asks you whether you want tea or coffee. The office building is called Maxwell House. The coffee is Nescafé.

When you are finally ushered into the seat of power, it's a spacious book-lined office. He puts his arm around you as he escorts you onto his balcony, which is the building's roof, inviting you as it were for a view of the City. An imposing man with mammoth hands that stay on your shoulder in a fatherly manner, he moves like an over-the-hill fullback.

'I want to show you something,' he says, as if you were the oldest of chums. 'Look at that.' He points to Liverpool Street Station. 'It's one of the rarest sights in London. See that? A train is actually running.'

Then he turns you around and points upwards. Could he really be about to say, 'And a plane is flying.' He asks, 'See that?' It's the top of his office building. 'I'm going to put a clock up there like you have in New York. And one of those digital read-outs that gives you the temperature too. We don't have anything like that in London. You will be able to seem my clock and my thermometer from all over the City.'

You nod. A clock and a thermometer. Why not. It's 10:29. The temperature is 58 degrees. Or will it be a centigrade thermometer? There's no time to ask because, still clutching your shoulder, he escorts you back to his office and sits you down. It's a big office with a couch and chairs and a cluttered desk with a large red-leather chair behind it. Some of the books on the wall of shelves even look read. More coffee? More tea? What can I tell you? What do you want to know? I am happy to meet you. You seem like a pleasant young man.

You say, 'So it's true about the Maxwell charm.'

He nearly blushes. 'Nah.'

'It must be. After all, what the hell was all that stuff about trains and clocks, except that you didn't want me to ask why you kept me waiting 45 minutes.'

He comes up with a great big smile. Even caught out he can be charming.

Robert Maxwell likes to think of himself as the British version of America's Armand Hammer. At least when someone says it about him, he doesn't argue the point.

Ask almost anybody and you'll soon learn that, for the most part, there are two things that most people know about him. The first is that he now owns the Mirror Group. The second is that he was once ruled unfit to run a public company. But not necessarily in that order.

In 1984 he used his considerable take-over skills to negotiate and win the *Mirror*. Sir Alex Jarratt, Chairman of Reed International, had announced a public flotation of the Mirror Group. Originally he had hoped to raise £75 million. But a re-evaluation by his advisers brought that figure down to £60 million. That's when Maxwell came along. He offered up to £100 million. It put Jarratt in the most uncomfortable position of not wanting to turn down the £40 million more while also wanting to keep his promise to spread the shares as widely as possible in a public sale. He fought it as best he could, determined that Maxwell should not have the group and that the public should. But he knew that one of the key attractions to flotation was the speculation that Maxwell might try to buy it that way, therefore running up the share prices. Without Maxwell hovering in the shadows of the public offering, Jarratt had to wonder if Reed might wind up with even less than the projected £60 million.

Timing is everything in life, and Maxwell's timing was perfect. Now he turned the heat up towards the boiling point. He raised his bid to £113 million. And now Jarratt understood that to refuse Maxwell would be financial suicide.

The deal was done by 2:30 a.m. It was July 13th. It was also Friday the 13th. The Mirror Group Chairman of six months, Clive Thornton, came to work at dawn, walked into his ninth-floor office and found Maxwell already sitting behind his desk.

A day or so later, Maxwell addressed the *Mirror* union members. He told them he wanted them to work with him to make the *Mirror* Britain's largest-selling daily. He told them he didn't want to go into battle with them. He told them, 'I don't want to spend years in trench warfare.' Then he asked rhetorically, 'Do you think I'm on an ego trip?' The audience shouted in unison, 'Yes.' But he reminded them, 'I have invested £90 million in this business. I don't belong to the Salvation Army.' Since then he's increased circulation, lowered the price, started a bingo war and got his picture on the front page with great regularity – although his mug is not easily confused with Princess Diana on page two or anyone, for that matter, on page three.

It was the culmination of a long march that had started on the wrong foot 15 years before.

It was 1969. He and the American wheeler–dealer Saul Steinberg decided it might be time to join forces. Steinberg's leased computers (Leasco) and Maxwell's magazines (Pergamon Press) were supposed to enjoy synergistic bliss. Steinberg had agreed to buy Pergamon shares at 173p.

'Somewhere in the middle of our dealing, Steinberg decided to pull out. I think he was probably short of cash.' (Steinberg's version is that Maxwell's profits were grossly exaggerated, that the share prices were inflated.) 'He turned on me to make me seem to be the villain. It is classic American business practice.' (So is something called subtle bookkeeping.) 'Steinberg had paid $6 a share for his interest in the partnership.' (No indication where that $6 figure came from because even at the 1969 average £1 = $2.39 the £1.73 price only equals $4.13.) 'I bought his shares for 25 cents.' (He actually paid 12p, which is what Steinberg eventually wrote them down to when he took a derisory loss on his own balance sheet five years later.) 'I spent $5 million. They say that he's only had two failures. Chemical Bank [a costly and bitter take-over bid Steinberg lost] . . . and me.' (Reached by phone in New York, Steinberg absolutely refused to make any comment about his Maxwell experiences. The impression his people gave was that he wanted nothing at all, absolutely nothing, really and truly nothing more to do, ever, with

Robert Maxwell. But, he was asked, is it true that Robert Maxwell is the only man ever to have got the better of Saul Steinberg? Not an easy task considering Steinberg's reputation. His public relations man, shielding Steinberg from any hasty comments, answered, 'Would you like it if he said, bullshit!')

The Stock Exchange had suspended dealings on Pergamon Press. The City Take-Over Panel was called in and they cited 'misgivings'. The Board of Trade ordered an investigation. Steinberg had used his shares to remove Maxwell from the Pergamon board. Leasco also filed a $22 million law suit against him in New York.

Throughout the investigation, Maxwell fought tooth and nail to change the methods used by the investigators. He saw it as a Star Chamber procedure and objected to many of the facts presented against him as being in disregard of the rules of natural justice. In particular, he claimed he had not been given the opportunity to confront, cross-examine and/or otherwise refute certain unfavourable testimony. He made several appeals, at times asking for injunctions against the inspectors. He lost. The report was published – critical of Maxwell. Today the case is one of those cited in great detail by the Department of Trade and Industry in their *Handbook of the Companies Inspection System*. The points raised and debated have set precedents and in some way changed the system. They also marked Maxwell for the rest of his career, because the inspectors ruled that, as he had been recklessly optimistic, he was therefore 'unfit to be a steward of a public-quoted company'.

*   *   *

Scene from the Life and Times of Chairman Bob: No 2.

The Chairman hates hotels so he keeps a suite behind all of his various offices around the world. Staff are on duty at all times when he is in residence. These days he's mostly in residence on the top floor of the Mirror Group headquarters at Holborn Circus.

It has been the custom at the *Mirror*, as it is around most newspapers, that editors will stock their offices with suitable liquid refreshments at the company's expense. But the Chairman has a great dislike for needless expenses and can get quite stroppy about expense accounts. So, when the Chairman took over, he decided to cut out such practices, and ordered that any expense account booze had to be personally approved by him. Discretion being the better part of Scotch on the rocks, most of the editors had the common sense not to push their luck. They paid for their own booze. But one editor figured, to hell with this, went to the Chairman's penthouse suite, banged on the door and found the Chairman relaxing in front of the television set. 'Here,' he said, pushing the expense voucher authorizing a bottle into the Chairman's hands, 'Sign this.' Much to the editor's surprise, the Chairman did not go into a tirade. He signed it. The editor went away. A week later the phone on the editor's desk rang. 'This is Robert Maxwell,' a voice boomed. 'Would you come upstairs to see me please.' Now worried for his job, the editor went to see the Chairman who met him at the door and said, 'Sit down. Would you like a drink?' Seems the Chairman was getting lonely and this editor was the only guy at the newspaper he knew who liked to drink.

*   *   *

Maxwell is a fighter.

The Leasco scandal had knocked him down. He took it square on the chin. But it didn't knock him out. He got up and he clawed his way back. In 1974 he re-took Pergamon Press, buying it off Steinberg, ending the case against him, ending the matter once and for all.

Except the inspectors' remarks about him are forever being repeated. And his come-back to the chairmanship of Pergamon created the reference that also won't go away – from that day forward he has been known as the Bouncing Czech.

He wheeled and dealed during the late '70s, but he was still, then, by international standards, small potatoes. Pergamon's pre-tax profits for 1979 were £1.5 million. He made the big time in 1981 when he went fishing, hooked and actually landed the British Printing Corp.

Losses at BPC were in the £10–£12 million range. But he knew the assets weren't being used to their fullest – it was the nation's largest printing company – and he had loads for them to print. He made a dawn raid. He spent £3 million to pick up 29.5 per cent of BPC's shares. He said at the time it was just an investment. But all you had to do was look at Pergamon to see how easily the two would meld together. He would literally be able to take money out of one pocket and put it in another. So he scraped around for the rest, and he took control.

Right from the start he made all the typical Maxwell moves. He tightened the management screws. He slashed a large chunk out of the work force. He renamed BPC the British Printing and Communications Corp. and, within a year, the company showed a tiny profit. These days Pergamon does over £375 million in turnover and brings in a pre-tax profit in the neighbourhood of 10 per cent. BPCC boasts sales in the area of £300 million and a pre-tax return also close to 10 per cent. Fair-sized fish swallows small whale and both live happily ever after.

It's a talent that has made him a fabulously wealthy man and, in a not always flattering way, a legend in his own time.

But he didn't start out rich and famous. Once upon a time he was a poor refugee on the run from the Nazis in his native Czechoslovakia. His father was shot by them. His mother died in a concentration camp.

'I worked for a time with the underground in Budapest helping to smuggle people to Yugoslavia when I was captured and sentenced to death. I escaped to France and fought there for a while until an American consul in

Marseilles offered me a chance to go to the United States. He offered me a scholarship and a visa. I turned it down because the war was on. This was 1940.'

His first sight of England came in September of that year. He arrived with, literally, not a penny in his pocket. He spent a brief period in a refugee camp, before enlisting in the Pioneers and North Staffs, thinking it was a fighting regiment. Four years later, he was in the British Army fighting in Normandy and earning himself a battlefield commission. 'It caused a lot of problems, not for me but for the War Office. Technically, I was a German or a Hungarian at the time. It took General Montgomery to personally intervene.' Monty himself pinned the Military Cross on Maxwell's chest. Actually, he pinned it on Jan Lodvick Hoch's chest. That was the name he was born with but, when the War Office found out that a foreigner was wearing the Military Cross, he was given near-instant British citizenship and a new name. From Hoch it became Du Maurier. He had seen it on a cigarette package and should probably count himself fortunate that today he isn't know as Bob Luckystrike. Then for a brief time it was Jones. Somehow it wound up Maxwell. To a 21-year-old Czech kid who had just fought a war, it had a terrific British ring to it.

Having shown a great ability for languages during those years – he says he speaks nine of them fluently – Maxwell spent a couple of years after the war in Berlin. Through a German publisher friend he discovered piles of technical studies done by German scientists. He decided a world-wide market for them might exist. So he bought the rights to as many of them as he could, and published them wherever he could. He says that by 1948 he was already a millionaire.

*　　*　　*

Scene from the Life and Times of Chairman Bob: No 3. The Chairman turned 60 years old in 1983 and figured it was reason to celebrate. He threw a party for his 2000 closest friends. It was a do to out-do even the annual Ewing barbecue. Seen at the birthday party were the Soviet Ambassador and the Bulgarian Ambassador. They were heard at the party too, as they read official tributes from their governments to the Chairman. Then the Chairman's wife Elizabeth took the microphone and read from a book she had prepared containing lots more tributes to the Chairman – these from a cross-section of the world's leaders who unfortunately were unable to attend. A photographer took pictures, and one of them turned out especially good. The Chairman liked it so much that he used it for his Christmas card. It was a party worth remembering so he wanted the several thousand people on his Christmas list to remember. In the picture on his Christmas card was a banner with the words, 'Happy Birthday Bob'.

And you thought Christmas had something to do with Jesus.

*   *   *

In 1951 he bought a small publishing company called Verlag Heidelberg from Butterworth & Springer for £13,000. He renamed it Pergamon Press.

By 1964 he was a Member of Parliament, best remembered by his colleagues on both sides of the House as the man on the catering committee who sold off their wine cellar. 'I spent seven years as an MP for the Labour Party for Buckingham. But that ended in 1970.' (A year after the Leasco scandal.) 'I got kicked out by the people. I lost an election.'

He has always been a staunch supporter of the Labour Party, even if they don't always let him wander around at leisure during their annual conferences. He vowed that the *Mirror* would be a Labour newspaper and it is. He is quite obviously very sincere about his socialist tendencies. However, with a personal fortune estimated to be worth over £150 million, the Labour Party doesn't know quite what to make of him. Some of the powerful print union factions have tried to kick him out of the Labour Party. But that may be less for his wallet and more for the fact that he's never hesitated to make severe cuts in his work force when he felt it necessary, has closed plants and made some very naked threats. The first day he met with the unions printing the *Mirror* papers, he told them if there was ever an illegal strike at the Mirror Group he'd shut down the paper. Just like that, he'd close the doors and walk away.

It hasn't won him a lot of friends in the union movement. But then again, he's stood up and played tough with the unions before so he probably didn't have too many friends in the union movement to begin with.

'I really have no time to worry or care. And that infuriates my enemies.' Then he justifies his actions by saying, 'I'm a socialist manager. But they have their job to do and I have mine. I still love them as brothers but business is business.'

Long before the *Mirror* came along, Maxwell was already claiming to be the world's largest publisher. Mainly through Pergamon, he publishes a list of some 600 technical magazines, annual subscriptions to which can cost hundreds and even thousands of pounds. *International Abstracts of Biological Sciences Monthly* is 11 separate magazines per month at the combined rate of £986 per year. *Computer State of the Art Reports* cost £1634 per year. While a combination subscription to *Insect Biochemistry* and the *Journal of Insect Physiology* is a bargain at £343. 'I'm the smartest publisher in the world because I do what none of the others do. I get writers to pay me.' Besides that, as all subscriptions must be paid in advance, he's got a positive cash flow in the £60–£70 million range.

He and his family trusts own 100 per cent of Pergamon Press – some of those trusts through off-shore holdings that are not discussed because he says they don't concern anyone. In turn, Pergamon owns 77 per cent of the publicly traded BPCC.

For many years, again before the Mirror Group came along, Maxwell had a dream of using BPCC to make him the Printer of Fleet Street. The theory behind his vision was to save Fleet Street from itself. In fact, he was so intent on putting his plan into action that in the summer of 1982 he actually announced he was giving up trying to buy a British daily newspaper in favour of this new scheme.

Maxwell's idea was to print under contract all of Fleet Street's newspapers. He felt that 'The way in which Fleet Street's proprietors have combined publishing and printing has been a disaster.' He offered to build a £37 million printing plant, which, when combined with additional facilities worth £65 million, could accommodate the nation's newspapers.

'It's not that I am looking to become the man who rules the British press,' he said at the time. 'Not at all. But the necessity is there for someone to become the printer of Fleet Street. The economics of the newspaper publishing business is appalling. Conditions are desperate. But all of this could be cured by someone undoing the source of the troubles. Let publishers publish and let printers print. Under the present system, as long as newspapers are in both the publishing and printing business, you've got problems. When a newspaper dies, you can't even set up a new one because the combination works against the new project. And it is all the more troublesome because Fleet Street's presses are 10 years out of date.'

Fleet Street didn't rush to break down his door to give him any business then. Now it's not likely that they ever will.

*   *   *

Scene from the Life and Times of Chairman Bob: No 4. The Chairman was having lunch with some friends. He was going on about how the British establishment had never taken to him. He slammed his great big fist on the table and said, 'I defy anyone who's ever done a deal with Bob Maxwell to say that he didn't get a full 12 annas for his rupee.'

There are, however, 16 annas to a rupee.

*   *   *

When you ring Maxwell House hoping to speak to some friends-of-a-friend who work there, hoping to ask them about Robert Maxwell, you get a strange amount of stammering and er, well, can you ring me at home tonight? The rumour around Maxwell House is that certain people can actually tap into any extension and listen to any conversation. Of course the implication that Maxwell listens in on everyone's calls is ridiculous. It would be much too petty of a man in Maxwell's position and much too demeaning for a man of Maxwell's stature to bother with such nonsense. But the interesting thing is that so many people working at Maxwell House believe the rumour to be true.

Blind faith and loyalty are not the top two qualities Maxwell inspires amongst his troops.

Even when you ring those friends-of-a-friend at home, trying to find out more about their boss, they're fast to say, please don't quote me or use my name. And that's interesting too. There is a very obvious hint of fear that surrounds many Maxwell employees.

It's no secret at all that he can be a bully, that he sometimes fires people in the most humiliating fashion and especially in front of their peers. Yet, after describing a man with that sort of temper, most of them will then have to admit that they admire him as a hard-driving entrepreneur who has attained great success. They admire him for being a workaholic, shrewd, astute, clever, at times charming, often brilliant with details, and also someone fortunate enough to possess a near-photographic memory. He has his critics. He has his enemies – in the nastiest sense of the word. But even they credit him for being someone who displays great love and admiration for his family. He's been with his wife for 40 years and they've had nine children – although two have died. He says that his main regret in life is that business has all too often kept him away from his family.

But business is business. And with Robert Maxwell it's almost as if there is an insatiable drive for the next deal. The game is the thing. He certainly doesn't need the money. He even says as much. 'I am not motivated by money.' As far as he's concerned, the best thing about money is being able to have someone drive your car for you. He tells people he lives in a Council House, but that council house turns out to be the biggest mansion on the block, on a hill overlooking all of Oxford. He claims he works as hard as he does because 'I wish to be of service.'

But that can't really be the only reason.

Some people say that his success is an ego trip. Others say the motivation is nothing but power. He denies both of those. If the past 40 years have been nothing but ego trip or a chance to play the game of power, it would certainly be understandable – the poor Czech boy who survives to do it all. Maybe that's why he puts his picture on the front page of the *Mirror*. Or writes those editorials in the *Mirror*. Or tells people, 'I'm the publisher. I'm involved in everything.'

Whatever he does, there's no denying that he does it with total commitment and élan. He is a sort of 'street kid' who knows how to scrap. When he takes on someone his own size, the odds are on him. How strange it was then in 1983–4 when he took on a little kid, and found the little kid just big enough to knee him in the groin. Maxwell wanted to take over a company called John Waddington, a Leeds-based printing business that happens to own the UK rights to games such as Monopoly, Lexicon and Cluedo. In June 1983 Maxwell launched a bid for Waddington that would eventually become worth £18.2 million. He came within a few percentage points of taking the company, although there was severe criticism at the time of certain people claiming that Maxwell had more shares pledged to him than he actually had. He had to wait a year for his second shot but, with 23 per cent of Waddington's shares in the coffers, he fired off a £44 million attack. This time David took aim at Goliath, and the stone found its mark. Victor Watson, the Waddington Chairman, said that as long as BPCC wanted to own his company, and as long as BPCC was 61 per cent owned by Maxwell's Pergamon Press Ltd, and as long as Pergamon Press Ltd was 100 per cent owned by a Liechtenstein trust called Pergamon Holding Foundation, he felt he had the right to know exactly who owned the Liechtenstein trust. After all, he argued, whoever owns the holding foundation would, in reality, own Waddingtons. That immediately raised questions the City's press found more important – such as, who then really owns the Mirror Group.

Maxwell instantly denied that he owned the *Mirror*. 'I am not a proprietor, I am a publisher.' To that he added, 'Look at the record for over 30 years. Every public statement I have ever made has made it clear that neither I, nor my wife, nor my family will inherit one penny of all the wealth that I have managed to create.'

Watson said that made it all the more important to know precisely who would be owning Waddington. And the press jumped on the statement too, asking, so who owns the *Mirror*? Watson didn't have to be told twice that he was onto a good ploy. Section 74 of the 1981 Companies Act gives public companies the right to demand that their shareholders disclose beneficial owner-ship of their stakes. Watson sent a letter to the resident director of Pergamon Holding Foundation in Liechten-stein, requesting such information. The official answer was one to stall Watson. I'll speak to my lawyers and let you know, the resident director responded. But, for Watson's purpose, he didn't have to wait. With his back slightly up againt a wall – a low one perhaps, but a wall nevertheless – Maxwell gave up on his Waddington bid. He conceded defeat and started selling his shares. As for who really owns the Liechtenstein trust and therefore the Mirror Group, the word is that it's a series of charities and members of Mrs Maxwell's family. She's French – they met in Paris in 1944 – and her relatives are not resident in the UK. That seemed to answer as much of the question as Maxwell intended – or might be required – to answer. The interesting point is that the ploy worked once. And, if that's Maxwell's Achilles' heel, it won't be long until the next take-over victim goes for the same spot.

Some people who know him well say that in the last 15 years he has had two dreams. The first is a Fleet Street newspaper. Now he's got that. The second is a peerage. Lord Bob of Coldtype. Alas, this one will probably never happen. The Labour Party isn't up to such things. And in getting as far as he's gone, he has never played the establishment's game. A life peerage is very much about playing that game. About having friends in high places, and markers that can be called in. With Maxwell, too many people fear him. Too many people mistrust him. And, maybe to his great credit, he has never really done much to change their minds. He says he doesn't care what people think about him. 'I'm the man everyone loves to hate.'

Some people who have done deals with him say that when you get into bed with Robert Maxwell you will always end up with the rumpled end. Others more generously suggest that he is a gambler. Yet perhaps the best description is the one that goes he is neither a cunning nor an evil man. He is not at all a calculating man. He is rather one who has an amazing sixth sense for a deal and when to go for it. He is, the theory goes, a man who has intimidated people into believing that his instinct is calculation which it's not – it is instinct. He's made his own victories. He's suffered his own defeats. There have been good deals that have worked out splendidly, and bad deals that have hurt him badly. He is a survivor in a game where it is not only the weak who are not permitted to survive. Yet if there is one chief weakness in the whole set up – one chink in the armour – it is the fact that he has become Robert Maxwell. The problem with being a legend in your own time is that you might start believing everything you hear about yourself. He has single-handedly, having started with nothing, built an empire. It is all the stuff of American soap on prime time TV. But, like Dallas without JR or Dynasty without Joan Collins, when he goes, the series could get cancelled.

*   *   *

Scene from the Life and Times of Chairman Bob: No 5.

The Chairman is an ardent non-cigarette smoker. He likes big cigars, but there are certain areas in his offices where smoking is absolutely *verboten*. One day while walking through a non-smoking area, he spotted a man sitting on a chair puffing away. In a rage, the Chairman bellowed that the culprit had been caught red-handed and should have known better. The penalty for such an offence was immediate expulsion from the firm. The Chairman demanded to know of the man how much he was earning. The man answered, £75 a week. The Chairman reached into his pocket and took out a month's pay – £300 – gave it to the man and said, 'You're fired.' The Chairman pointed to the door and the man sheepishly left.

The only problem was that the man was merely there making a delivery.

Index